COUNTERCULTURES
A Sociological Analysis

COUNTERCULTURES
A Sociological Analysis

WILLIAM W. ZELLNER
East Central University

ST. MARTIN'S PRESS
New York

Editor: Sabra Scribner
Managing editor: Patricia Mansfield-Phelan
Associate project editor: Nicholas Webb
Production supervisor: Alan Fischer
Art director: Sheree Goodman
Cover design: Rod Hernandez

For information, write:
St. Martin's Press, Inc.
175 Fifth Avenue
New York, NY 10010

ISBN: 0-312-08084-0

Acknowledgments
Excerpts in Chapter 1. "Skinhead Reich" by Jeff Coplon. From *Rolling Stone,* December 1, 1988. By Straight Arrow Publishers, Inc. All rights reserved. Reprinted by permission.
Excerpt in Chapter 4. Reprinted with permission from *Occult Crime Control: The Law Enforcement Manual of Investigation, Analysis and Prevention* (Las Vegas: San Miguel, 1989) by William Edward Lee Dubois.
Table in Chapter 4, p. 86. Reprinted with permission from: Hicks, Robert D. "The Police Model of Satanic Crime," in *The Satanism Scare.* Edited by James T. Richardson, Joel Best, and David G. Bromley. (New York: Aldine de Gruyter) Copyright © 1991 Walter de Gruyter, Inc., New York.
Excerpts in Chapter 5. "Scientology" (series of articles) by Joel Sappell and Robert Welkos. Copyright 1990, *Los Angeles Times.* Reprinted by permission.
Excerpts in Chapter 5. Reprinted with permission from Robert W. Lobsinger, Publisher, *Newkirk Herald Journal,* Newkirk, Oklahoma.

To the memory of two men who loved books:

Maurice A. Zellner   1915–1994
Lloyd W. Goss   1933–1993

This book is also dedicated to the living:
my wife, Pamela, and my children, Zachary and Chelsea

PREFACE

A *subculture* is part of the dominant culture, but some aspects of the subculture's value system and life-style set its members apart from the larger culture. The Amish are a good example of a subculture. Their horse-and-buggy life-style has changed very little since the 1700s. The Amish are not part of the world that most of us inhabit. For example, they do not have churches as we know them. Services are conducted in members' homes. For the most part, education is considered a family function. Perhaps what is most unique about the Amish is that they have retained the economic system of a bygone era. The Amish family is a self-sustaining economic unit. They build their own homes, make their own clothing, and grow and process their own food.

The Amish interact as little as possible with the turbulent world outside their communities, but they are not at war with the larger American society. Their life-style was not created in reaction to the way in which most people live, nor is it sustained in opposition to American cultural patterns. As a consequence, the Amish are not viewed as a threat to the dominant culture. In fact, non-Amish tend to view Amish ways as a healthy alternative to the fast-paced life-styles of most Americans.

A *counterculture,* on the other hand, is deliberately opposed to certain aspects of the larger culture. For example, the Ku Klux Klan has been a cancer in the United States since the time of the Civil War. The cultural norm of "equality for all" shared by most Americans is challenged by Klan organizations, which argue that unwitting nonwhites, prodded by Jewish overseers, are the root cause of most of America's problems. The Klan is a prime example of a counterculture that, despite overwhelming mainstream opinions against it, retains its core audience and attempts to teach its "truths" to others.

Of the multitude of different countercultures, I have chosen six for inclusion in *Countercultures.*

Skinheads   Satanism
Ku Klux Klan   The Church of Scientology
Survivalists   The Unification Church

These groups are interesting and lend themselves well to sociological illustration. Many students will have had firsthand experience with one or more of the countercultures described in this book and will want to know: Why do people join such groups? What kinds of people devote their lives to groups that, because of their extreme beliefs and behaviors, are regarded in our society as bizarre, radical, and even dangerous?

An examination of countercultures makes it possible to illustrate major sociological concepts in concrete form. In this book, concepts such as scapegoating, alienation, anomie, and differential association are given life through the words and experiences of people like "Dave," a college student and skinhead, and Anton LaVey, founder and self-labeled black pope of the Church of Satan. Robert Merton's typologies of deviance serve to illustrate the tenuous balance between culturally approved means and goals and those considered deviant. Attention is also given to the work of C. W. Mills and Herbert Marcuse and their concerns about the nature and direction of modern society.

Chapters 1 through 3 (skinheads, the Ku Klux Klan, and survivalists) address societal problems caused by three hate groups. The lines that distinguish one of these groups from another are not always clear.

Skinheads, the least organized of the groups in question, often act as soldiers for more sophisticated hate groups such as the Ku Klux Klan and Aryan Nations. The effects of the skinhead *argot* (language), dress code, and music are examined in Chapter 1 to determine how each serves to bind young people together in hate-group activity. Included in the chapter is an interview with Dave (a pseudonym), a nonracist skinhead.

The Ku Klux Klan is not the threat to society that it once was, but it remains a potential threat. As we see in Chapter 2, Klan activity has been tempered by civil law suits that have reduced Klan financial holdings and caused Klan leaders to eschew violence in favor of political action to promote their causes. The chapter includes an interview with Thom Robb, national director of the Knights of the Ku Klux Klan. Robb is a successor to David Duke, the former Louisiana state representative who recently ran unsuccessfully for governor of Louisiana.

Chapter 3 describes two kinds of survivalists, "retreatists" and "rebels." Among the rebels are some of the most dangerous hate groups in the country. Those that have made headlines in recent years include Posse Comitatus; the Order; and Covenant, Sword, and Arm of the Lord. Perhaps the best-known survivalist is Kurt Saxon, a retreatist who claims to hate no one. He is interviewed in Chapter 3.

Chapter 4 addresses Satanic cults as a social problem. Social problems become societal issues when a significant number of people, concerned about problems such as crime, drug use, or abortion, demand change. In recent years, Satanic cults have become a much discussed social issue. Is this a real problem requiring greater attention and mobilization for action, or is our society suffering from psychosomatic fears? This question about the real or perceived threat of Satanism is addressed in a discussion of W. I. Thomas's theorem that states "when situations are defined as real, they are real in their consequences."

Chapters 5 and 6 address religious countercultures. Unlike the groups discussed in earlier chapters, the Church of Scientology and the Unification Church are highly sophisticated, structured institutions. Each does business by operating a variety of front organizations. In the case of Scientology, the fronts make money—a lot of it. L. Ron Hubbard, founder of Scientology, was fond of saying, "Make money, make more money, make others produce so as to make money."

The Unification Church appears to be, in one sense, the opposite of the Church of Scientology. While Scientologists follow the admonition of Hubbard to *make money,* Unificationists *spend money,* alarmingly large sums of it. Yet sources underpinning the financial empire of the Unification Church and its founder, Sun Myung Moon, are, at best, obscure. Chapter 6 relates the history and practices of the corporate institution called the Unification Church. The theories of C. W. Mills and Herbert Marcuse are used to characterize the Unification Church as a powerful force that influences business, government, and public opinion.

Acknowledgments

During the late 1970s I read William Kephart's book *Extraordinary Groups,* which examines the unconventional life-styles of a variety of subcultures such as the Old Order Amish, the Oneida Community, and Father Divine. Near the South Dakota State University campus at Brookings was a Hutterite community, a Mennonite group with many similarities to the Amish, whom I had studied. My subsequent interaction with the Hutterites as a research assistant further enlivened my interest in subcultures. During the dozen years since earning my doctorate, I have continued my interest in subcultures and countercultures, and in 1989 William Kephart asked me to join him as coauthor of the fourth edition of *Extraordinary Groups.* The relationship continued until his death in 1993.

At St. Martin's Press, I wish to thank Louise Waller, Lynnette Blevins, Nick Webb, and Alan Fischer for their help.

WILLIAM ZELLNER

CONTENTS

COUNTERCULTURES
A Sociological Analysis

CHAPTER ONE

SKINHEADS

In February 1988, during a segment of *Oprah Winfrey,* Winfrey's guests, a group of white supremacist skinheads, trashed the set and called her a "monkey." In response Winfrey said, "I have never felt such evil and hatred in my life."

Winfrey was more fortunate than talk-show host Geraldo Rivera. She suffered only the stings of name-calling. Rivera was hit by a chair when a fight broke out between Roy Innes, representing the Congress for Racial Equality, and a group of skinheads—invited guests on the same program. Rivera's nose was broken. Both Winfrey and Rivera, however, were more fortunate than many who have encountered skinheads.

In July 1988 a black female schoolteacher, attempting to cross a footbridge in a park in San Jose, California, was accosted by a band of a dozen or so teenagers with shaved heads. She was told that to cross the bridge she would have to pay a "nigger toll." Her skinhead assailants said that if she did not pay, she would be hung from a tree. After scaring the wits out of her, they allowed her to pass by.

A few months later in Portland, Oregon, a group of skinheads encountered an Asian American leaving a Chinese restaurant with his white wife. After taunting him with shouts of "Go back to Hong Kong!" the skinheads knocked him down and kicked him until he was unconscious. In the same city, in November 1988, members of the East Side White Pride skinheads group attacked a group of Ethiopians, killing one with a baseball bat.

In December 1988 a homeless black man, asleep in a bedroll on the balcony of a museum in Tampa, Florida, was discovered by two skinhead brothers, nineteen-year-old Scott and sixteen-year-old Dean McKee. The transient was brutally beaten, then stabbed through the heart. Scott McKee turned state's evidence and was sentenced to five years in prison. The younger brother, Dean, was convicted of first-degree murder and given a life sentence.

Skinheads do not confine their hatred to racial minorities. A common Saturday-night sport for them is gay-bashing. Also victimized are so-called anarchists and what skinheads define as long-haired, hippie types. Pleasure is taken in knocking a hippie to the ground, sitting on his chest, and cutting his hair off with a straight razor.

The incidents cited here are representative of a much larger number of hate-motivated attacks by skinheads. In recent years the number of racist skinheads in the United States has grown exponentially, from an estimated 300 in 1986 to about 5,000 today. Skinhead activity is no longer just a nuisance. Their hate crimes constitute a social problem. To counteract the problem, it is necessary to understand who the skinheads are, what they believe, and how they came to such beliefs.

Skinhead History

Beginnings in England   In the early 1950s, when England was still recovering from World War II, rebellious working-class youths began sporting Edwardian knee-length coats, tight pants, and very short hairstyles. Commonly known as *teddy boys* or *teds*, these young people seemed to want nothing more than a job, plenty of beer, sex, and rock-and-roll music.

By the early 1960s the *teddy boys* had split into two distinct groups, the *mods* and the *rockers*. The mods considered themselves elite, above the moral codes that shaped the lives of their parents. The rockers were content with leather jackets and loud bikes.

According to British writer Nick Knight, it was from the mod element that the skinheads emerged. Knight notes that "in establishing their own style, the younger brothers of the *mods* adopted certain elements of the *mod* style, combined them with items from traditional working clothes, borrowed some influences from the West Indian blacks and became Skinheads."[1] Clearly, the first wave of skinheads was not racist. Journalist Paul Mulshine notes that "the thing that set them apart from other kids, aside from their short hair, was their love for Jamaican reggae music. They were some of the first white people to take notice of reggae, and they helped make it an international success."[2]

To keep the bugs and dirt of the factory out of their hair, young, working-class Britishers shaved their heads. Moreover, it was a fashion statement. Journalist Sarah Wood writes that it "was simply a way for young workers to take pride in being working class."[3]

Short hair had another practical advantage: it couldn't be grabbed in a fight. Even before large numbers of skinheads adopted a racist ideology, the group was violent, always spoiling for a fight. Their preferred

---

[1]Nick Knight, *Skinhead* (London: Omnibus Press, 1982), p. 10.
[2]Paul Mulshine, "Head Games," *Philadelphia*, April 1989, p. 184.
[3]Sarah Wood, "These Skinheads Aren't Racists," *Sassy*, December 1991, p. 52.

method of attack was to knock their victims down, then gang-kick them with steel-toed work boots.

According to educator Patti McCall, the first skinheads "were kids with concrete and immediate values. They did not want to philosophize on how to save the poor; they merely wanted to avoid becoming poor and homeless themselves."[4]

In the late 1970s meaningful laboring jobs were scarce in Great Britain. During this period of economic unrest, skinheads turned right-wing and racist; many accepted the ideology of a newly formed political party, the National Front. Mulshine describes what happened:

> The National Front rose to notoriety in England by blaming the chronic unemployment there on immigrants from colonies such as India, Pakistan and Jamaica. The already belligerent, snarling Skinheads latched onto that, and suddenly a new term —"Paki-bashing"— entered the English vocabulary. The National Front developed links to far-right groups on the Continent. . . . Then the fascists got together with some radical leftists and formed a philosophy called the "Third Position." This view, embodied in the slogan "Hitler and Mao United in Struggle," calls for a racially pure and socialist Europe.[5]

Scapegoating Theory   Sociologist Richard Schaefer writes that "prejudiced people believe they are society's victims. . . . The term scapegoat comes from a biblical injunction (Leviticus 16:22), telling the Hebrews to send a goat into the wilderness to symbolically carry away the people's sins. Similarly, the theory of scapegoating suggests that an individual, rather than accepting guilt for some failure, will transfer the responsibility for failure to some vulnerable group."[6]

Schaefer goes on to say that the "downwardly mobile usually are more prejudiced. People who lose a job and are forced to accept a lower-status occupation experience increased tension and anxiety. Who is responsible, they ask, for their misfortune? At this time a scapegoat, in the form of a racial, ethnic, or religious group, may enter the picture."[7] Many out-of-work British toughs accepted the National Front ideology and willingly blamed immigrants, using them as scapegoats for their feelings of frustration and anger.

Skrewdriver   Ian Stuart, lead singer for the British rock band Skrewdriver and part-time organizer for the National Front, uses his "white

---

[4]Patti McCall, "Skins," unpublished manuscript, p. 2.
[5]Mulshine, "Head Games," p. 184.
[6]Richard Schaefer, *Racial and Ethnic Groups*, 4th ed. (New York: Scott, Foresman/Little Brown, 1990), p. 61.
[7]Ibid.

power" band to bond skinheads to the cause of racial purity. Unfortunately, Skrewdriver's hate music produces as much fervor at a skinhead gathering as "Rock of Ages" does at a tent revival. The racist periodical *WAR* states that "Music is one of the greatest propaganda tools around. You can influence more people with a song than you can with a speech."[8]

A number of skinhead rock groups, such as Storm Troop Five, have appeared on the American music scene in recent years. Most are second-rate imitators of Skrewdriver and have had little impact.

Beginnings in the United States   In the late 1970s skinheads began to appear on the American music scene, mostly in California. Observers viewed them as shaven-headed versions of the punk rockers. The first California skinheads were multiracial; anyone with the right haircut— black, Hispanic, Jewish—was considered an equal. It wasn't until the mid-1980s, with Skrewdriver albums appearing in record stores, that "white power" skinhead groups developed.

Jeff Coplon, writing for *Rolling Stone*, notes:

> The Nazi Skinhead ascendance first became evident in the summer of 1985, in the weathervane city of San Francisco. In two scant decades Haight-Ashbury had changed from a semi–skid-row to Peace and Love Central to a mellow model of gentrification, and now it was changing again. Swastikas were carved on patches of pink sidewalk. Buena Vista Park was expropriated and became known as Skinhead Hill. Packs of Skins swaggered down Haight Street, punching out longhairs and interracial couples.
>
> "That was a bitchin' summer" [a skinhead told Coplon]. "We'd get in fights with bunches of hippies and blacks and punks and anarchists. Kids were coming in from the suburbs, and other Skins from Los Angeles and Seattle, and everyone was hanging on Haight Street—it was like a big party. And any time anyone gave us any lip, we just bashed 'em, because this was our street."[9]

Argots   Skinheads arriving on Haight Street from different parts of the country had little difficulty recognizing each other. Argots are a special language peculiar to a group that sets them apart from other people. For example, young women associated with the skinhead movement are called skinbirds, and the shout "Skins' Night Out!" is a cry for skinheads to attack an enemy.

Much of the skinhead argot is embodied in a silent language. For example, a committed skinhead may sport tattoos over much of his

---

[8]Jeff Coplon, "Skinhead Reich," *Rolling Stone*, December 1988, p. 65.
[9]Ibid.

body. Some have the word "Skins" or a swastika tattooed on the insides of their lips. The German Eagle is a popular body marking.

The skinhead wardrobe adds to the desired feeling of separation of "us" from "them." The uniform consists of a nylon bomber jacket, jeans, skinny suspenders called braces, and steel-toed work boots. Not just any work boot will do. A real skin owns a good pair of Doc Martens. (The typical outfit for a skinbird is a shaved head in back with a little fringe of bangs, a bomber jacket, and Docs.)

Certain nuances of dress say much about a skinhead. For example, the color of the laces worn in the Doc Martens tell a story. Red laces stand for "white power"; white laces for "white pride" (a more moderate position); and yellow boot strings signal a hatred for cops—or indicate that the wearer has killed a cop. Watch out for skinheads wearing their braces low. It means they are spoiling for a fight.

Why They Join

Many young men become skinheads because they cannot find meaningful work. Much like the British teds, they are victims of a new kind of industrial revolution. The following observations are from *Dollars & Sense* magazine:

> Beginning in the 1970s, the economy began losing thousands of higher-wage manufacturing jobs as corporations closed plants and relocated production overseas to take advantage of low-wage labor in the third world. These economic shifts . . . have decimated the unionized manufacturing sector, especially durable goods industries such as autos and steel. This drop in well-paying manufacturing jobs chiefly affects young men without extensive education, who have traditionally moved into these jobs.[10]

With manufacturing jobs becoming difficult to find, young men have been looking to the rapidly expanding service industry for employment. Although such jobs are still dominated by women, many men now work at low-paying sales and service jobs. Coplon postulates that "Skinheads are casualties of a Burger King economy with no room at the top."[11]

Certainly not all unemployed young men join gangs. Some accept what they can get in the work world, and others seek to erase educational deficiencies. However, Eva Sears, a program associate at the Center for Democratic Renewal in Atlanta, Georgia, notes that

[10]"The Roots of Skinhead Violence: Dim Economic Prospects for Young Men," first printed in *Dollars & Sense* magazine, reprinted in *Utne Reader,* May/June 1989, p. 84.
[11]Coplon, "Skinhead Reich," p. 56.

Disaffected young whites often feel that the future has little to offer them. For many of these youth, the cynical, materialistic sentiment of the upper middle class ("He who dies with the most toys wins") not only is repugnant to their work ethic, but also is a goal likely to be beyond their economic reach. Many such youngsters see themselves as being forced to compete with nonwhites for the available minimum wage, service economy jobs that have replaced their parents' unionized industry opportunities.

For the first time in the history of most white families, there is no guarantee that life will be better for the younger generation.[12]

As used by sociologists, the term *alienation* refers to a sense of futility and insignificance. Alienated persons feel that those in power have neglected them and there is nothing they can do about it. They believe that they have little or no control over their own destiny, and that—in effect—they have become dispensable. Sears describes the effects of such alienation: "In many cases blue-collar youth have little respect for their teachers, schools, law enforcement agencies, or religious institutions, and often they become part of the Skinheads. Some middle-class youngsters join Skinhead organizations as an escapade and later find themselves drawn into white power ideology and criminal activity."[13]

Social scientists have not done extensive studies of the skinhead counterculture. Skinheads are not likely to respond to questionnaires; and there are obvious hazards associated with participant observation. In order to participate, the social scientist would have to become involved in antisocial activities. Refusal to participate could involve intolerable sanctions.

Based on a limited number of interviews, Coplon observed that skinheads "are as likely to be middle-class as working poor. But in other respects they are typical gang members. They tend to come from broken homes, and a high proportion were abused as children."[14]

The Anti-Defamation League of B'nai B'rith presents an interesting hypothesis:

anger at their plight has led them to identify with the most violent and offensive image they could imagine—Nazism, which most youngsters have seen on television, in the movies, [and] in comic books. . . . In addition, Skinhead gangs, like all street gangs and cults, provide their members with a substitute family composed of their peers. This is particularly true for those Skinheads who live communally, in rented apartments or houses, as many do. "We care about each other," said one Skinhead, "we're family." That sense of kinship is strengthened even further if the

---

[12]Eva Sears, "Skinheads: A New Generation of Hate-Mongers," *USA Today,* May 1989, p. 25.

[13]Ibid.

[14]Coplon, "Skinhead Reich," p. 56.

gang has been involved in violence together. Military sociologists have long known that soldiers who have fought together develop a deeper sense of solidarity.[15]

Where They Are

The Anti-Defamation League of B'nai B'rith estimates that there are about 3,000 skinhead activists in thirty-one states. The greatest concentration is on the West Coast, followed in order of strength by the South, Midwest, Mid-Atlantic, and New England. No section of the United States is completely free of skinheads.

Racist skinhead groups often take names associated with Nazi Germany, for example:

The National Socialist Skinheads of Houston, Texas
The National Socialist Youth Corps, Vancouver, Washington
National Socialist Skinheads, Naperville, Illinois
Nazi Skinheads of Indianapolis, Indiana
New Aryan Front, Rhode Island
Reich Skins, Spokane, Washington
SS of America, Charlotte, North Carolina
The Youth of Hitler, Milwaukie, Oregon; Vancouver, Washington
Blitzkreig, Harrisburg, Pennsylvania

Other names reflect a white supremacist ideology: East Side White Pride, Portland, Oregon; National White Resistance, Cincinnati, Columbus, Indianapolis, Metairie (Louisiana), Lawrence (New York); United White Youth, Racine (Wisconsin). Still other skins find a way to incorporate a violent theme in naming their groups: BASH, Birmingham, Baltimore; Confederate Hammer Skins, Dallas, Memphis; Romantic Violence, Chicago; SMASH, Baltimore. A few skinhead groups adopt vulgar names. All three of the following gangs are based in Orange County, California: Fuck Shit Up Skins, Crazy Fuckin Skins, Peni Skins.

Organizing Skinheads

Of great concern to those who monitor racist activities is the mobilization of skinheads as front-line troops for old-line racist organizations. Klanwatch, a project sponsored by the Southern Poverty Law Center in Montgomery, Alabama, reported in 1989 that skinheads, acting as soldiers for

[15]"Skinheads Target the Schools," (New York: Anti-Defamation League of B'nai B'rith, 1989), p. 29.

such groups as the Klan, were the most dangerous of the supremacist groups: "Not since the height of Klan activity during the civil rights era has there been a white supremacist group so obsessed with violence or so reckless in its disregard for the law."[16] During 1988, skinheads were linked to four racially motivated murders and two-thirds of all racial assaults.

In recent years skinheads have taken part in virtually every important hate-movement rally, march, and conference. The Klan, the Idaho-based Aryan Nations, and White Aryan Resistance have all forged links with the skinheads. Tom Metzger, founder of White Aryan Resistance (WAR), has been the most successful at recruiting skinhead troops.

Tom Metzger   From his TV repair shop in Fallbrook, California (about halfway between San Diego and Los Angeles), Tom Metzger runs WAR. For Metzger, radical right-wing activism dates back to the 1960s when he joined the John Birch Society. During the 1970s he was active in the anti-Semitic Christian Identity movement and California's Knights of the Ku Klux Klan. In 1980 he ran a David Duke–style campaign in the Democratic primary for Congress and won, only to be beaten badly in the general election.

Today he produces and hosts *Race and Reason,* a program seen on public-access television that reaches millions of cable subscribers in thirty-five cities. An advocate of the "third position," as he calls it, Metzger proposes to overthrow "ZOG," the "Zionist Occupational Government" of the United States. According to Coplon, there is little new in the third position:

> Metzger kept the old whine—the dog-eared myths that "race mixing" is cultural suicide, that Jews control the media, and that blacks are congenital parasites—but poured it into a shinier, sleeker bottle. Where the Old Right was aging, isolated, rural-based, and mindlessly patriotic, Metzger's New Right would be dynamic, hip, urban, and the champion of a white working class against a treasonous white ruling elite. It would not work politely within the system; it would demand a white separatist state. It would be a place where alienated skinheads could feel right at home.[17]

Skinheads show up at Metzger's meetings and act as his bodyguards. In return, they are given free anti-ZOG literature and the sense that they are part of something big.

On his television show, Metzger appears the soft-spoken intellectual, ready to divide the nation into black and white states without a blood-

---

[16]Peter Applebom, "New Report Warns of Alliance of Racist Groups," *New York Times,* February 6, 1989.
[17]Coplon, "Skinhead Reich," p. 58.

bath. All he claims to want is a good environment for future generations of whites. His newspaper (also called *WAR*) depicts a different Tom Metzger. In the tabloid, WAR members, skins, Klansmen, and other haters involved in violent racial incidents are canonized. The pages of *WAR* leave no doubt that Metzger is a dangerous hatemonger.

Metzger admits to having difficulty in organizing the somewhat nomadic, often capricious skinheads. But he does believe they are necessary to his WAR effort. It may be as Coplon speculates: "Metzger knows that the present generation of Nazi Skins will eventually grow out of the scene, into college and marriage and outward respectability. But he also sees their younger brothers—children as young as twelve years old—already picking up their razors and enlisting in the cause. And he's betting, too, that the older ones will remain on his side long after they've shed their boots and braces."[18]

John Metzger   Following closely in his father's footsteps, Metzger's eldest son, John, at the age of nineteen, assumed the presidency of the Aryan Youth Movement (AYM) following the resignation of Greg Withrow, founder of the organization's predecessor, the White Student Union (WSU). Soon after leaving AYM, Withrow renounced his racist attitudes. Some months later he was found in a nightclub parking lot, bleeding. A board had been tied across his shoulder blades and his palms had been nailed to the board. His assailants were identified as skinheads. Neither Metzger was ever tied to the incident.

His father's best recruiter, John Metzger heads the largest of the skinhead organizations (WAR Skins), numbering some 1,400. The younger Metzger has pulled together some of the largest California groups, and he has known ties with skinheads in Detroit, Cincinnati, Dallas, Tulsa, Oklahoma City, Portland, Toronto, and several cities in New Jersey. At any time he can summon support for AYM-WAR rallies.

John Metzger travels to high schools and colleges, recruiting members. *Scholastic Update* reports that "If you just look at him, you'd never know that he was a violent neo-Nazi. Clean-cut, with rosy cheeks and plenty of blond hair, John looks like an all-American boy. . . . But you don't have to listen to John speak long before he blows his cover." John told *Update*, "I'm the nicest guy you ever want to meet, but I have no trust in our ability to change things by voting. I'll probably end up out there one day with a machine gun, with a lot of others, blowing away the people who are problems."[19]

Like WAR, AYM has a newspaper. Coplon notes that it directly addresses skinheads and that "its pages are filled with the most primitive

[18]Ibid., p. 94.
[19]David O. Relin, "Harvesting Young People's Hate," *Scholastic Update*, April 7, 1989, p. 6.

comic strips—depictions of 'ritual murders' of Jews, of black children burned at a stake, of a communist teacher and a mixed-race class bombed to bits."[20] But the paper goes well beyond comic strips. Skinheads guilty of violent assaults on Jews, blacks, or gays are treated as heroes in the younger Metzger's press.

Antiracist Skinheads

As mentioned earlier in this chapter, the first skinhead gangs in the United States were multiracial. Some still are. They dress no differently than their Nazi counterparts, and in a sense they live in the worst of two worlds. Racist skinheads see them as weaklings and punish them just as they do members of minority groups. Because they look the same as racist skinheads, law enforcement officers keep close tabs on them.

In 1968 the first nonracist skinheads were organized in London. Skinheads Against Racial Prejudice (SHARP) is still the largest of the antiracist groups, with branches in many American cities.

Nonracist does not necessarily equate with nonviolent. Chicagoan Sarah Wood interviewed a group of antiracist skins and drew the conclusion that "verbal persuasion is simply an introduction to violence—they go through the motions of trying to talk it out with racists, knowing full well that it will probably end up in a fight."[21] Wood concluded:

> even if violence is not the only means used by the anti-Nazi Skinheads to fight injustice, it is still the most common. . . . It's the old "end justifies the means" argument that vigilante groups . . . use: Unpleasant methods are okay if they achieve a positive result. But I believe Skinheads are not the eradicators of racism they believe themselves to be. They are merely the defenders of victims of prejudice. Ultimately violence only begets more hatred. It does nothing to reeducate or change attitudes, which is the only way to end racism. [22]

Racist, nonracist, black, white, brown—it is fair to say that young people today are more violent than at any other time in this nation's history. Violence is often predicated on alienation, and alienation is often predicated on anomie. First used by theorist Emile Durkheim and now a part of the standard sociological vocabulary, *anomie* refers to a sense of powerlessness or worthlessness, leading eventually to a feeling of alienation. An anomic person feels left out of the mainstream of society;

[20]Coplon, "Skinhead Reich," p. 62.
[21]Wood, "These Skinheads Aren't Racists," p. 54.
[22]Ibid., p. 53.

because of this state of normlessness, his or her very survival comes into question. Even highly intelligent people can be affected by anomie.

Dave

The following interview with "Dave," a pseudonym, was conducted in the summer of 1992. At the time, Dave, age twenty-five, was a sophomore at a regional state university. He described himself as the product of a dysfunctional family. In defining *dysfunctional* he said, "that means there is someone there to blame." For his own reasons (as you will see), Dave was a member of SHARP from "the tail end of 1987 to September 1989." His vocabulary is a mix—street and country club. His intelligence is reflected in his schoolwork; he is a nearly straight "A" student.

Dave has an engaging personality and an intellectual curiosity, and he was cooperative with me. Nevertheless, I was uneasy throughout the conversation. I knew there was a handgun in his book bag.

Zellner: How did you become involved with SHARP?

Dave: It started at an underground music club in Florida. I was part of a heavy-metal combo that frequently played there. The club was closer to where we (the band and its followers) lived than any of the other places we played, so we decided to make it our base of operations for selling dope.

Unfortunately, Nazi skinheads were intent on keeping that from happening. They would come to the club and stir up trouble. The cops would show up and that wasn't good for business.

Zellner: Sounds like the Nazis were the good guys, and you were the bad guys.

Dave: We certainly weren't white knights in shining armor. The Nazis don't sell or do drugs. They're into booze. But drugs wasn't the reason why they were trying to shut the club down. They hated the "anarchist peace punks" that hung out there.

Zellner: Your joining SHARP had nothing to do with combating racial prejudice, did it?

Dave: Not a thing. You got to understand where we were coming from. The band was small but we always had an entourage of from twenty-five to thirty "heavy-metal punks" at any given time. There were a couple of Hispanic followers, a couple of Orientals, and a few blacks, but most were white, rural, southern—and probably, to some extent, racists themselves. Our group had no expressed racial ideology, nor had we ever had any concern for bettering society. We wanted a safe marketplace for our drugs. Ours was not a humanitarian organization.

Zellner: What kind of music did you play? Any of Skrewdriver's music?

Dave: None of Skrewdriver's music. I was the drummer. Musicians come and go, but we always had a standard guitar and a bass guitar. One of the songs in our repertoire was a piece called "White World." The lyrics were about white noise or static. When the Nazi skins heard the song announced the first time, they thought it was a white-power song. They cheered before they heard the words.

Zellner: Did you and the band's groupies join SHARP simply to outnumber the Nazis in a fight?

Dave: It wasn't quite like that either. SHARP was there, but they weren't interested in fighting. Most of them were young— sixteen to nineteen years old—and most of them were scared of the Nazis. The owners of the bar were scared of them too, but they did nothing to keep them from busting up their club. We asked management for a shot at solving the problem, and they said go ahead if you think you can. We really didn't join SHARP; we more or less took the Sharpies over.

Zellner: Were you selling drugs to the Sharpies?

Dave: No. Most of the Sharpies were also members of "Straight Arrow"—no drugs, no alcohol, no immoral sex. The Sharpies were mostly into the music scene. The club was divided into two parts—an adult section and an underage section. Most of the Sharpies couldn't even buy alcohol, and we didn't sell our drugs on the other side of the wire mesh.

Zellner: What kinds of drugs were you selling—crack, marijuana?

Dave: Believe it or not—mushrooms. There is a mushroom that grows wild in Florida that will really lay a psychedelic high on you.

Zellner: You've got this big tattoo of the Grim Reaper on your right arm and around it, "Death Is Certain—Life Is Not." What's the significance?

Dave: Nothing really—a hangover from my biker days.

Zellner: What about the cross earring?

Dave: Nothing, except it pisses Christians off to see a guy like me wearing it.

Zellner: You have hair now—did you back then?

Dave: No.

Zellner: How could one tell you from a Nazi skin?

Dave: The first time I went to the club, three skinheads came up to me and asked me if I was a Nazi. Usually it is just as blatant and up front as that. "Are you a Nazi?" If there are three of them and one of you, you had better be a Nazi.

Zellner: What do you know about Tom Metzger and his "White Aryan Resistance"?

Dave: In the spring of '88, I went to one of his meetings. We had a sort of homemade, skinhead magazine, and we read that he was having a meeting near San Diego. I joined with other protesters and stopped cars going to the rally site. There were more of us than there were of them, and we pretty much shut down the rally.

Zellner: Did you rely on your Doc Martens to stop them?

Dave: No, we had some pretty sophisticated weaponry. Assault rifles—stuff like that. Incidentally, there is a really neat store in Fort Walton Beach that used to carry nothing but fully automatic weapons. When Florida passed a gun law, they converted it to a semiautomatic weapons store. Florida law permits fairly sophisticated hardware, so long as people can see it.

Zellner: In other words, if I could find some way to strap a bazooka from my shoulder to my ankle and then find some way to bend my knee, that would be legal?

Dave: That's the Florida law. I swear to God, I have been in bars where you had to check your guns at the door. They're big on concealment—not much else.

Zellner: Did the band have much control over its fans?

Dave: We always had reasonably intelligent band members. Most had training beyond high school. One of the guys had completed a two-year vo-tech program in drafting. Another had been to GIT—the Guitar Institute of Technology.

Zellner: (Laughing) Hell, I didn't know there was a GIT.

Dave: And a PIT and BIT, too. PIT is the Percussion Institute of Technology and BIT is the Bass Institute of Technology.

Zellner: Where are they?

Dave: There are two schools and each has all three, BIT, PIT, and GIT. One is in Atlanta; the other in Hollywood.

Zellner: Getting back to the original question, did the band pretty much control the groupies?

Dave: In a word—no! I had a lot to say about what the group did. The other band members didn't. Let me tell you a story about what some of the guys did.

Zellner: What story is that?

Dave: How we got rid of the Nazi skins. We started by keeping them out of the bar altogether. There were a few fights outside of the club; guns were shown and a lot of threats were made. But the Nazis wouldn't fight and we knew it. If they don't have you outnumbered by quite a bit, they don't want a fight. And we made sure we always had superiority of numbers. You know, Metzger really doesn't know the skins, or he wouldn't want them for his soldiers.

Zellner: Why is that?

Dave: They're not going to fight you if there are two of them and only one of you. One of them might get hurt. They're cowards. The band had a lot of psychotic, long-haired followers who were pulling guns and making threats. The Nazis didn't want to fight, so they quit showing up.

Zellner: That was the end of your trouble with the Nazis?

Dave: Pretty much the end of our trouble but the beginning of theirs.

Zellner: How so?

Dave: The young kids had a clubhouse, separate from the bar where we played. All the peace punks and Greenpeacers went there after the bar closed. The kids that used it ranged in age from about twelve to twenty. They were hippie types and not into fighting. One kid's father was a realtor and he gave it to the long-hairs to use as a safe house. The place could have been condemned, it was so run down.

Zellner: What time did the bar close—some of those kids were really young?

Dave: Two in the morning. One morning a group of young punks went to the safe house, about eight of them. And three carloads of skin-heads showed up with baseball bats and trashed the place. They beat up everyone in sight, even the little kids.

Zellner: You got even?

Dave: Our guys met the next day and mapped out a strategy we called "Justified Terrorism." We wanted to be sure that the Nazis would never try anything like that again—or somebody was really going to get fucked up.

Zellner: What was considered justified terrorism?

Dave: We did a couple of drive-bys on the skins' safe house and put a couple of bullets into it. We put Molotovs under their cars. And we did a lot of psych stuff.

Zellner: Explain psych stuff.

Dave: A lot of the punks went to school with the Nazis so we had them find out where they lived. Then we called their parents and told them that their kids were part of the Nazis involved in beating up the punks. It was in all the newspapers.

            If the parents showed no interest in what their kids were doing, we followed them around until we found out where they [the parents] worked. Then we called their bosses. On occasions, when our calls were met with indifference we would threaten to blow the business up. All we insisted on was that they fire the person we were calling about.

Zellner: How long did this terrorism last?

Dave: A month to six weeks, but there was a crowning coup—a real jewel.

            The skinhead leader worked at a Kettle restaurant as a dishwasher.

Zellner: Some leadership qualification.

Dave: We caught him one night after his shift and forced him into a van. We beat him until he was nearly unconscious and took him to where the band rehearsed—a mini-storage building in a really rural area.

            For the first few hours we kept him in submission. We had a guy standing over him, and every time he moved his arms, the guy would kick him. After that we stripped him and padlocked a logging chain around his neck. Then we padlocked the chain to a

Zellner: tree. We kept him chained to the tree for three days. We sat out there and flipped cigarettes at him, shot him with a BB gun, and shit like that.

Zellner: What kept him alive?

Dave: We didn't deprive him of food or water. We gave him a fresh canteen every day and each day we stopped at a convenience store that sold hot dogs, three for 99 cents, and we fed them to him.

On the last night, we beat him up again and put him back in the van, naked. Then we took him to a city park and chained him to a bench. We never had a problem with the Nazis again.

Zellner: You didn't get caught?

Dave: No.

Zellner: Do you have any felony convictions?

Dave: No.

Zellner: Lucky?

Dave: No, careful. I've never even been convicted of a misdemeanor. In fact, I've never had as much as a parking ticket.

Zellner: Why did you leave the group?

Dave: As I said, I'm careful. I was afraid that some of the groupies were about to get involved in things that could result in heavy-duty jail time. I felt that I had to get out when I did.

Zellner: Do you ever miss the life?

Dave: Sure I do—the camaraderie. We all had so much on each other that we couldn't roll over on the next guy. Your criminal past almost makes you brothers. We were different from the skinheads.

Zellner: What do you mean?

Dave: The skins are the first to roll over. Tell everything they know. And they won't fight. That's what I meant when I said that Metzger doesn't really want them.

Zellner: You once told me that you are a violent person. Are you done with that? Did that end when you left Florida?

Dave: I think that in the way that I think about political ideology, I am a revolutionary. I think that sometimes violence is the easiest way to get your point across. As for political heroes—I often think of Malcolm X.

Zellner: He softened his position on violent activity before his death.

Dave: Yeah! I agree with that to a point. Use the system if you can, but you know. I don't go anywhere without a gun. I live in the country, and I don't even go out to my mailbox without a gun. If I take my trash out, I take my gun with me.

Zellner: Don't you feel safe?

Dave: No, I don't feel safe at all. Not in any aspect. I don't feel safe at all.

Zellner: You don't even feel comfortable here at school?

Dave: I feel comfortable everywhere. I don't feel safe anywhere. If I don't have my gun with me I feel uncomfortable. Even in class, I peer out into the hall and see what is going on out there. I don't know what that comes from. Some paranoia maybe.

Zellner: Were you that way before you became a gang member? Or did it come from being part of a gang?

Dave: You had to watch where you stood in your house; we were always afraid of drive-by shootings. But we really didn't have any enemies.

Zellner: You still miss being part of that scene?

Dave: I still miss it.

Solutions to the Problem

There is nothing new about young people dressing and adopting behaviors that offend the adult community. The skinhead counterculture offers a support network for teens rebelling against parental control and the accepted mores (strong norms) of the community. Unfortunately, disenchanted youth often blindly follow the "isms" of charismatic adults such as the Metzgers. For example, skinhead novitiates with no sense of history often do not understand Nazism, the racial epithets associated with the dogma, and the symbolic meanings attached to the swastika, the yellow Star of David, and other odious artifacts of the movement. On a number of occasions, young skinheads arrested for defacing synagogues have claimed no racial prejudice whatsoever.

Law Enforcement and the Courts   Most sociologists seek to understand social disruption in terms of structural failures—for example, breakdowns in the economy, family, and agents of social control such as the church. However, sociologists do not excuse the actions of deviants. When gang members violate the law, law enforcement officers and the courts have a duty to uphold the law.

An important step that police departments must take to curb gang activity is a return to neighborhood policing. Well-trained police officers walking a beat learn their neighborhoods and are often able to prevent trouble. There is considerable merit in the old saying, "an ounce of prevention is worth a pound of cure."

Only in recent years have police departments recognized or admitted to having "gang" problems in their communities. Greater emphasis, energy, time, and money are now being directed toward controlling gangs. Some police departments have set up separate units specializing in bias-motivated crimes. At the federal level, during January 1992 the Federal Bureau of Investigation (FBI) reassigned three hundred former spy-chasers to cities across the nation to monitor gang activities and work with local law enforcement agencies.

By the early 1990s, forty-seven states and the District of Columbia had passed hate-crime legislation. The statutes vary from state to state, but most prohibit paramilitary training and religious desecration, along with mandating stiffer penalties for hate-motivated crimes.* Klanwatch reports that "the overall effectiveness of such legislation in deterring hate crime is still undetermined."[23] Nevertheless, the same report cites a number of cases in which laws have proven effective. The following is an example:

> In Santa Ana, Calif., on Jan. 13, 1989, three Skinheads were given the maximum prison sentences (4 to 7 years) for state civil rights violations in the beating of a man they believed to be gay. The Skinheads were convicted under a state law that makes it a crime to assault someone "because of their sexual orientation," and increases the criminal penalties for acts of violence motivated by the victims' race, color, religion, ancestry, national origin or sexual orientation.[24]

In 1993 the Supreme Court reviewed lower court rulings that "struck down a Wisconsin hate crime law in 1992. . . . The case involved a sentence that was doubled in connection with an assault conviction. Todd Mitchell was sentenced to four years in prison instead of two for the 1989 racially motivated beating of a fourteen-year-old white youth in Kenosha, Wisconsin."[25]

The Supreme Court unanimously upheld the double sentence. Chief Justice William H. Rehnquist, writing for the Court, said that bias-motivated crimes are "thought to inflict greater individual and societal harm. . . . The state's desire to redress these perceived harms provides an adequate explanation for its penalty-enhancement provision over and above mere disagreement with offenders' beliefs or biases."[26]

Many skinheads are in jail, and others on the outside belong there. Unfortunately, however, the penal system is notorious for allowing gang activity to continue behind bars. Little effort is put forth to change the aberrant racial attitudes of prisoners. Emphasis in prison is on control, not education. Many former inmates leave the penal system more hardened racists than when they entered.

Civil Law Suits   In recent years the activities of the largest and most organized hate groups have to some extent been curbed by civil litiga-

---

* The three states that do not have such legislation are Alaska, Nebraska, and Wyoming. See *Intelligence Report: Special Year-End Edition, 1992,* (Montgomery, AL: Southern Poverty Law Center, March 1993), p. 9.

[23]"Hate Violence and White Supremacy," (Montgomery, AL: The Klanwatch Project of the Southern Poverty Law Center, December 12, 1988), p. 18.

[24]Ibid., p. 19.

[25]"Hate Crime Legislation under Attack," in *Intelligence Report: Special Year-End Edition, 1992,* (Montgomery, AL: Southern Poverty Law Center, March 1993), p. 9.

[26]"High Court Upholds 'Hate' Sentencing," *Oklahoman & Times,* June 12, 1993, p. 1.

tion. The most effective litigator has been attorney Morris Dees, executive director of the Southern Poverty Law Center. In the opening paragraphs of this chapter, it was noted that a young Ethiopian student, Mulugeta Seraw, was killed with a baseball bat, beaten by skinheads.

Filing suit on behalf of the Seraw family, Dees proved that "publications supplied by the Metzgers served as teaching tools in training Skinheads. One issue reportedly included a story with the headline, 'Clash and Bash,' which described hunting parties where white youths seek out nonwhites and break their bones."[27]

A Special Report issued by the Southern Poverty Law Center states that "On October 22, 1990, after two weeks of testimony, the jurors reached their decision. They ordered Tom Metzger to pay $5 million to the Seraw family, John Metzger to pay $1 million, the White Aryan Resistance to pay $3 million and the two Skinhead defendants, Kyle Brewster and Ken Mieske, to pay $500,000 each. In addition, the jury awarded $2,475,000 in compensatory damages."[28]

Neither the White Aryan Resistance nor any of the individuals charged with damages can pay. Nevertheless, despite the fact that the Metzgers are still operating their hate machine, it is at a slower pace. The judgment insures that the defendants will not accumulate enough assets to increase the scope of their operation.

Education   In part, the solution to hate gang–related problems is education. Sears argues that "educators must admit that simply placing children of different races or cultures in the same classrooms automatically does not abrogate prejudice."[29] Children must be taught early on that tolerance and harmony are in the best interest of all groups.

Sears further states that every segment of society, not just the schools, has a part to play in combating prejudice, discrimination, and violence:

> To protect young people from victimization, it is essential that parents teach their children the true meaning of democratic ideals. . . . Clergy and the community of faith will teach and preach against hatred and bigotry . . . when congregations demand it. Civic leaders and elected officials must articulate clear opposition to any hint of exclusionary, discriminatory behavior; law enforcement must be sensitive to hate crime; and the business community must combat institutional racism.
>
>   . . . Most important, young people themselves must choose whether to allow a new Hitler state to be built on their backs, or make sure that their

---

[27]"Metzgers Seeking Reversal of $12.5 Million Judgment," in *Intelligence Report: Special Year-End Edition, 1992*, (Montgomery, AL: Southern Poverty Law Center, March 1993), p. 8.

[28]"Murder in Portland," in *The Ku Klux Klan: A History of Racism and Violence*, 4th ed., (Montgomery, AL: Southern Poverty Law Center, 1991), p. 51.

[29]Sears, "Skinheads: A New Generation of Hate-Mongers," p. 26.

world has people who show respect for each other's differences. Youth can be challenged and taught in school settings, church or temple organizations, civic or ethnic clubs, or within the counterculture music "scene."[30]

But is education and a more concerned criminal justice system enough? Scapegoating is to a great extent based on the faulty perception that unqualified minority groups are acquiring jobs at the expense of qualified members of the majority. Full employment would do much to relieve racial tensions.

Spending the Peace Dividend   Since World War II, much of the nation's energies and resources have been devoted to developing a military power sufficient to destroy, many times over, the so-called "evil empire." To that end, the United States spent its enemies into submission. In an effort to keep pace with our military preparedness, developing nations such as the Soviet Union (and they were that), spent themselves into bankruptcy. Our sluggish economy in the years since the fall of the Berlin Wall is in part due to government's failure to redirect money spent on the Cold War toward peacetime initiatives.

For the past fifty years we have paid government contractors to produce "military junk": tanks, planes, bombs, warships, chemical and biological weapons, stores of ammunition—an endless list of nonutile goods. At the time of manufacture, it was known that these items would be of no value to humankind other than, perhaps, to provide peace of mind to a frightened public and line the pockets of politicians and the manufacturing elite. During these years, millions of American men and women were trained in the use of this hardware; were paid, housed, and fed at taxpayers' expense. None of their work was productive in the sense that we can now point to it with pride and say, "That was good for humanity."

With the Cold War at an end, the perceived need for military expenditures has ebbed. Taxpayers and politicians alike no longer see the necessity for turning over large sums of money to such "super defense contractors" as McDonnell Douglas, Texas Instruments, and Teledyne in exchange for military hardware. Nevertheless, not paying for what we do not need is having a profoundly negative effect on the economy. Skilled and unskilled nonproductive workers have been laid off, and more cuts in the nonproductive work force are anticipated in the near future.

With a reduction in military personnel, another large group of nonproductives has returned to an overcrowded, private-sector work force (as it is presently structured). Most of these people are still young and have

---

[30]Ibid.

some technological skills. Their return to civilian life will force a large number of young, marginal workers out of the work force. A poor economy has traditionally led to increases in hate-group activity. The Ku Klux Klan, for example, thrives during periods of economic recession and depression.

Do marginal workers have a right to a job, too? Most are marginal, not because they are lazy but because they do not have the skills to compete in a highly technocratic, service-oriented society. And many cannot obtain, for one reason or another, the necessary skills. Should we doom these people to poverty because they lack the tools to survive without help?

Perhaps what is needed is a new kind of army, a peacetime, productive army subsidized by the government. Furthermore, government contractors must retool for peace. If we can afford a nonproductive army, we can certainly afford an army that will improve the nation. What the private sector cannot provide, the public sector must. Especially needed is work for the marginally employable—back and muscle work. Let the new army fix highways, repair bridges, keep our cities clean, in return for a decent wage. Both the worker and society will benefit.

CHAPTER TWO
KU KLUX KLAN

Incredible as it may seem, the Ku Klux Klan started as a joke. Six young Confederate veterans, out of work and with few prospects, met on Christmas Eve 1865 in Pulaski, Tennessee, and decided to form a club. Their intent was to add a bit of levity to their dreary, postwar life.

Their first act was to name the club. Journalist Fred Cook described the process: "One suggested 'Kuklio,' from the Greek word meaning band or circle. Since all were of Scotch-Irish descent, another suggested adding the word 'Klan.' Ideas were tossed back and forth; and as their thoughts were running to Ks, someone suggested 'Ku.' Putting it all together, the group came up with the name . . . Ku Klux Klan."[1]*

In keeping with their intent to amuse and entertain, the veterans decided to masquerade as ghosts, covering their heads with pillowcases and their bodies with bedsheets. While they were at it, they draped sheets over their horses. The first "night-ride" of the Ku Klux Klan was nothing more than a lark. The veterans played pranks on their parents and serenaded their girlfriends.

No one could have guessed that from such simple beginnings, four chronologically separate and organizationally different Klan movements would emerge as national plagues: the Reconstruction Klan, the Patriotic Klan, the Anti–Civil Rights Klan, and, as it exists today, the Kareful Klan.

The Reconstruction Klan

It was Abraham Lincoln's intent to end the Civil War with General Robert E. Lee's surrender at Appomattox. With the preservation of the

---

[1]Fred Cook, *The Ku Klux Klan: America's Recurring Nightmare* (Englewood Cliffs, NJ: Julian Messner, 1989), p. 10.

*The Klan argot emphasizes the letter K. A klavern is a local Klan den; a klonclave is a secret Klan meeting; a klavalkade is a parade. Other colorful terms, apart from "K" words, include the following: Invisible Empire, the universal jurisdiction of the Klan; Realm, a subdivision of the Invisible Empire (usually a state); Province, a subdivision of a Realm (usually a county or region); Imperial Wizard, chief officer of the Invisible Empire; Grand Dragon, chief officer of a Realm; Great Titan, chief officer of a Province; Exalted Cyclops, chief officer of a klavern.

Union assured, Lincoln willingly accepted promises of loyalty offered by Southern political and military leaders. It was his expectation that these men would lead the South to full peacetime recovery.

Congress, however, being dominated by radical Republicans, was unwilling to treat established Southern leaders as equals. Nevertheless, Lincoln's popularity was such that he was able to control those members of congress who disagreed with him. His assassination shortly after the war changed the course of recovery in the South.

Andrew Johnson, Lincoln's successor, himself a Southerner from Tennessee, shared Lincoln's views on reconstruction; but lacking Lincoln's popularity, he was unable to control Congress. During May 1865, with Congress adjourned, he issued a proclamation of amnesty, that allowed Southern states to adopt new constitutions and elect governments. In response, Congress passed the first radical "Reconstruction Act," which in effect disenfranchised white Southern leaders.

Scalawags and Carpetbaggers   The Reconstruction Act barred the old white leadership from voting and practicing law. Many even had difficulty defending themselves in court. A new coalition was in charge in the South: unscrupulous Southerners called scalawags, and carpetbaggers from the North.*

Carpetbaggers and scalawags recruited followers from the Negro population and armed them. To the chagrin of Southerners, their former slaves were seen parading up and down the streets with guns on their shoulders. Former slaves were put in charge of local administrative offices, but for the most part they were abysmal failures. Prior to the Civil War, it had been against the law to educate a Negro—and thus few blacks could read or write.

With the Reconstruction Act, the South was turned upside down.

Alienation   Alienation is the experience of powerlessness in social life—a feeling that life is out of control. It is little wonder that the white Southerner felt alienated after the war. His enemies (carpetbaggers), in collusion with Southern traitors (scalawags) with their armies of former slaves, controlled every aspect of life in the South.

Legitimacy   Political sociologist Seymour Martin Lipset defines *legitimacy* as the capacity of a society "to engender and maintain the belief that existing political institutions are the most appropriate for the soci-

---

*A scalawag is an animal that is unfit, small, and unworthy, usually because it hasn't been fed properly. Northern profiteers were called carpetbaggers because it was said they could put all they owned into small carpet valises, which were commonly used as traveling bags during this era.

ety."[2] Citizens may disagree with some aspects of their political institutions, or with political leaders. For a government to be legitimate, however, most citizens must share a basic belief in the norms that specify how power is to be exercised.

Most white Southerners during Reconstruction did not consider the government imposed on them legitimate. There is an old saying that "you can't sit on bayonets." In other words, without the consent of the governed, the use of force will always be necessary. But government by coercion cannot last forever. Ultimately it will lead to chaos rather than to a society that functions smoothly.

Hatred for the government in Washington grew in the South during Reconstruction. A second civil war was out of the question. Federal troops were stationed in every part of the South. To combat what they saw as illegitimate government, white Southerners resorted to guerrilla strategies. It fell to Klan organizations patterned after the Pulaski "night-riders" to carry out this warfare. The Pulaski veterans had stumbled across a unique method for controlling African-American populations, which most southern whites considered a threat.

Psychological Control   During the early 1800s there were several significant slave revolts. The most notable of these insurrections were led by Gabriel,* Denmark Vesey, and Nat Turner. The rebellions led by Gabriel and Vesey were thwarted before white blood was shed. Turner's insurrection of 1831 in Virginia, however, began with the slaying of his master and his master's family. The revolt gained momentum, and before it was over some sixty slaves were involved in killing whites within a twenty-mile radius of the first murders.

Southern planters lived in fear of such revolts. They studied the insurrections and determined that Gabriel, Vesey, and Turner had three characteristics in common: they were extremely intelligent, had been privy to some education, and were religious. Thereafter, policy was established to control slaves by eliminating educational opportunities and controlling religious beliefs.

Psychological control was exacted by playing down Christianity and playing up superstitious beliefs: fear of ghosts, witchcraft, and the unknown, which were prevalent in the African cultures from which most of the slaves descended. Gladys-Marie Fry noted:

> Fear of the supernatural in particular was a vague, indefinite kind of fear which kept slaves so constantly occupied with thoughts of impending disaster and misfortune that ideas about insurrection were stifled before

---

[2]Seymour Martin Lipset, *Political Man* (Baltimore: Johns Hopkins University, 1981), p. 64.

*Gabriel's owner was named Prosser. Historians state, however, that Gabriel rejected Prosser as a surname.

they were born. Psychologists tell us that this kind of all-pervading fear becomes an important mechanism of social control, paralyzing actions and even undermining personal safety and well-being. Under such circumstances, everybody and everything become possible threats.[3]

Laws of assembly were enacted by southern legislatures to keep Negroes from meeting and conspiring against their masters. Mounted patrols, called *paterollers*, were formed to observe and intimidate the African-Americans. Ghostly tricks were played on the fearful slaves, who were led to believe that the only safe place for them at night was in their huts.

This type of psychological control was so effective that slave owners used it to control even minor indiscretions such as stealing foodstuffs. Fry's interview with an informant is revealing: "Dey used to skeer us out 'bout red 'taters. Dey was fine 'taters, red on de outside and pretty and white on de inside, but white folks called 'em 'nigger-killers.' Dat was one of der tricks to keep us from stealin' dem 'taters. Der warn't nothin' wrong wid dem 'taters; dey was jus' as good and healthy as any other 'taters."[4]

The Invisible Empire

The Pulaski pranksters soon noticed that their ghostly night-rides were having a strange effect on the black population. African-Americans, emancipated from the yoke of slavery, had not been freed from a mindset that would enslave them for years to come. On seeing the ghostly apparitions, credulous blacks spread wild stories about ghostly visitations. According to Cook, "white figures were reported sailing in the skies on white-clad horses above the roofs of towns. Their leader was always a superhumanly terrible figure—'ten feet high, his horse fifteen.' He carried 'a lance and a shield.' Could anyone escape his vengeance? Not a chance. These sky-riding spirits would pursue an enemy wherever he went, and he would be snatched away never to be seen again."[5]

The Klan was quick to capitalize on what seemed an opportunity to undermine the carpetbagger-scalawag government. Political rallies were disrupted. Frightened blacks were told not to attend such meetings, vote, or participate in the Reconstruction government. If they did—they were told—they would suffer retribution from the spirit world. Once again, African-Americans were hiding behind closed doors at night.

[3]Gladys-Marie Fry, *Night Riders in Black Folk History*, (Knoxville: The University of Tennessee Press, 1975), p. 46.
[4]Ibid., p. 50.
[5]Cook, *Ku Klux Klan: America's Recurring Nightmare*, p. 13.

Klansmen used trickery to prey on the fears of the gullible African-Americans. For example, they would ride to a black's hut pretending to be the ghosts of Confederate soldiers killed in battle and ask for water. They would claim not to have had a drink since leaving hell. The Klansmen would then appear to drink buckets full of water. Concealed under their robes were rubber bags to catch the water.

Another common trick involved offering the victim a detachable hand carved from wood. When the fake hand came off in the black's hand, he was expected to shriek and run for cover. Blacks who did not show fright were often beaten and some were killed.

There is no doubt that a great many former slaves were intimidated by the ghostly night-riders and yielded to their demands because they feared the supernatural. But how many feigned fright because the alternatives were worse? This question can never be answered. There is no doubt, however, that the night-riders were effective.

In 1869 Imperial Wizard Nathan Bedford Forrest, a former general in the Confederate Army, officially disbanded the Invisible Empire. By 1871 changing conditions, including the assurance of white supremacy and martial law, combined to virtually halt all renegade Klan activity.

Considering all the attention given later Klan organizations, there is no doubt that more crimes were committed by the Reconstruction Klan than by all later Klan organizations combined. Historian David Chalmers reminds us that "Klansmen were occasionally hurt, but the death toll of Negroes and Republicans probably ran close to a thousand."[6]

The Patriotic Klan

Stimulated by Thomas Dixon's romantic novel *The Klansman,* (1905) and D. W. Griffith's motion picture *The Birth of a Nation* (1915), a new Klan emerged in the first part of the twentieth century. Its selling point was the protection of traditional American values. Chalmers writes that "the changing world of the 1920s, which saw post–World War I restlessness and new waves of immigration combined with the Prohibition-accented erosion of both the small town and fundamentalist morality, brought the Klan millions of recruits. The Invisible Empire was soon a factor to be considered in the communal and political life of the nation from Maine to California."[7]

Fueled by a variety of new anxieties—black Americans were effectively under control during this period—such as fear of immigrants,

---

[6]David M. Chalmers, *Hooded Americanism: The History of the Ku Klux Klan* (Chicago: Quadrangle, 1968), p. 2.
[7]Ibid., pp. 2–3.

Catholics, communists, Jews, and unions, white Protestants joined the Klan in record numbers. In Texas 75,000 robed and hooded Klansmen turned out on "Klan Day" at the state fair. In Oklahoma a governor was impeached after imposition of martial law following hundreds of violent Klan incidents. In Arkansas Klan primaries were held prior to Democratic Party primaries to determine which Klansmen would be supported by their hooded brothers.[8]

Every county in New Jersey was organized. Colorado elected two Klan-supported senators. One Klan stronghold, Indiana, under the leadership of the notorious D. C. Stephenson, elected a U.S. senator and the governor and won a majority of seats in the state legislature. Fear generated by a drift away from the small-town, Anglo-Saxon culture that most Americans had grown up in generated a variety of frenetic behaviors. For example, Chalmers reports that "one small town [in Indiana] went down to lynch the Pope when the rumor got abroad that he was coming on the train from Chicago."[9]

Klan successes in the 1920s were not mirrored in the 1930s. Indeed, Klan leaders

> were out for money and ruled irrationally and dictatorially in its pursuit. The fight over the spoils wrecked the organization in nearly every state and practically every community. . . . Klan terror went too far, the extremists ranted too loudly and the leaders were too immoral. The affluent and civic-minded came to realize what a divisive force it actually was in a community. When a young woman whom the Klan's most dynamic northern leader, Indiana's D. C. Stephenson, had kidnapped and assaulted gave a full deathbed testimony, it cost the Klan thousands of members.[10]

By the time of the Great Depression in the 1930s, Klan membership had dwindled to about one hundred thousand nationally, approximately the same number as was on the rolls in sparsely populated Oklahoma in the 1920s. Except for a few feckless remnants, the Klan disappeared in the northern states and became again a southern phenomenon. By the mid-1930s, Klan organizers were emphasizing un-American activities, stressing a need to fight communism and organized labor. For many Klansmen, unions and communism were the same things. Despite publicity, or perhaps because of publicity associated with cross-burnings and floggings, Klan recruitment efforts did poorly; and by the end of World War II the organization was nearly dead.

In 1949 Klan leader Dr. Samuel Green, an Atlanta obstetrician, died. No leader emerged strong enough to control the Klan, and it broke into a

---

[8]Ibid.
[9]Ibid., p. 3.
[10]Ibid., p. 4.

variety of factions. Uncontrolled, many Klansmen committed acts of mindless violence and ended up in jail. Pressed to curb the activities of the Klan, many states enacted antimask laws and instituted grand jury investigations even though such juries were reluctant to return indictments against the Klan. Nevertheless, in the years that followed, the Klan and its sympathizers were unable to stem the growth of a new racial tolerance in the South.

Anti–Civil Rights Klan

A Klan resurgence occurred in the South when civil rights workers attempted to force southern communities to comply with the Civil Rights Act of 1964. There were numerous instances of bombings, floggings, and shootings attributed to Klansmen.

Some of the most heinous Klan crimes were semi-official in nature. For example, in Philadelphia, Mississippi, in 1964 three civil rights workers in their early twenties—James Chaney, Andrew Goodman, and Michael Schwerner (Chaney was black, Schwerner and Goodman white)— were arrested on false charges and confined in Philadelphia's jail until nightfall. After their release, members of the White Knights of the Ku Klux Klan, along with a deputy sheriff, stopped their car on a country road. The three were murdered and their bodies buried under a dam that was being constructed in the area. The case received national media attention, but it was only one of hundreds of semi-official acts aimed at terrorizing civil rights workers.

Although most semi-official acts against civil rights workers were carried out by local officials, there is evidence of complicity by high-ranking federal officials. Editors of a handbook prepared for use in secondary schools point out the following:

> evidence indicates that the F.B.I. director, J. Edgar Hoover, knew in advance that the Birmingham police and the Klan were plotting to ambush Freedom Riders arriving at the Birmingham bus terminal in May 1961. Hoover was informed that the police had promised the Klan 15 to 20 minutes to beat the riders and that police commissioner "Bull" Connor wanted the riders beaten until "it looked like a bulldog got hold of them." Not only did the Bureau take no action to prevent the attack, but an F.B.I. informer, armed with a lead-weighted baseball bat, was a leader in the Klan's vicious beating of the Freedom Riders. In addition to his possible implication in the 1963 church bombing in Birmingham,* this same in-

*One of the most despicable Klan crimes committed during the civil rights era involved the bombing of a church in Birmingham, Alabama, in 1963. Four choir girls, ranging in age from eleven to fourteen, were killed in an explosion shortly after Sunday school ended. Three of the four girls were children of schoolteachers.

former was one of four Klansmen in the car from which a bullet was fired, killing Mrs. Viola Liuzzo, a white civil-rights worker from Detroit, as she was driving between Selma and Montgomery, Alabama, after a . . . demonstration in 1965.[11]

To give civil rights workers protection under federal law, the U.S. Congress passed the Voting Rights Act of 1965. By the end of the 1960s, with pressure from the African-American community (which had the support of many whites), black people's civil rights were established. Nevertheless, institutional discrimination still persists.

Institutional Discrimination   Sociologists have learned that legal equality may have little effect on people's behaviors and attitudes. This form of discrimination can be quite complex. Sociologist William Kornblum, for example, notes that the conditions that led to rioting in the Watts section of Los Angeles were such that

> African-Americans were trapped in a self-perpetuating set of circumstances that almost inevitably resulted in discrimination: Blocked educational opportunities result in low skill levels, which together with job discrimination limit their incomes. Low income forces them to become concentrated in ghettos, which lack adequate public services such as transportation, making the search for work even more difficult. In those neighborhoods, also, the schools do not stimulate achievement, thereby repeating the pattern in the next generation. At the same time, the police patrol ghettos "to the point of harassment," with the result that young African-Americans are more likely to be arrested—and to be denied jobs based on their arrest records.[12]

Klan Broken in Civil Court   The Klan fragmented after World War II. No group had more than four thousand members, and no strong leader emerged to pull the various factions together. Restrictions barring Catholics from membership were dropped by most groups, but all Klan groups maintained a belief in white supremacy; were anti-Semitic, anti-gay, and anti-immigrant; and opposed equal rights for women.

The largest of the Klan groups in the early 1980s was the United Klans of America, whose estimated membership was 3,000 to 4,000.[13] In the spring of 1981, Klansmen in Mobile, Alabama, learned that a jury had deadlocked after a trial in which a black man was accused of killing a

[11]*Violence, the Ku Klux Klan and the Struggle for Equality,* (published jointly by the Connecticut Education Association, Hartford: the Council on Interracial Books for Children, New York; and the National Education Association, Washington, DC, 1981), p. 17.

[12]William Kornblum, *Sociology in a Changing World,* 2nd ed. (Ft. Worth, TX: Holt, Rinehart and Winston, 1991), p. 406.

[13]*Violence, the Ku Klux Klan and the Struggle for Equality,* p. 17.

white police officer. Bennie Hays, titan in charge of Klavern 900, United Klans of America, is purported to have said to his followers, " 'Get this down: If a black man can kill a white man, a white man should be able to get away with killing a black man.' "[14]

Two days later Klansmen James (Tiger) Knowles, age seventeen, and Henry Hays, age twenty-six, son of the Klavern leader, randomly kidnapped nineteen-year-old Michael Donald, an African-American, at gunpoint. After beating and torturing him, Hays cut Donald's throat—three times. He was taken to the Hays dwelling and hung from a camphor tree in the front yard. The elder Hays is alleged to have called it "a pretty sight."

Despite the fact that Donald's body was hung in the yard of the local Klan leader, and that a cross was burned on the lawn of the Mobile courthouse that same evening, prosecutors refused to tie the Klan to the lynching. The Klan does not promote such activities in its bylaws, they contended. From this premise, it was argued that Donald's murder was committed by two men who just happened to be members of the Klan.

Ultimately, suit was brought for damages in civil court by Beulah Mae Donald and the NAACP against the United Klans of America. The idea was to secure a judgment large enough to bankrupt the Klan. Attorney Morris Dees of the Southern Poverty Law Center acted on behalf of the plaintiffs. Dees convinced the court that Knowles and Hays were influenced by the Klan to commit murder. Included in the testimony against the Klan was a statement by Tiger Knowles that he took his orders from Bennie Hays and that Hays took his orders from the Klan's top man, Imperial Wizard Robert Shelton. After four hours of jury deliberation, Mrs. Donald was awarded $7 million. Journalist Richard Meyer reported that "the Klan could not pay. It had nowhere near that kind of money. So in addition to a quarter of the wages some of the Klansmen will earn for the rest of their lives, and in addition to Titan Bennie Hays' house and farm, Beulah Mae Donald accepted every penny of the several thousand dollars that the United Klans of America had to its name—and the deed and keys to its national headquarters. She shut it down."[15]

The Kareful Klan

The downfall of the United Klans of America taught other Klan groups a lesson. In essence, the court's ruling told Klan organizations that they were responsible for the actions of their members, just as a corporation

[14]Richard E. Meyer, "The Long Crusade," *Los Angeles Times Magazine*, December 3, 1989, p. 16.
[15]Ibid.

is responsible for the actions of its employees when they carry out its policies.

Today's Klans tend to be "Kareful Klans," at least in rhetoric. Violence is rarely mentioned openly. The focus of Klan efforts in recent years has been to promote institutional discrimination through political means. For example, the Klan proposes to close the nation's borders so that people of color cannot immigrate. Klansmen lobby to end quota laws and play to the fears of white, working-class men. Their slogan: *Rights for Whites.*

The Knights of the Ku Klux Klan, formerly headed by David Duke—who resigned to head the NAAWP, or National Association for the Advancement of White People—is perhaps the largest and most successful of the current Klans. The unctuous Duke, who was a state representative in Louisiana, preferred slick to violence, even before the fall of the United Klans of America. Since leaving the Klan, Duke has built a career on racist politics. His unsuccessful bids for governor of Louisiana, the U.S. Senate, and the presidency of the United States have been vehicles for generating enormous contributions from racist constituents nationwide.[16]

When Duke resigned his position with the Klan, Don Black, a young man noted for little more than a quick temper, took charge. Soon after, he was arrested for conspiring with a neo-Nazi group to overthrow the government of the Caribbean island of Dominica. On Black's imprisonment, Thomas Robb, an ordained Baptist minister, assumed leadership of the Knights of the Ku Klux Klan.

Knights of the Ku Klux Klan   Two weeks before the general election in 1992, I traveled to Zinc, Arkansas, a nearly abandoned shell of a community that once mined the ore for which it is named. Robb lives a few miles down a dirt road from the town. The path is lined with board shacks and ancient trailer houses; most bear "no trespassing" signs. I said to my wife, Pam, "I'm glad we have an appointment; a stranger could get lost in here and never be seen again."

We missed the lane that leads to Robb's house and drove instead up a hill and into a KKK campground. There was a guardhouse at the entrance with "KKK" in large letters painted on the structure. The only other building on the grounds is a small kitchen facility. There was a volleyball net and a dozen or so picnic tables. An unusual amount of litter at the site attested to the fact that there had been a meeting there of some magnitude. It was also evident that the meeting had been some time in the past: the printing on potato chip boxes and the like was faded with age.

A year earlier, Ginny Carroll had interviewed Robb for *Newsweek:*

---

[16]Jason Berry, "Louisiana Hateride," *The Nation*, December 19, 1991, pp. 727–29.

The Rev. Thom Robb has a dream. Robb and his wife recently bought 40 acres of scenic Ozark Mountain greenery near Zinc, Ark., a few miles north of legendary Dogpatch. The couple envisions transforming the meadow-land into a small Bible-camp resort with family-size cabins, recreational facilities such as volleyball, and, eventually, a video-production center for the Robbs and their guests to make movies. Three flags already fly over the campground: the Stars and Stripes, the Confederate battle flag and the white and gold Christian Banner. Robb . . . wants to create a mecca for white supremacists—and a national headquarters, with a Kleagle in every cabin, for revitalizing the Klan.* "People still think of the Klan as running through the night shooting black people," he says. "This is the '90s. . . . We don't hate anybody."[17]

I backtracked and found Robb's house on a nearby hill. Guarding his yard was a German shepherd the size of a small but well-fed horse; I moved slowly toward the grand dragon's porch. The dog was glad to see me, but not because he was friendly. He ran to the end of his chain with such force that he was turned completely around before coming to a full stop. The man who came to the door in response to his barking dog was less threatening than his animal.

"He won't bite," Thomas Robb said. Right, I thought, but I didn't stop to pet the nice doggie.

The first thing that impressed me about Thom Robb was that he is not as the press pictures him—perpetually scowling. He is, in truth, polite, affable, and easy to talk to. I found him to be the stereotypical small-town minister—that is, until he started talking about the Klan. Before beginning the interview, I was introduced to Thom's wife, Muriel; their younger son, Jason; and their only grandchild, Charity (still a toddler), their daughter's child. Robb is forty-nine years old.

The cedar home, which Robb built himself, is nicer than most of the surrounding homes, but it is something less than I expected. After all, Robb is grand dragon of what is purported to be the largest Klan organization in the United States. The house was cluttered, filled with boxes full of Klan promotional items: T-shirts, lock-blade KKK knives, ball-point pens, KKK buttons and pins, baseball caps, and much more. Perhaps the most impressive item was what is described in Klan publications as a beautiful, ceramic "Klansman Statuette," ten inches high, with red eyes that light up, only $20.00.

After exchanging gifts (I gave Robb a copy of my latest book, and he gave me a "Robb for State Representative" baseball cap and T-shirt, along with a KKK pen and tie stud), I began the interview.

---

*A kleagle is a paid Klan organizer who keeps a portion of membership dues (sometimes called the klecturn) as a fee for his services.

[17]Ginny Carroll, "Coming Soon: Klub KKK: A Dream Resort for White Supremacists," *Newsweek*, July 8, 1991, p.30.

Thom Robb

Zellner: I took a wrong turn coming here and ended up in the campground. Have you made any progress on Klub KKK?

Robb: I don't understand.

Zellner: An article in *Newsweek* said you were building a Klub for the
KKK.

Robb: Oh, that. The article was an exaggeration. We plan the camp-
grounds as a temporary place until we move into the White
House. Right now we are soliciting funds to build an office, and
we plan to build a room for producing our own videos.*

Zellner: Are you the largest Klan in the United States?

Robb: I don't care to speculate. Let the ADL [Anti-Defamation Lea-
gue] do that. If you want to say that there are ten thousand of
us or ten million of us, or that I am the only one, that's OK with
me. None of the other Klan groups report their numbers either.
But I can say we appear to be the largest. We have three or four
people around here all day long; we have a newspaper; we
travel the world over; and I don't know of any other Klan that
does that.

 We are the only Klan that has successfully moved out of the
South into the North and the West. As head of the Klan, I try
to develop leaders. Leadership depends on spokesmen who
can articulate out in the field. We now have very powerful
leaders in Florida, Alabama, Colorado, Illinois, Texas, and
other places.

Zellner: What is the history of your Klan [Knights of the Ku Klux Klan]?

Robb: This particular Klan started out as a very small group in New
Orleans, I think in the mid-1950s. I believe the founder's name
was Jim Lindsay. It remained small until David Duke took it to
the national level. There is no original Klan, of course, but what I
say that sometimes gets me in trouble with other Klans is that
our Klan has been the only one able to capture the spirit and
idealism of the original Klan.

Zellner: Most Klans call their leader the "Imperial Wizard." Why do you
call yourself the "Grand Dragon"?

Robb: The original Klan used "Grand Dragon." We just went back to
that. Actually, I prefer to be addressed as "National Director."†

Zellner: What is your history with the Knights?

---

*The following is from a solicitation letter given to me prior to the interview: "Donors
who give $100 or more will have their names on a plaque in the office. $250 donors get their
names on the plaque and a flag that has flown over national headquarters. $500 donors get
their names on the plaque, a flag, and a beautiful 11 × 14 photo of the 'Grand Council' and
a videotape of the dedication ceremony."

†Robb is much more comfortable in a suit and tie than in a hooded robe. The Knights
rarely don robes other than for naturalization ceremonies (inducting new members into the
order) and for cross burnings.

Robb: I have been involved with patriotic, racialist groups since 1963. I
           was proud to be a member of the John Birch Society.* In 1979 I
           joined the Klan. I became editor of the newspaper in 1982 and
           was appointed Klan chaplain the same year.

Zellner: I understand that you are an ordained Baptist minister. How do
           you justify your racist attitudes with your religion?

Robb: I was raised Baptist; attended a small, conservative seminary in
           Colorado; and was ordained a Baptist minister when I was
           twenty-one. I still adhere to the fundamental teachings of the
           Baptist church. I don't disagree with them historically, but in a
           modern sense I believe that race is a very important issue.

Zellner: How is the issue important?

Robb: The strength and foundation of a nation does not rest on its
           economy but on the race of people who make up the country.
           Communism is based on economics. Economics is a very impor-
           tant issue, but I believe that there is something even more im-
           portant than economics—and that is race. Race determines the
           society, the religious faith of the nation, and ultimately the eco-
           nomics of the nation. You know, for example, our free enterprise
           system was born in Europe. Our whole system of justice, our
           whole idea that man is innocent until proven guilty, was born in
           Europe. The ideas of free speech and freedom of religion were
           born in Europe. All these things are concepts that came out of
           the race of people of Europe.

Zellner: Are other people inferior to people with European ancestry?

Robb: Our founding fathers came here and established the Mayflower
           Compact, and other charters and various state constitutions, and
           eventually the Declaration of Independence and Constitution of
           the United States. This concept of America did not just spring
           out of the ground but came forth out of our blood. You could
           have put our founding fathers on any other continent—Africa,
           South America—these same ideals would have come forth and
           they would have been just as successful. So people who come
           here from places other than Europe can enjoy the benefits of our
           society, but they can never contribute to America in a spiritual
           sense. They might even contribute in an economic sense, but
           never in a spiritual sense. They might even contribute in a physi-
           cal sense like carrying a gun into battle, but they were not given
           the ability to contribute in a spiritual sense.

*John Birch was an obscure army captain killed by Chinese communists near the end of
World War II. The Society, founded in 1958 by candymaker Robert Welch, memorializes
Birch as the first casualty of World War III. The Society believes that communist conspirators are at the root of most of America's problems. Supposedly among the conspirators was
former president Dwight Eisenhower. At its apex in the mid-1960s, the Society had nearly
100,000 members. The civil rights movement was viewed as a communist conspiracy to set
black against white to create internal dissension in the United States. This position was
accepted by many Klansmen.

Zellner: Can you use scripture to justify any of what you just said?

Robb: As far as the Klan would work? The Klan, although established on religious beliefs, is more secular than religious in nature. A lot of people of many different religions are part of the Klan. I can discuss what I believe in a personal way, but I can't speak for the Klan. My purpose as national director is not to convert Klansmen to my religious beliefs.

I know what you are fishing for. You did research before you came here. Yes, I adhere to "Christian Identity" beliefs, which are in tune with what I have said about our European forefathers.*

Zellner: Are you a separatist?

Robb: I think that the difference between us [KKK] and most conservative politicians is the issue of race. Taking a stand on race is what makes us unique. Race is an important issue to us, more important than a new car, a new home, and how much money we have in the bank. We are separatists.

Zellner: Would you divide up the nation into black and white states? A number of Identity ministers have suggested this be done.

Robb: I don't have that kind of power. Only an insane man would want that kind of power.

Zellner: If you had that kind of power?

Robb: Nobody should have that kind of power. Not me nor anyone else, but I know what you are referring to. Some separatists believe that we should declare the states of the Northwest—Washington, Oregon, Idaho, Montana, Colorado—white property, and separatists should move there. I do think a white separatist state is ideal. Whether it can be achieved or not is up to future generations.

Zellner: Would you accept the old "separate but equal" ideology?

Robb: No, that's impossible. First, there is no such thing as equal. There is no such thing as equality between races—or, for that matter, there is no equality within races. You know, I get kind of a lark out of people who say "appreciate our differences." (Laughing) They don't know what side they want to be on. They say appreciate our differences, our diversity, and then they say that everybody is equal. You can't have it both ways. We either are the same with no differences, or we are different. I think we can appreciate our differences, and saying someone is different doesn't make them bad.

In times past, some Klan members have opened themselves up to charges from the liberal media that we consider ourselves good because we are different and others are bad. Just because we are different doesn't make us good and other people bad. For

---

*Christian Identity is a religious philosophy rooted in the belief that the Aryans are the true descendants of Israel, those who had been earlier chosen for world domination in Hitler's "master race" philosophy. Although a fair number of Klansmen subscribe to this ideology, Christian Identity is discussed more extensively in Chapter 3, "Survivalists."

example, just because a man is different from a woman doesn't make the man good and the woman bad. Because a child is different from a parent doesn't make the parent good and the child bad. It's like the manager of WalMart and an employee. The manager isn't holy because he is the manager and the employee bad. It just means the manager is in charge. I think we can learn to appreciate our differences. Just because we want to stay separate doesn't make us bad.*

There is an element of truth to our thinking that we are superior to other groups. I think it is only nature to be loyal to your own kind. Every animal, for survival, is loyal to its own kind. I don't think that is necessarily bad.

I don't believe in integration, but that doesn't mean that I think black people are bad or should be held back. If I am a true white supremacist as I am called, then I don't need to believe that black people should be held back. A white supremacist would believe that his people will rise to the top naturally, without interference. There are a lot of blacks and others who want special privileges, you know. I believe in equality for all and special privileges for none. I am a white supremacist in that I am loyal to my race.

Zellner: What do you think about David Duke? Is he a traitor? Politically, at least, he seems to want to sweep his Klan past under the rug.

Robb: I haven't talked to David Duke in years, so I don't know if he's a traitor or not. I'm not privy to his inner thoughts, and he doesn't call me up to confer with me. Nevertheless, I have listened very carefully to what he has been saying.

First, let me say that people in the public spotlight—I can tell you this from my own experience—often say things they wish they hadn't said or wish they had worded things differently. For example, Dan Quayle. I'm quite confident that he wishes he had never made a statement comparing himself to John Kennedy.

Everyone in the public eye from time to time wishes he had said something differently, so I'm not going to denounce Duke for that. I kind of look at what he says from that standpoint. As far as his renouncing the Klan, what he more or less denounced was hatred, and I denounce that too. I denounce hatred. As far as I know, David Duke has always believed that all people should be treated with respect.

But people say that the Klan doesn't believe those things, so it is probably easier for him to say as a politician that he renounces the hateful things in his past, rather than defend the Klan.

*At rallies and in Klan publications edited by Robb, he is often less careful with his words than he was during this interview. For example, in one issue of the *White Patriot* he defines freedom from a black man's perspective: "Dat's when A'hs does what A'hs want. . . . Dat's also when A'hs kin have da white girls, da free food stamps . . . " Reprinted in the *White Patriot*, Issue no. 91, undated, mailed January 1993.

I think that Duke has always believed that black people have a right to be proud, that Mexicans have a right to be proud, that other cultures have a right to be proud of their race and that white people have the same right, and I don't see anything wrong with that.

Zellner: What about skinheads? Do you involve them in your activities?

Robb: As far as I'm concerned, I like skinheads. As far as I'm concerned, Tom Metzger does not like skinheads. I know that sounds like a twist to what you read, especially in his publications. In reality, I'm probably the only one who does like skinheads. I care about them. I don't want them to get in trouble. I want them to have a prosperous, fruitful life. I want them to be successful, not just with their movement but with their lives in general. I don't want them to waste their lives because they walked down the street and got mad at some black person and kicked his teeth in. To me, Metzger uses the skinheads to promote his newspaper and his organization.

I don't care who people are, how long or short their hair is, how many tattoos they have—Klansmen, skinheads; if they conduct themselves in a dignified manner befitting our people, I don't care what they look like. If they do not abide by our rules, we do not want them at our rallies. Some skinheads are good, and I like those who are, and some of them are bad. I don't dislike the bad ones, but I let them go their own way.

Zellner: What was your background before the KKK?

Robb: I'm from Detroit, Michigan—a Yankee. My dad was in the building business. I'm the product of a working-class background. We weren't affluent, but we weren't poor either. It was just a middle-class, average home. (Laughing) Psychologists are always looking for what twisted your mind up. Ours was an average home—no drinking, no drugs, no abuse, no divorce.

In 1961 my family moved to Arizona, and of course I moved with them. My mom was always interested in politics and supported conservative candidates and positions. They say the acorn doesn't fall far from the tree, so in 1962, the year I graduated from high school, I joined the John Birch Society.

My plans included going to law school and then getting into politics in some way. I decided to go to a Bible school for one year first, and ended up in the ministry. I met my wife in Colorado; she was at the same school.

We went back to Arizona, and I opened up my own print shop. I was concerned with all the illegal aliens crossing over from Mexico, and I began printing up literature trying to get people and the government to understand that it had to stop. And it was nothing in those days, nothing like it is now. Everybody thought I was crazy, but I could see the handwriting on the wall. It finally got to the point where we couldn't stand

	Arizona anymore, so in 1971 we packed up and moved to Arkansas.
Zellner:	Why Arkansas?
Robb:	I had a friend who said it was a good place.
Zellner:	And that's all it took?
Robb:	I wanted to raise my kids in a rural environment. I didn't want to raise them in the city. The cities were becoming alien to what we considered the traditional life.*
Zellner:	Are you happy with where you are in life today? Are there any regrets that you chose the Klan as your life's work?
Robb:	I'm a happy fellow. (Laughing) I'm very optimistic, and I see a lot of good things happening. By 1982, in my mind, maybe a little earlier than that, I could see things were changing in this country. Not in the government structure, but at the grassroots level. A window of opportunity opened that we [the KKK] could enter. Our movement has now reached a point where it is unstoppable.
Zellner:	The ADL says your numbers are dwindling.
Robb:	I've been associated with racialist movements for thirty years. The ADL is lying and they know they are lying, but I think they put out that propaganda to give the appearance that we are not reaching people. I know how strong the racialist movement was thirty years ago, and it is much stronger today.

Our organization is probably the best established white racialist organization in the world today. When you are associated with something, it is only natural that you want it to grow. We operate on what I am going to call the leadership principle. That is how Sam Walton made so much money off the WalMart stores.†

I was in the post office in Harrison one day when WalMart was celebrating its fortieth or forty-fifth anniversary. I overheard one gentleman tell another that he had opened a store the same year that Sam Walton opened his. He couldn't understand how his store had not done as well as Sam's. Well, I knew. It was because

---

*The *London Sunday Times* reported the following on October 11, 1992: "Some folk say that if you could buy a drink in Boone County you'd get tourists in, but heck, who wants strangers poking their noses in everywhere? Ask the old men who sit in the shade of the oak trees around the courthouse in Harrison and they'll tell you that people don't take too kindly to strangers in Boone County. They'll also tell you they don't take too kindly to 'nigrahs,' either. That's why Boone County is white and that's why Thom Robb chose it as an ideal place to live twenty years ago."

†Headquarters for WalMart is in nearby Bentonville, Arkansas. During my visit, I learned very quickly that Sam Walton was much admired and respected in northwest Arkansas, a near folk hero. It is interesting that there is a common misconception among many area residents that Walton was an uneducated, pickup-driving hillbilly from Arkansas who became a success by having "good old country, common sense" as his only tool. Walton, an air force officer during World War II, was born in Oklahoma and held a degree in economics from the University of Missouri.

Sam Walton followed certain principles. You must follow principles to be successful.

I am a great believer, for example, in the writings of Norman Vincent Peale and Zig Ziglar.*

Zellner: How have such principles been applied in the Knights of the Ku Klux Klan?

Robb: I didn't write the laws for success. They are ingrained in the sands of time. Other Klans are just like us. They want to grow. Take, for example, some guy in Tennessee who wants to start a Klan. He develops a membership form, and he sends it to a guy in Missouri or Oklahoma or whatever. Invariably, that guy becomes state leader just because he is there, regardless of abilities or leadership qualifications. That way the Klan leader can put in his newsletter that he has a state office in Missouri. We don't do that. We have members in every state in the country, but we have very few state offices. We will not appoint someone a state leader until they have proven to us that they have leadership abilities. They must be with us four or five years and demonstrate strong leadership abilities. They must organize for us, and they must work as a leader before we appoint them a leader.

A good example is Shawn Slater in Colorado. We can't appoint him a state leader overnight, but the national office can't ignore the fact either that he does a good job of organizing rallies and public events. In a sense he is like a leader in Colorado, but he is not *the* leader. That way, if something [negative] should happen, our endorsement would not be quite as strong.†

Zellner: How autonomous are the state offices?

Robb: We don't do all the work here [National Headquarters]. For example, Michael Lowe down in Texas does a tremendous job. And we are interlocking our leaders with fax machines. We have fax machines in Ohio, Illinois, Texas, Colorado, and Alabama. We recognize that these are not the 1860s. Things change. Propaganda changes. We have to appeal to the American people as they are today.

Zellner: The Klan has been involved in violent activity in the past, even in the recent past. What is your position on violence?

Robb: I am a totally nonviolent person.

Zellner: Nothing could cause you to become violent?

Robb: Everybody has a right to defend themselves. You know, I was at a Klan function one time, and I probably made the speaker ahead

---

*Norman Vincent Peale, who died in 1994, had a television and radio ministry but is best known for his book *The Power of Positive Thinking* (1952). Megan Rosenfeld described Zig Ziglar for the *Washington Post* as the "high priest of Up-beatism, a preacher of Candoism, and an exorcist of negativity," November 1, 1992. Prior to achieving success as a motivator, Ziglar spent fifteen years as a salesman of pots and pans.

†The January 1993 issue of the *White Patriot* notes that Shawn Slater has been promoted to Grand Titan.

of me mad because I contradicted his whole method of propaganda. He stood up there with his legs straddled about three feet apart, his hands on his hips, and a cocky look on his face. He said, "I am the biggest, meanest, toughest Klansman in the whole state of"—I won't say which state it was—and that's the way he started out his speech.

That's not the way to communicate with people today. When it came my turn to speak, I told the crowd that I'm not the toughest and I'm certainly not the biggest Klansman. What I am is simply a man who loves his family, his children, and loves America. I think those are the qualities that Americans want to see in leaders. You have to understand the problems of the average American. I think I have experienced those problems. I think I am more in tune with the problems of the average white American, not blacks or Mexicans, than either George Bush or Bill Clinton.*

Zellner: Your political career as a Republican candidate for state office made national news. Would you tell me about it?

Robb: It was one of those things. I ran unopposed in the Republican primary for state representative in the 39th District. The law clearly says that if a candidate files and is unopposed or if he wins the primary, he is by law the candidate. Apparently the Republican Party doesn't like me. They sued to get me off the ballot. My attorney read the law to the judge. The law is clear and simple, but the judge said in effect, "Well, maybe that is what the law says, but I feel the Republican Party still can decide who they want as a candidate."

You know, that is absurd. That's like going before a judge and the judge says, "Well, I know there is a law against murder, but in this case I will overlook it."

Zellner: Have you sought your last political office?

Robb: I'm a young man. I'll be around a few more years.

Zellner: You have a chance to make one of your own, an Arkansan, president of the United States next week. But I'm going to guess that you are not going to vote for Mr. Clinton.

Robb: You guessed right. I'm not going to vote for Bill Clinton. I may vote for George Bush because he says more of the things I like to hear. I don't think he believes what he says. I don't think he's honest. The only one to really address issues has been Quayle. All the political fluff is meaningless. For example, which candidate is not going to say, "Get America back to work"? He would be stupid not to. Whichever one says it more convincingly is going to get elected.

Perot has been the only one to come out against free trade. Free trade and immigration are going to be the issues of the next

*This interview was conducted one week before the general election in November 1992.

decade. Free trade is going to be devastating. Countries that are homogeneous like Japan have an advantage over us.

Diversity in America breeds mistrust in the corporate world. People here shake hands with each other with smiles on their faces; and we know and you know that in private circles whites are telling nigger jokes, while publicly they say they don't have a prejudiced bone in their bodies. You know, and I know, and they know that whites are telling jokes about the blacks. And of course blacks, in their own circles, don't trust honkies at all. I don't know if we can compete against cultures like the Japanese where people can trust each other.

I don't know if I can describe it the way I want to. I was born in 1946. *Time* magazine, back in April 1990 I think it was, had an article on America's changing colors. In the 1950s America was 92 percent white. Today it is a little bit below 70 percent white. European Americans are not fewer in number today than they were in the 1950s; it is just that the country is being inundated with foreigners. Politicians in the 1950s were loyal to the white Americans who had established this country, not to Mexicans who crossed our borders, or Koreans, or people from Vietnam. Just crossing our borders doesn't make them Americans. Politicians today should show their loyalty to white Americans, just as they did in the 1950s.

Zellner: You said before that you were still young, that you would be back politically. Where do you go from here?

Robb: I think white Americans are getting tired of blacks on welfare and paying for illegitimate children. At least when they were slaves, they paid their own way. They did something for their keep. Americans are tired of the outrages, the demands of homosexuals and Jews.

You saw how fast things changed in Europe with the fall of the Berlin Wall—how the Soviet Union collapsed. Suddenly those that were in were out, and those that were out were in. It can happen in the United States the same way. We will be ready when the time is right. I have no immediate political aspirations, but I do not rule out the possibility of running for office again.

A New Beginning

The January 1993 *White Patriot* announces in bold red letters on page one, "Knights of the Ku Klux Klan . . . A New Beginning!" Unquestionably, the contemporary Klan exists as it is described in their newspaper:

The Knights of the Ku Klux Klan have, most certainly, entered a *new beginning*. Gone are the days of dead propaganda that was unable to pinpoint the source of our national ills. The original Klan knew that the heart of the problem was not coming from the recently freed slaves, but was coming from the tyranny of federal troops occupying the South. Likewise, the Klan once again recognizes that it is the federal government that has created the laws that has forced Negroes into our schools, homes and lives. It is the federal government that permits the open borders which allows millions of illegal aliens into our country. It is the federal government that is betraying our trust and the trust of millions of good hard working people with its promotion of the North American Free Trade Agreement which will suck thousands of jobs out of the U.S. into Mexico. Negroes and other minorities would be *controllable* if it wasn't for the powerful fist of the federal government posed . . . ready to lower its deadly might upon anyone who does not *willingly* support integration.[18]

The new Klan provides a vehicle for haters like David Duke and Thom Robb to enter the political arena. And Robb is right. Given current circumstances, a poor economy, and increasing competition for jobs, a window of opportunity does exist for hatemongers and scapegoaters to enter the political arena. It must be remembered that David Duke was an elected member of the legislature in Louisiana, and that he did draw 44 percent of the vote in his unsuccessful bid for governor in 1991.

The new Klan, at least for now, is content with building a political machine. The civil suit that broke the United Klans of America did have an effect. The following is excerpted from the *White Patriot*; similar disclaimers appear in all publications of the Knights of the Ku Klux Klan:

> The Knights of the Ku Klux Klan does not encourage, teach, direct, support or suggest publicly or privately, violence or illegal activities which include, but may not be limited to: murder, robbery, peddling drugs, mail fraud, etc.
>
> The Knights of the Ku Klux Klan is not engaged in:
>
> 1. Seeking to overthrow the United States government,
> 2. Harassing Negroes or other "minorities,"
> 3. Paramilitary camps, or
> 4. Paramilitary training.
>
> The Knights of the Ku Klux Klan wishes to see the national government and the people of this nation (the children of the Republic) return to the laws of God in fulfillment of II Chronicles 7:14.
>
> If my people, which are called
> by my name, shall humble themselves,
> and pray and seek my face, and

---

[18]From an undated edition of the *White Patriot*, mailed January 1993, p. 1.

turn from their wicked ways; then will
I hear from heaven, will forgive their
sin and will heal their land.[19]

The disclaimers do not mean that the Klan is not spreading hate. The purpose of such announcements is to provide the Klan with plausible deniability. It is much more difficult to tie either Klan organization or Klan leadership to members who commit violent acts if such activity is publicly denounced. For example, the Republican Party, the Daughters of the American Revolution, the Catholic Church do not advocate violence. Hence, if a member commits a crime, the organization can reasonably deny blame.

Solutions to the Problem

Journalist Fred Grimm believes the Duke-type Klan leader is more dangerous than the half-stupid, backwoods types of the past: "I could never find them as frightening as David Duke, who can disguise racist ravings as acceptable political discourse. And who can stir community support for his hateful ideas."[20]

Although the Knights of the Ku Klux Klan is just one of many Klan organizations, some more violent than others, it has been the trend in recent years for most Klan organizations to eschew violence in favor of political activity. This does not mean that they are not dangerous. Indeed, David Duke is the only Klansman who has won political office in recent years. But, as Robb pointed out, "political winds change quickly." If indeed such people are elected to office in significant numbers, bigotry will find political sanction.

The new, slicker Klans can raise money to fund their activities. Ralph Bennett, writing for *Reader's Digest*, regards Duke as a fund-raiser:

> In 1975 he appointed himself Grand Wizard of the Knights of the Ku Klux Klan, the pinnacle of the organization's power. But as he moved more into the world of thousand-dollar lecture fees, he found less and less time for speeches from the backs of flatbed trucks to handfuls of Klansmen. He was growing tired, he was to say, of being associated with "all those guys with green teeth". . . .
>
> In a midnight meeting at an Alabama farmhouse in July 1980, Duke was videotaped apparently trying to sell his own Klan's membership list to a rival Klanleader for $35,000—breaching an oath not to disclose members' names.

---

[19]Ibid., p. 4.
[20]Fred Grimm, "Asian Killing Recalls 1979 Attack in Greensboro," *Miami Herald*, October 18, 1992.

[During his 1991 race for governor of Louisiana], Duke spent $2,000,000, $300,000 less than he took in. His finance report listed more than 26,000 contributors—a breathtaking jump from the 2,500 contributors to his 1988 state race. Almost half were from out of state.[21]

Duke has denied attempting to sell his group's membership list.

As noted earlier, my visit to Arkansas took place the week before the November 1992 general election. Ever the researcher, I asked many people in Harrison how they felt about the possibility of a native son, Bill Clinton, becoming president of the United States. Some were proud and planned to vote for Clinton, but what appeared to be a nearly equal number were very anti-Clinton. At a WalMart store, I asked a checkout clerk what she thought about Clinton's candidacy. Apparently uncomfortable with the question, she mumbled something unintelligible. The giant of a man in line behind me, however, had no trouble telling me what he thought: "The only people in this part of the country that will vote for Clinton are niggers and queers." By a very slight margin, Clinton did win in Boone County. According to the *Harrison Times*, he had not carried the county in any of his gubernatorial campaigns.

A good many of the people I visited with knew Thom Robb personally or had heard him speak. More than a few thought highly of him. On the other hand, a fair number thought he was an embarrassment to the community. Few were ambivalent. Their feelings appeared to be either very positive or very negative.

It might be argued that Chris Piazza, the circuit judge who denied Robb the right to run for state representative, erred. Indeed, it might serve the community well to know how many support bigotry in order to know how much education is needed to counteract such thinking.

Educating Bigots   Timothy Jones, writing for *Christianity Today*, reported that a judge in the U.S. district court in Huntsville, Alabama, ordered four Klansmen guilty of disrupting a civil rights march to sit down and talk with Joseph Lowery, president of the Southern Christian Leadership Conference, and four other march organizers. "While some commentators called the plan naive when it was first publicized . . . the meeting showed that sitting down to talk and listen can change attitudes. Indeed, sociologists find that when people increase their interaction with one another, a corresponding increase in regard and appreciation follows. When it comes to distrust and distance, small steps toward understanding can lead to impressive strides."[22] Lowery reported that

[21]Ralph Kinney Bennett, "David Duke: Racial Politics for Profit," *Reader's Digest* 140, no. 839 (March 1992), pp. 43–48.
[22]Timothy K. Jones, "Klansmen Wise Up," *Christianity Today*, July 16, 1990, p. 13.

"all but one of the participants joined hands at the end of the two-hour meeting."[23]

Disrupting Klan Rallies and Parades   The Klan conducts rallies and organizes parades as much to draw a crowd of anti-Klan demonstrators as it does to perform for sympathizers. For example, in early 1992, Klansmen, neo-Nazis, and skinheads met in Janesville, Wisconsin, to demonstrate and vent their rage. Michael Riley, reporting for *Time* magazine, described the scene:

> The placid town of Janesville, Wisconsin (est. pop. 52,000), never asked for a Ku Klux Klan rally. But the Klan considered the town perched on the Rock River ripe for recruits. So there in the middle of Rockport Park stood a massive burlap-wrapped, kerosene-soaked cross surrounded by Klansmen, and even a few Klanswomen, their robes billowing in the soft breeze.* The loud twang of country music mixed with the angry chants of protesters jousting with police a few hundred yards away: "Death to the Klan!"
>
> The Kluxers kept a wary eye as the demonstrators repeatedly charged the police line, only to be repulsed by chilly blasts from a fire hose. Eventually the frustrated crowd began to pelt the cops with mud, rocks, bottles, and obscenities. The police made eight arrests. For the man whose presence triggered the violence, no outcome could have been better. "Oh, yeah," said Grand Wizard Thom Robb of the Knights of the Ku Klux Klan. "I couldn't have bought this advertising for a million bucks."[24]

Attacking Klansmen can have the effect of making the Klan look like a group of peace-loving, law-abiding citizens, and those who demonstrate against them appear as thugs. For example, a march by twenty-seven members of the Christian Knights of the Ku Klux Klan in October 1990 drew 1,200 demonstrators to a Washington, D.C., mall. Mary Jordan and Linda Wheeler, writing for the *Washington Post*, described the scene:

> Fourteen people were hurt and forty were arrested when rock-throwing protesters skirmished with police who guarded a small group of Ku Klux Klan members as they marched from the Washington Monument to the Capitol. Eight of the injured were District police officers, including one whose neck was fractured by a brick that officials said was thrown from the anti-Klan crowd. The windshields of twelve police cars were shattered in the melee, along with the windows of several buildings on Pennsylvania Avenue, police said.

[23]Ibid.
*Although the Reconstruction Klan used a variety of mechanisms for frightening former slaves, cross burning was not among the methods used. Cross burnings first appeared in Thomas Dixon's romantic novels and in a film, *The Birth of a Nation*, around the turn of the century.
[24]Michael Riley, "White and Wrong: New Klan, Old Hatred," *Time*, July 26, 1992, p. 25.

No Klan members were hurt, and police characterized the protesters' injuries as minor.[25]

The cost of protecting the Klan's constitutional right to march was tremendous. The D.C. police chief, Isaac Fulwood, Jr., said that 2,000 city police officers in riot gear, 800 U.S. Capitol police officers and 325 U.S. park police lined the parade route. While the march was in progress, all 4,750 district officers were put on call. The cost of protecting the Klansmen was $800,000.

Durham-based North Carolinians Against Racist and Religious Violence tallies racial assaults and harassment, as well as marches and rallies by white supremacist groups. Gaston, North Carolina, had eight marches during 1991 and ranked number one on the organization's hate-activity list. Ann Helms and Sharon White, reporting for the *Charlotte Observer,* interviewed Christina David-McCoy, executive director of the group. "There needs to be a balanced, contrasting message from the powers that be," she said. "If you don't stand against something, people believe you are for it."[26]

Laurie Wood, a researcher for Klanwatch, "recommends that people who oppose the Klan stay away from their rallies to avoid violence and publicity for the Klan. But opponents should consider making public statements of condemnation or holding alternative events, such as unity celebrations, at another location during Klan rallies."[27]

A Christmas Cross in Cincinnati   During 1992 Marge Schott, owner of the Cincinnati Reds, was accused of making racist remarks related to the work ethic and intellect of blacks.* In December, as Christmas approached, racial tensions caused by her remarks seemed to be ebbing. But the U.S. Knights of the Ku Klux Klan would not let the opportunity to foment trouble pass.

During the Hanukkah season, Rabbi Sholom B. Kalmonson's Lubavitch congregation applied for and was granted a permit to display an eighteen-foot menorah on Cincinnati's Fountain Square. Based on law, the Klan could not be denied access to the city park:

> After years of litigation and legal hair-splitting, courts have settled on a formula for constitutionally permissible municipal holiday displays. Some

[25]Mary Jordan and Linda Wheeler, "14 Hurt as Anti-Klan Protesters Clash with Police," *Washington Post*, October 29, 1990, p. A1, A8.
[26]Ann Helms and Sharon White, "Whether Threat Is Real or Not, the Klan Still Stirs Emotions," *Charlotte Observer*, July 12, 1992, p. 4.
[27]Ibid.
*At the baseball owners' meeting in winter 1993, Mrs. Schott was suspended from baseball for one year, fined $25,000, and required to take a course in multicultural education before she could return to baseball.

religious content, like nativity scenes or creches, is acceptable as long as it is garnished with a dollop of religious pluralism and a trace of secularism, like reindeers or elves. But private groups have a First Amendment right to erect explicitly religious displays in public places, at least once that forum is opened to other groups.[28]

Noting the success of the Jewish congregation, the Klan applied for a permit to erect a ten-foot cross in the park. Access could not be denied. Grand Titan Gary Orick of Cincinnati contended that "his group was placing the cross not to sow racial or religious divisiveness but 'to put Christ back in Christmas.' "[29]

Because of doubts about the Klan's sincerity, there was much disagreement as to what the city's response should be. Dwight Tillery, the first elected black mayor of Cincinnati, acknowledged that Schott's remarks and the Klan cross indicated that some racism existed in the community, but that it was not a redneck town. He cited his own election as evidence—only four of every ten city residents are black. Tillery said, "If you put up a cross and no one pays any attention to it, they won't be back. But if you make a big deal, they'll say, Hey, it works, and they'll be back next year, maybe before Christmas."[30]

While the Klan was erecting its cross, Tillery attended a prayer vigil at a Catholic church several miles from Fountain Square. Apparently the mayor's example worked. No serious racial confrontations occurred as a result of the Klan's actions. However, as Klansmen are wont to do, they were back in Fountain Square with their cross during the Christmas season of 1993. According to sociologist Robert Carroll at the University of Cincinnati, less attention was paid to their activity than the year before.

[28]David Margolick, "Klan's Plan for Cross Stokes Anger in Cincinnati," *New York Times*, December 18, 1992, p. B10(N), B14(L).
[29]Ibid.
[30]Ibid.

CHAPTER THREE
SURVIVALISTS

The term *survivalist* was coined by Kurt Saxon in the early 1960s to describe "superior" people who would survive an apocalypse brought on by what he then perceived as an inevitable nuclear war. With international tensions abating in the 1990s, Saxon has shifted his emphasis from nuclear holocaust to a worsening economy brought on by worldwide overpopulation. Saxon predicts that hordes of starving, urban survivalists will be forced to leave the cities to search the countryside for food and shelter. In his many publications, Saxon demonstrates how it is possible for rural survivalists to fight off urban invaders and live without the trappings of modernity, using what would now be considered outdated technologies.

Since the term was coined, *survivalist* has come to mean more than Saxon intended—self-protection from attackers. For some it means avoiding divine judgment of this wicked world by turning to escapist religious orientations. Often such religious enclaves are armed: the Branch Davidians, for example, held federal officers at bay outside their compound on the outskirts of Waco, Texas, for fifty-one days during the spring of 1993. There are others who band together to fight perceived governmental machinations aimed at destroying important American institutions such as the traditional family, religion, and education. Groups such as neo-Nazis, Aryan Nations, and Posse Comitatus, along with violent Ku Klux Klan organizations, fall into this category; and it is not uncommon for individuals to hold membership in a number of such organizations at the same time. Why people join together in "survival groups" is of interest to social scientists.*

---

*Not all survivalist groups are racist. A directory in *The American Survival Guide* (September 1991, p. 69) includes numerous nonracist ads, parts of which are worded as follows: Australia: "If you are racist, don't bother . . ."; Alma, Georgia: "Have a 150-acre retreat. No Klansmen or crazies"; Bakersfield, California: "I will answer any and all who might be interested. . . . No phonies, druggies, gays or racists."

Merton's Theory of Anomie

Robert Merton, a prominent sociologist at Columbia University, developed a theory of *anomie* to explain why people accept or reject the goals of society and, at the same time, accept or reject the socially approved means to achieve those goals. For example, it would appear on the surface that a bank robber and a bank teller have very little in common. Yet in fact each is putting forth an effort to acquire money, which can then be used to buy desired goods.

The difference is that the teller is conforming to the socially approved norm of "hard work" to achieve his or her goal and the bank robber is not. Although there are many established cultural goals, Merton maintains that one such goal is success, which is often measured in terms of money. As I mentioned in previous chapters, scapegoating, or blaming minority elements for a lack of success, is common practice. How does this mesh with the theory of anomie?

Conformity involves adapting to culturally approved means to achieve culturally approved goals. Not following culturally approved means results in deviance. Merton identified four deviant modes of adaptation:

Mode	Institutionalized Means	Societal Goal
Conformity	+	+
Deviant adaptations		
Innovation	−	+
Ritualism	+	−
Retreatism	−	−
Rebellion	$\left[\begin{smallmatrix}+\\-\end{smallmatrix}\right]$	$\left[\begin{smallmatrix}+\\-\end{smallmatrix}\right]$

Note: + indicates acceptance; − indicates rejection; [±] indicates replacement with new means and goals.

The bank robber is an innovator. Indeed, the robber's goals are the same as the bank teller's; but the robber, perhaps blocked from the goal by circumstances beyond his or her control, turns to illegitimate means to achieve the goal.

The ritualist is one who has abandoned the cultural goal of success, usually because it is perceived as unobtainable. This person tends to keep plugging on, perhaps at a dead-end job, committed to the institutional means. There is only so much financial success possible in society, and the means of achieving success through approved institutional channels are limited. Ritualists, unlike innovators, prefer to avoid deviance that would put them at odds with the law.

The retreatist, according to Merton, has withdrawn or "retreated" from both the goals of society and the prescribed means to achieve such goals. Success in the way that most people view success is abandoned, as are the conforming means to achieve success. A hermit is the ultimate retreatist. Such a person, going it alone, is one kind of survivalist. He or she has abandoned both the goals prescribed by society and the means to achieve such goals. Such survivors, whether alone or in small groups, are not aggressive and present little danger to society. On the other hand, some survivalists are rebels, and they present a clear danger to the social order.

Rebels, like retreatists, reject the existing social order. Unlike retreatists, rebels would, if they could, replace society's existing goals with goals of their own. For example, in our society the ideal of equality for all is considered an important cultural goal. Some rebels, those guilty of scapegoating, see no value in this goal and would replace it with "white domination." The illegitimate means to achieve this goal would be the elimination or subjugation of their scapegoats.

Aryan Nations

Based on a nineteenth-century Anglo-Israelite theory that the British people are descended from Israelites who were carried into captivity by the Assyrians in 721 B.C., Wesley Swift, a former rifle team instructor for the KKK, founded the Church of Jesus Christ Christian in 1946. By concluding that Christ was an Aryan who was put to death by the Jews, Swift laid the groundwork for a racist theology that supports what is now known as the Identity Church movement. Thanks to Swift, it became possible to be a follower of Christ and an anti-Semite at the same time. In fact, Swift, from his church in Lancaster, California, mandated revenge against the Jewish people who had crucified Christ.*

Michael and Judy Newton comment on the irony of this ideology:

"the true" Israel—are the Teutonic, Scandinavian, and white Anglo-Saxon races of the world, those who had been earlier chosen for world domination in Adolf Hitler's "Master Race" philosophy. Both Klansmen and neo-Nazis find themselves attracted to this doctrine, which today has become an underlying theme connecting groups such as the Aryan Nations, Christian Defense League, Christian-Patriots Defense League, Posse Comitatus, the Mountain Church of Jesus Christ, the New Chris-

---

*In this theological framework Anglo-Saxons, not the Jews, are considered God's chosen people. Black and other nonwhite races are called "mud people" and are believed to be on the same spiritual level as animals.

tian Crusade Church, various Klan factions, and the Covenant, the Sword, and the Arm of the Lord . . . [1]

Aryan Nations, officially entitled the Church of Jesus Christ Christian–Aryan Nations, is a direct offshoot of Wesley Swift's church. When Swift died in 1970, Richard Butler took over the congregation and moved it to Hayden Lake, Idaho. Butler, who believes that a race war is imminent, says, "If you believe in the Bible, you know that there is no peaceful solution."[2]

Each year rallies are held at the Hayden Lake compound; they are attended by skinheads, Klan elements, neo-Nazis, Posse Comitatus members, and other militant groups. Although Butler claims 6,000 followers nationwide, "observers place attendance at rallies at between 150 and 200."[3]

Butler requires that members contribute 10 percent of their annual incomes to the church to support its causes. Other income is generated from the sale of his taped sermons.

The Order

The most militant survivalist group, the Order, was founded by Robert Jay Mathews and named for a terrorist gang of right-wing fanatics found in the hate novel *The Turner Diaries*. Mathews was impressed by its author, William Pierce, founder and leader of the anti-Semitic National Alliance. Nevertheless, despite his respect for Pierce, Mathews discontinued his own membership in the Alliance, because he felt it was not militant enough. He then joined Butler's group at Hayden Lake. When he found the Aryan Nations too tame as well, he formed his own band of action-oriented haters.

The new group was a cross-section of extremists culled from far-right gangs. Among the twenty or so members were violent elements of Aryan Nations; National Alliance; KKK; and the Covenant, Sword, and Arm of the Lord (CSA). Mathews also recruited as his top lieutenant Gary Yarbrough, a professional criminal known for his membership in the Aryan Brotherhood (not associated organizationally with Aryan Nations) while he was in an Arizona prison.

The Order's first raid, on a Seattle porno theater in April 1983, netted only $369. But their skills improved. Following a run of bank robberies in

[1]Michael Newton and Judy Ann Newton, *The Ku Klux Klan: An Encyclopedia* (New York: Garland Publishing, 1991), pp. 281–82.
[2]Ibid., p. 25.
[3]Ibid.

early 1984, the gang robbed an armored truck on April 23, 1984, fleeing with $500,000 in cash.

The money was used to finance other terrorist activities. Homosexuals were attacked in Portland, Oregon. A synagogue was bombed in Boise, Idaho. On June 18, 1984, an Order hit team assassinated Jewish talk-show host Alan Berg in Denver, Colorado, in keeping with an episode in *The Turner Diaries*.

Then, in July 1984, the Order attacked an armored car in Ukiah, California, getting away with $3.6 million. Only $600,000 of this money was ever accounted for. Michael and Judy Newton report that "authorities believe that large sums of the money were distributed to leaders of the racist right."[4]

Lured into a trap set in Portland, Oregon, by an FBI informant, Mathews escaped a shootout with the FBI on November 24, 1984, only to die in a second shootout twelve days later at a hideout on Whidbey Island, Washington. Most members of the Order were captured within a year, convicted of their crimes, and are now serving lengthy prison sentences.

Posse Comitatus

With Christian Identity as its religious underpinning, the Posse Comitatus is politically neo-Nazi with a survivalist bent. The first Posse was founded in Portland, Oregon, in 1969 by Henry Lamont Beach. According to Michael and Judy Newton, the "Posse Comitatus—literally, 'power of the county'—draws its inspiration from the post–Civil War Posse Comitatus Act, which forbade federal troops from intervening to enforce domestic laws."[5]

Posse members recognize no government higher than the county level. For them, the highest ranking public official is the county sheriff, "and even that authority is disregarded if a sheriff is suspected of cooperating with the 'Zionist Occupational Government' in Washington, D.C. Devoid of any meaningful nationwide organization, local Posse units have been identified in California, Colorado, Delaware, Idaho, Illinois, Kansas, Michigan, Nebraska, North Dakota, Oregon, Texas, Washington, and Wisconsin."[6] It is common for Posse members to also hold membership in the KKK and other ultraconservative groups.

Despite the group's apparent lack of organization, "Posse members were active enough by the mid-1970s to prompt creation of a special IRS

4Ibid., p. 442.
5Ibid., p. 467.
6Ibid.

Illegal Tax Protester Program."[7] By 1983 federal agents were able to identify between fifty and sixty thousand dedicated tax protesters. One such protester was a North Dakota farmer, Gordon Kahl.

Journalist James Corcoran describes the economic situation confronting Kahl and thousands of other farmers in mid-America during the late 1970s and early 1980s:

> Farmers organized to press their demands. The American Agricultural Movement, and later Groundswell, called for higher commodity prices, guaranteed loans for spring planting, and long-term debt restructuring. They also demanded a moratorium on farm, home, and small business foreclosures as a way to stop the hemorrhaging that was bleeding the rural economy dry. Buoyed by the success of those who had led similar movements in the 1930s, farm leaders expressed optimism. In 1978, Elmo Olson, head of the North Dakota chapter of the AAM, told a reporter for *The Forum* of Fargo-Moorhead that he was certain the government would take notice and bring farm prices in line with production costs. But the farmers didn't have the political clout that they had in the 1930s.
>
> By 1983, North Dakota alone was losing three farmers a day, as its farm debt nearly doubled from $2.5 billion to $4.9 billion, and the interest paid on the debt tripled to $555 million. Foreclosure or debt reduction accounted for nearly 40 percent of all land sales. Other states in the farm belt were harder hit, losing ten, twelve, up to fifteen farmers a day and a bank a month. The farm debt for the nation exceeded $215 billion, a quarter of that deemed uncollectible. And by 1987, reported the Center on Budget and Policy Priorities, nearly 17 percent of rural Americans lived below the poverty line, a rate that was nearly as high as the 18.5 percent in the inner cities.[8]

It was against this backdrop that Kahl, a decorated war veteran and spokesman for the Posse, took his stand against what he believed was an illegal government controlled by Jews, intent on sucking the lifeblood from true Americans.

Jailed once for tax evasion, Kahl was on probation when two federal marshals came to arrest him for parole violation. A shootout followed during which Kahl, his son Yorivon, and a friend, Scott Faul, killed the marshals. As a fugitive, Kahl found refuge with sympathizers throughout the Midwest until the daughter of a friend he had stayed with near Smithville, Arkansas, reported his whereabouts to the FBI.*

After Kahl killed a county sheriff, who ignored orders not to attempt to take Kahl alone, two SWAT teams and a small army of state and federal officers stormed the house where Kahl was staying. Thousands

---

[7]Ibid.

[8]James Corcoran, *Bitter Harvest: Gordon Kahl and the Posse Comitatus: Murder in the Heartland* (New York: Viking, 1990), pp. 18–19.

*Smithville is near the community of Evening Shade, Arkansas, the setting for the popular TV sitcom *Evening Shade* starring Burt Reynolds.

of rounds were fired into the frame dwelling before it was set on fire by a smoke grenade hurled by one of the officers. The grenade touched off ammunition stored in the house and Kahl was killed in the blast.

Before putting the house under siege, law enforcement officers had feared that Kahl might have accomplices recruited from the ranks of the Covenant, Sword, and Arm of the Lord. The FBI informant reported that Kahl had been in touch with the group and was trying to buy weapons from them. Except for Kahl's hosts, an elderly married couple who left the house before the shooting started, Kahl was alone at the hideout.

Covenant, Sword, and Arm of the Lord

Founded in 1971, CSA was a collection of paramilitary survivalists about 100 strong, including women and children, who lived on a 200-acre compound near Mountain Home, Arkansas.* The Newtons report that "CSA believed that U.S. society was near the point of collapse into chaos and racial warfare and they were preparing for the breakdown by stockpiling weapons, food and wilderness survival gear."[9]

The group was blatantly racist and anti-Semitic; its members followed the Identity religion. Corcoran quotes an FBI agent who said, "if Kahl had been accepted into the bosom of such a group, it would not have been an easy feat to extract him without a lot of people getting hurt in the process."[10] According to Corcoran,

> CSA followers believed that mankind had entered Tribulations—that period of war, famine, and economic collapse which will end with the Battle of Armageddon and be followed by Christ's return to earth. The CSA members believed they were chosen by God to spearhead the fight during this period against the Jewish-led anti-Christ forces that repeatedly violated God's law. Such violations included allowing blacks to marry whites, homosexuals to practice sodomy, and communists to speak and move freely in society. To fulfill its duty in the struggle, the CSA established itself as the paramilitary arm of the Identity movement, and assumed the responsibility of training its members and other Identity followers in the art of guerrilla and urban warfare. Seminars on Christian military truths, as well as courses in the use of automatic weapons, explosives, and small

---

*On April 19, 1985, federal agents and Arkansas police surrounded the CSA compound. CSA leader James Ellison was arrested after a three-day standoff. Inside the compound authorities found illegal weapons, landmines, explosives, cyanide, a rocket launcher, and an armored car. Ellison was indicted on weapons and racketeering charges. He and six other CSA members were charged the following month with additional crimes, and CSA was effectively shut down.

[9]Newton and Newton, *The Ku Klux Klan: An Encyclopedia*, p. 140.
[10]Corcoran, *Bitter Harvest*, p. 238.

arms, were regularly offered at the compound, which had a shooting range that included wooden, pop-up targets of state troopers who wore badges shaped like the Star of David. Along with food, water, and other essentials for survival in event of a holocaust, the group also stockpiled large caches of weapons and ammunition.[11]

Perhaps the best-known survivalist—at least among survivalists—is Kurt Saxon, publisher of *Survivor*, a monthly newsletter.* Saxon, who lives at Alpena, Arkansas, about seventy miles from what had been the CSA encampment, complains that law enforcement officers invariably attempt to tie him to such groups as CSA, Christian Identity, the Order, or Aryan Nations, just because he is a survivalist. Saxon claims he has no ties to any organized group. He states, "my only interest is in teaching intelligent people how to survive." To emphasize that he has never been affiliated with the Order, or any group like it, he gave me during an interview a 1985 edition of one of his publications, *The Gun Runner*. The following is excerpted from a lengthy article:

> The Order's activities make them similar to the Aryan Brotherhood, a prison-originated cult. They may be one and the same. At any rate, their acts of banditry are more akin to those of the left than the right.
>
> Racketeering, bank robbery, armored car holdups, murder, bombings, etc. are not the tactics of right-wingers, who for the most part plan to move when the red flag goes up over the Capitol dome. Until a takeover is obvious, rational rightists don't trust themselves or each other to begin an offensive.
>
> The Order spokesmen justify their robberies by claiming the loot was for training patriots in guerrilla warfare. Yet, any lad can join the National Guard, get better training and get paid for it.
>
> They claim to be fighting for the white race and against the Jews. Nothing they've done has served even the most radical objectives of the most racist of rightists. Killing a Jewish radio talk show host, Alan Berg, a grizzled mediocrity, who did more for the right by demonstrating a need for it, was no service. Nor is any amount of synagogue bombing even a service to anything but the fantasies of the most warped anti-Semites . . .
>
> All on the far left have good reason to cheer the activities of the Order and the CSA. They have dealt the right wing a blow from which it will not soon recover. Moreover, only the most irrational of self-styled patriots will now act against those chipping away at the foundations of our republic.[12]

---

[11]Ibid.

*Saxon, a journalist by profession, is a prolific writer and editor. He claims that his newsletter, *Survivor*, is nothing more than a catalog advertising his many publications, audio and video cassettes (some of which provide instructions for building bombs and making use of poisons), tools for survival, and the like.

[12]Kurt Saxon, "The Covenant, the Sword, and the Arm of the Lord, or the Pooped Patriots," *The Gun Runner* (Harrison, AR, 1, no. 6 (1985), pp. 81, 83.

In the opening passages of this chapter, I discussed Robert Merton's theory of anomie. Survivalist groups such as Aryan Nations and Posse Comitatus are rebels who would prefer that the existing government be overthrown and replaced with an all-Anglo order. On the other hand, Kurt Saxon is a retreatist with a bent for self-preservation. He insists that he has no burning urge to overthrow the government.

I visited Saxon during the same week that I interviewed Thom Robb, Knights of the Ku Klux Klan. Robb lives on a dirt road seven miles east of Harrison, Arkansas. I had directions to Robb's house before I left my home in Oklahoma, but I would not have needed them. Many I spoke with in Harrison were able to provide me with precise directions to where he lives.

Saxon lives seven miles west of Harrison in Alpena, population 319. I asked him on the phone if he lived right in town; he said he did, so I didn't bother to get directions to his house. Alpena is a tourist town with a chamber of commerce and a small business district. I asked a volunteer at the chamber of commerce for directions to Saxon's home, but she didn't know him. I asked passersby on the street and shopkeepers, but nobody seemed to know him. I reminded people that he had been on David Letterman's show and the Phil Donahue show twice, and that he had testified before a Senate investigating committee; it didn't help. It wasn't until I asked at an appliance store where the bookkeeper doubled as collector for the city water department that I got directions to his house. And, indeed, it was right in the middle of town.

Saxon is a big man who has a way with words. He warned me before the interview that he had seventeen cats and several dogs. I was led to an upstairs study for the interview; had I been asked then how many cats lived under his roof, my nose would have prompted me to guess more than a hundred.

I told him of the difficulty I had finding directions to his house. He said that he wasn't surprised, that he intentionally keeps a low profile. "Besides," he asked, "have you ever taken the time to speak to the rednecks that live in small towns like this? I'm delighted you are here. I am starved for stimulating conversation."

Kurt Saxon

Zellner: Let me start out with a curiosity question. Are people around here going to vote for Bill Clinton?

Saxon: No, people in this part of the country aren't going to vote for Bill Clinton. He's just a total politician, a grinning idiot. Arkansas is the second poorest state in the United States and he hasn't done anything but loot it. He has the biggest dope-pushing operation in the country at Mena [west central Arkansas]—at his airport.

The people from the Medellín cartel fly in their stuff, and he has to know about it. There is a great deal of corruption in this state.

Zellner: Give me an example of the corruption.

Saxon: It's like the system they have between here and Branson, Missouri. They sell liquor at a place on the Missouri border. There is an unwritten limit on what people can buy and take with them into this part of Arkansas, which is dry. You can buy, say, a fifth of hard liquor or a gallon of wine. But if you buy a case, then the people in that liquor store will call the highway patrol. They already have their money, so it doesn't hurt them a bit when the highway patrol confiscates the booze and sells it to a private club in Arkansas.

This is about the crookedest state in the union, the poorest state in the union. There is little intelligent life in Arkansas. It's the Bible belt, of course, and if you don't believe that two and two is five, you are going to burn in hell. Incidentally, how did you connect me with Thom Robb? [Saxon knew I had interviewed Robb the day before.]

Zellner: I didn't connect you with Thom Robb. It's just that you are in the same locale. And I . . . .

Saxon: Oh! You sent me a book that you wrote with another fellow that had a chapter in it on the Amish. Yes, yes, I got that book a few days ago. I stopped at an Amish restaurant one time in Ohio, the food was just wonderful, and it wasn't expensive. But the Amish don't have much survival potential. They're pacifists, and, of course, I'm not.

Zellner: I mentioned to Robb that I was going to visit with you today, and he said you told him that you have no more religion than the cats you keep.

Saxon: I am an atheist and a reincarnationist.

Zellner: (Laughing) Reincarnation—you don't seem the type.

Saxon: (Laughing) Well, I believe it, but if I'm wrong, I can live with it after I die. It doesn't matter that much. I don't believe that any belief system is worth fighting for. A belief is not a virtue as some would have it; it is actually a vice. I was baptized in the Church of Christ [ultra-conservative church, found mostly in the South], and you can't get more hardline than that. I remember asking my mother when I was a child how many Church of Christ members there were in the world, and she said about two million. And she thought that everyone who wasn't a member of the Church of Christ was going to burn in hell. I thought that was nonsense.

I had an argument with a minister a couple of months ago—I think he was a Baptist. He didn't care much for my line about the collapse of civilization, and he thought I ought to get right with God. I said look—I teach people how to make corn meal mush. I teach them how to eat for a penny a pound. What does the Bible teach? He told me that it teaches people how to be saved. I said it

certainly does not. You got about 400 Christian sects in this country and just about every one of them is telling you how people
who belong to the other ones are going to hell. If it did teach you
how to be saved, there would be just one Christian church.

Zellner: They started with just one.

Saxon: And most of the first Christians were lunatics. Bill, I can't understand how people who know that man has landed on the moon
can accept as religious philosophy a bunch of threats and impre-
cations handed down from a bunch of dirty, belligerent lunatics
from 3,000 years ago.

I don't think that anything was written earlier than about 2,500
years ago, and it has been interpolated to the point where none
of it makes any sense. If you read the New Testament, you'll see
that Jesus was an ignorant, primitive, bigoted, paranoid, schizo-
phrenic, Jewish peasant—and not a thing more. I can quote chapters and verses—take for instance John 8—where he's talking to
these Jews, who else could he talk to—that's where he was; it's
what he was. These Jews believed in him and were hanging on
every word he said. And then he said, "You want to kill me."
They didn't care to kill him. The guy [Jesus] was paranoid!

And all that stuff about me and my father are one, and my
father this and my father that. I like his last line, though: "My
God, my God, why hast thou forsaken me!" That says it all. It
wasn't his father, and it wasn't ever his God. If it had been his
God, it wouldn't have forsaken him. I told that to a lady one
time, and she said, "God didn't forsake him," and I said, "Look
lady, if you were hanging buck-naked on a cross fouled by your
own waste, you'd know what the term *forsaken* means."

Zellner: I can understand how what you believe would be offensive to
most of the people in this community.

Saxon: When you talk about religion, you really rattle my chain. I'm not
like most of the people in this town. My parents were born in this
state, and I was raised partly in this state. My dad was a peanut
roaster, and during the Depression he was out of work most of
the time, so he'd send us kids to Arkansas to the grandparents.
So I more or less grew up with these people. I know them. I sort
of like them. But I despise them just the same, and I'm sure they
despise me too. We're even. And if you write down what I am
telling you, which you are privileged to do, you'll have everyone
in the country hating me. And that's okay too.

Zellner: What do you think is the greatest threat to the world today?

Saxon: In 1850, for the first time, the population reached 1 billion. About
thirty-five years later the population doubled. Then in about
1975 it got to be 4 billion, and by now it is 5.5 billion. There
comes a time to stop, but there is no stopping. Most people live
lives of denial. They are hung up on equality, the myth of religion. You would be surprised how many people believe that this

would be the best of all possible worlds if it weren't for a few greedy people. Of course, you know Thom Robb's version of this [reference was to God and race], and I say there is no God and there is no ethnic group causing problems; it's just that there are too many stupid people and these stupid people are having too many children.

Zellner: If overpopulation is a social problem, what solutions are possible?

Saxon: I am interested in sociology. When I was an early teenager I started thinking about people, so I made a graph—actually a pyramid—and about this far down (pointing to near the top of a figure he had carved in the air) are intelligent, functional people. Then you've got the middle class: they're the workers, they keep the streets clean and the boxes packed. And at the bottom of the pyramid you have the mental defectives. And, of course, the pyramid is flattening. In fact, it's just about flat now. So there are very few people left that I am reaching out to.

People don't have to respond to what I have to teach. If they want to eat, drink, and be merry—hey, that's OK with me. I'm a nice guy. I'm not going to force myself on someone's consciousness and cause him to be worried to death about something that he is unable to handle. That person is just going to go along with the herd. These are people with bovine intellects. Unfortunately, they are in the majority, and they are having as many children as biology allows. Hey, I don't want to rock their boat. There is going to be a massive die-off. Most people will die. And when that happens, the few of us who do know what is happening and why it is happening will know better than to let it happen again.

If there were just a few good laws on the books. It's too late now—they would have had to have gone on the books fifty years ago. Then . . .

Zellner: What kind of laws?

Saxon: For example, if everyone applying for welfare had to supply a doctor's certificate of sterilization, if everyone who had committed a felony were sterilized, if anyone who had mental illness to any degree were sterilized, then our economy could easily take care of these people for the rest of their lives, giving them a decent living standard—but getting them out of the way. That way there would be no children abused, no surplus population, and, after a while, no pollution. The race of Homo sapiens has simply outbred the carrying capacity of our environment and socioeconomic system.

Survivalism makes sense. I've never done anything to give it a bad name. Others have done that for me.

Zellner: You coined the term. If survivalism has a bad reputation, who is responsible for that?

Saxon: Yes, I coined the term. I'm not inordinately proud of it. Actually, we are not really survivors yet. We are preparing to survive the collapse of civilization, but we haven't done so yet, so we are not yet survivors; we are survivalists. The term has gotten a bad reputation, however, because of those idiots—the CSA, Aryan Nations, such trash as that—they call themselves survivalists, too.

Zellner: You have never had anything to do with these groups?

Saxon: The leaders of some of these groups are such phonies. I knew a bunch of these people when they first started out. They were nothing but comic relief. The reason they called themselves survivalists was because the term was just catching on, and some took it to mean people who live out in the woods and try to be self-sufficient. The Identity people lived out in the woods and it was easier for them to say "I am a survivalist" rather than "I am from one of the ten lost tribes of Israel, and Jesus wasn't a Jew." So instead of saying that and getting spit in their face, they just said, "we're survivalists."

These people have been a headache to me. Take that Ng character, an Oriental guy and his friend up in Washington state.* They had a little house out in the woods and they allegedly took women out there, where they raped and butchered them. And they told everyone they were survivalists. I got calls from Washington authorities, day after day after day. They would ask, "Are these your people? Are they your subscribers?" There was no connection whatsoever. These idiots used *survivalist* as a cover term because they had a place in the woods. *Survivalist*, as I view it—and remember, it's my term so I can define it any way I want to—has no religious, political, or racial connotations. We are just people who want to be prepared to survive the collapse of civilization when that happens. Our only goal is to become more self-sufficient.

Zellner: What preparations have you made? Your home here looks like an ordinary house.

Saxon: By next season, I'm going to trample down all that garden out there, and I'm going to cut out several hundred tires and make tire gardens. You can take tires, say for the average size car, and drill a hole just at the tread. You take a saber saw and you grind the saw so that it is sharp and jagged, and it will cut around a tire like it was butter. You can cut a whole tire in just five minutes. You lay it down and put two-thirds soil and one-third compost in it. [Mr. Saxon, an obvious authority on many subjects, spent a good deal more time discussing tire gardens. The preceding is included here to exemplify just one of his many survival techniques.]

*Charles Ng is a former Marine who was charged in 1985 with twelve murders involving sexual abuse and torture. Ng fled to Canada, where he was captured and held in custody. Because Canada does not allow capital punishment, Ng was able to delay his extradition to the United States for several years, arguing that he would probably be given the death penalty (which, under Canadian law, would constitute cruel and unusual punishment). Ng is currently in a California prison awaiting trial.

Zellner: Would you say that you are closer to Thom Robb or Euell Gibbons?*

Saxon: That's a good question. I suppose I am somewhere in between. I don't say that you should try to live like an Indian. Even the Indians couldn't make it as Indians. But you have to be self-sufficient. If you think you're going to live off the land, you're not. All I'm interested in doing is teaching people how to survive. And surviving doesn't mean hating Jews or making scapegoats out of any minority.

Zellner: How did your career as a survivalist begin?

Saxon: In the 1960s I was an anticommunist, but there is no point being an anticommunist today.

Zellner: Were you a Bircher?

Saxon: Oh yeah, I was a Bircher. I was kicked out of the John Birch Society. I've been kicked out of about everything. My curiosity gets me into things, and my skepticism gets me into trouble. I was even kicked out of the Church of Satan.

I went to college for a while and I majored in journalism, but before that I worked in the Arizona state nuthouse as an aide.

About the time that I was involved with that sort of thing, Senator Thomas Dodd was acting to push some restrictive gun laws. That panicked the patriots. One of my friends who was a Nazi at that time—he was later caught for bank robbery and spent several years in jail—was a real clown.

He was typical of the type I hung around with then: ineffective, neurotic, borderline psychotic. But having worked at the nuthouse and having worked for a time as a reporter, I was terribly bored with run-of-the-mill people. They held no fascination for me. My friends were interesting. It was like being on duty at the nuthouse all the time. You can't get a better bunch of drinking buddies than Nazis. You wouldn't want them for neighbors, but to party with, they are supreme.

One of my Nazi friends was so crazy. One day he asked me how he could make a good living. I told him he could sell terry cloth towels to wetbacks. And he was really planning to buy a bunch of towels and go down to the border—no brains at all.

But associating with Nazis put me in contact with the modern Identity movement, and I was able to watch it as it grew. Since those early days, it has taken over almost every ultra-right-wing organization there is. If I were Jewish and I wanted to emasculate the Right, I would encourage people to become Klansmen. I can't get that through to Thom Robb. When you become a member of the Identity religion or the modern Klan, you drop out. You

*Euell Gibbons was a popular naturalist who often appeared on the Johnny Carson show. His discussions and demonstrations included topics such as edible tree bark. Gibbons died in 1975.

don't do anything. You are isolated physically and insulated from reality. How many people can you look in the face without grinning and say that Jesus was not a Jew—that white people are from the ten lost tribes of Israel and Jews are scum? Everyone that you don't lose, you are ensconced with. You cannot communicate with anyone outside your own little society and you cannot function outside your little group.

You effectively isolate a person who might become a troublemaker by turning him on to Identity. The paranoia in these groups is just oppressive. They end up doing nothing because there just has to be a Jewish spy at every meeting. If the Anti-Defamation League knew what it was doing, it would promote the Identity religion. There is less effective anti-Semitism and political violence today than there was in the 1960s. If someone sets off a firecracker now, it's headlines.

Zellner: I understand that you testified before a Senate committee relevant to your publishing activities.

Saxon: In August 1970 I appeared before a Senate committee because I had published the *Militants Formulary*, a precursor to my *Poor Man's James Bond* series. The biggest seller was not one of mine but a book called the *Anarchist Cookbook*. Along with publishers of other radical materials, I was called on to give testimony to the Senate so they could determine if such publications were directly affecting the violence that was going on in the country at that time.

On the way to the hearing, I stopped and bought a copy of *Newsweek* that had in it all of the bombings done about that time and who did them. It showed that over 50 percent were from the Left, and I was considered a right-winger. Some bombings were done by unions, some were just criminal acts, but only 11 percent could be considered right-wing. They had never met anyone like me in the Senate before. They didn't know what to make of me, and I had a ball. They were halfway thinking about banning books. And I assured them they couldn't constitutionally do that.

My name was Don Sisco during that period. I didn't want to embarrass my relatives in Arkansas, so I changed my name to Kurt Saxon. I have been accused of coming up with a real Nordic, Nazi-type name, but my favorite TV show was *Along Came Bronson*, and Bronson's first name was Kurt. I liked it, so I took it. Also, my favorite actor at that time was John Saxon, hence—Kurt Saxon. Very simple—nothing Nordic about it. People are always taking simple things and trying to twist them into something ominous.

Zellner: I think I understand your right-wing background. But how did you come to "invent" survivalism?

Saxon: I think my experience in college may have gotten me started as a survivalist. I didn't go to high school, but I did manage to get into a junior college. Because I didn't have a high school diploma, they made me take bonehead math. I found out that kids just out of high school couldn't count to eleven without taking off a shoe. I looked around me and thought: if people could get to this level being this ignorant, and if these people are our future, we don't have one.

I started thinking. With all these dumb people having as many children as they can, what are we going to do when the bottom drops out of everything? So I thought, the best thing we can do is go back to a kind of genteel life-style that would allow intelligent people to fend for themselves. I picked up a formula here and a formula there until I really got good at it. I have the best collection of formulas and processes from the nineteenth century for laymen: things that can be applied, that your wife can do, that your kids can do. I am setting up a system; you don't have to believe in anything, or you can believe anything you want. You can feed yourself, make money, your oldest boy (age ten) could be working with tires, and you could start your garden that way.

Zellner: Survivalism—including your brand—hasn't met with a great deal of success. What is the resistance to, specifically, your ideas?

Saxon: The media hates me. I've been on the Donahue show twice. Oh, they hate me. Audiences hate me. They love to hate me. This Disneyland for dummies is about to shut down forever. You are going to learn to take care of yourself or you are going to die. It's as simple as that. They don't like to hear that. The city is where they have their jobs, it's where they own a home; it's where their kids go to school. They want to discredit me as some kind of nut. So I say, "Eat, drink, and be merry, sweetheart; go ahead." So the media writes about me and tries to associate me with haters. There is nothing in my program that has anything to do with hate.

If you read urban newspapers, I'm responsible for urban flight, the brain drain, and the erosion of the urban tax base. So if they can say, this guy is a hater—fine. It doesn't really bother me, but I do get impatient with people like that because they are so stupid. I have to consider the source; they are trying to protect their own little environment, what little there is left of it.

Incidentally, I can't even win over the right-wing crazies. The people in the Identity movement in general are a bunch of kids in adult bodies. I try to win them over, but it's like talking to five-year-olds. They are satisfied with using Jews as scapegoats. There are only a handful of Jews in Arkansas, I think under a thousand. And I imagine that a good many local Identity people don't even know a Jew. It's really themselves that they hate. They have nothing; they are losers; they don't have the motivation or the stick-to-itiveness to finish anything.

I'm trained in journalism, but I think my first love was sociology. You're interested in social movements. So am I. I joined them

all, and I participated in them, and it was fun. A person who is
ready to give his life for a cause he doesn't really understand is the
most interesting. He's better than studying the corner grocer or
someone who works at McDonald's or whatever. He won't settle
for anything but the worst. He thrives on it. He's a case study, and
he is fun. I have learned a lot from people like that.

Zellner: I agree—but give me an example of something you learned from
such people.

Saxon: I remember an Identity meeting in Hollywood, California, with
Wesley Swift.* Now this is sort of funny. I had gotten back from
New Mexico where I had been a reporter in Taos, and I met some
friends I had gone to college with. They sat me down and told
me that I was an Israelite.

They started heaping all this garbage on me before I had ever
heard anything about Identity. I knew I wasn't an Israelite; I was a
hillbilly. One of my friends—he later went to prison for selling automatic weapons to the Feds—asked me if I had any guns. Well, I
had guns when I was in New Mexico, but I had left them behind.
He said, "You better take a gun to the Hollywood Women's Club
to hear Reverend Swift." I told him I didn't think I would need one.

My friend tried to convince me that the Jews had the place all
spotted out and that they were going to have the niggers attack
the club, so all of us younger guys were supposed to go armed so
that we could fight them off. As I was a reporter, I thought, hey,
there's a story in this someplace, so I went with them. They had
a Volkswagon bug, and in the back of the back seat in a storage
space was an M-1 carbine and 1900 rounds of ammo. My buddy
had a .45 automatic with about ten clips under the seat, and the
guy next to him had a .22 pistol. My pal's brother had a .357
magnum in a case. So, decked out in this fashion, we went to the
Hollywood Women's Club. There was a mob of people milling
around—all white, naturally. It was mainly a geriatric event with
a lot of denture breath evident—mainly old people.

We young people were supposed to scout the area and make
sure the niggers and Jews didn't attack. This is an aside. Several
of us were up on a porch part, and I was with one of the storm
troopers. He looked down at Wesley Swift, who was just coming
in, and said, "Who's that ugly little Jew?" And a little old lady
standing nearby said, "Oh, that's not a Jew, that's Wesley Swift."

Well, you watch the guy; he's all hands when he's talking. He
must have learned his speaking from the Talmud, or whatever.
He was such a liar. One time he said, "There are 60,000 niggers
training in the Arizona desert to take over Los Angeles." He said

*For a discussion of Wesley Swift and his movement, see this chapter's earlier section,
"Aryan Nations."

there were 60,000 Chinese communists in Baja, California, who had come over by submarine. At that time the Chinese had about ten World War II submarines, and Baja couldn't hold 60,000 field mice. He seemed to be hung up on 60,000. He was such an obvious liar. But I looked around at the people at the meeting, and they were taking it in—believing every word of it.

Anyway, we young guys were patrolling the area. There were no blacks, no Jews, except as figments of lively imaginations. It would only take one rumor spread among that bunch of chickens to get them all cackling in unison. I couldn't resist conducting an experiment. I happened to walk by an open side window that was right by the stage. I looked in, and there was my friend's brother sitting up against a back wall with his gun case cradled on his knees. I said in a loud whisper through the screen, "Hey, dair's one ub dem mothas in here." Then I ran like hell because he could have shot right through that wall with his .357 magnum.

Within three minutes, a buzz got around everybody. The guys had their guns out and they were putting ammo in. I guess I could have gotten someone killed, but it was the funniest thing. For months after, people were talking, saying a nigger had gotten right up to one of the windows.

This was the element I lived with. You've got to love them. You can't hate them, because they're too stupid to hate. Little children. I could write a book. In fact, I was going to write a book and call it *Nazi Dogs Don't Bite*. This stems from an experience I had in southern California.

I went to visit Nazi headquarters with a clean-cut type I had met. I can't remember the name of the town or the name of the guy. The headquarters was just a house. We went inside and they had this big Doberman. It was very embarrassing. He stuck his nose up everybody's crotch. It was his way of getting acquainted. When we got there, the storm troopers were getting ready to go to church, Colonel Gale's Identity church.*

Anyway, this Doberman, when people came around the place screaming epithets at the Nazis, would crawl under the bed and whimper. So that's why the title, *Nazi Dogs Don't Bite*.

I didn't go to church that day, opting instead to stay back with a Nazi who had also opted not to go to church. We had a conversation and the Nazi explained to me that when civilization collapses, we will need to cordon off the area around the compound and take care of the white survivors. He said, "We'll feed them.

---

*Colonel Gale, an Identity follower, founded the California Rangers, a paramilitary group, in the late 1950s. According to Newton and Newton, *The Ku Klux Klan: An Encyclopedia* (p. 219), one of his favorite sayings was "turn a nigger inside-out and you've got a Jew." He claimed that the six million Jews purported to have been killed by the Germans during World War II were actually living in the United States.

We'll feed them niggers; they won't know it. There is nothing wrong with cannibalism as long as you don't do it with your own race." I remember, those were his exact words. The guy was bouncing off the walls in front of my eyes. I had to know more about these guys, so I hung around with them for about a year. They were fun! I couldn't resist. Could you?

Zellner: Indeed, I am fascinated by people with unique ideas just as you obviously are.

Saxon: What people want to believe about these people is that they're sinister, they're organized, and they're dangerous. The biggest danger they are is to themselves. The only vicious fights I ever saw were among themselves. The only killings I saw were among them. Leave them to their own devices and they'll wipe each other out.

Zellner: Of the myriad problems facing the world today, what are the most important problems?

Saxon: As I said before, overpopulation is a major problem; the other is stupidity.

Let me say a bit more about overpopulation. When I first moved to Los Angeles in 1953 there were eleven theaters in downtown. Two were Mexican theaters. And there was one all-night theater for winos who slept through three pictures at a time. When I went back six years ago, there was only one theater for whites, and it was a porno house. There was still a theater for winos, but all the rest were Mexican.

The Mexicans are taking over. Who can blame them? Look at world populations. Most people are born with no purpose, except to consume and pollute. There is no longer any reason to be born. Look at the wastage of life. People are becoming desensitized to people.

Now let's talk about stupidity. The level of intellect in this country is going down, generation after generation. The average IQ is always 100, because that is the accepted average. However, the kid with a 100 IQ today would have tested out at 70 when I was a lad. You get the concept. Hence, the marching morons. We have people believing and accepting, basing their lives on such fallacies as religion. Dangerous fallacies. When the end comes, they are not going to know what hit them. Unlike in Somalia or Bangladesh, there just isn't anyone who is going to be able to send us aid.

Zellner: I got the distinct impression when I asked you what you thought of Bill Clinton, that you do not plan to vote for him. Are you willing to say who you will vote for?

Saxon: I don't vote. The last time I voted, I voted for George Wallace, and I really didn't like it. Besides, I think that voting is a hypocritical act. If you have enough knowledge of what is actually going on in the world, then you know it is pointless to vote.

Zellner: Have any of the candidates impressed you at all.

Saxon: The only one that has actually mentioned population problems is Al Gore. Maybe if he were running for president, I might vote for him. OK, the guy is a politician. He's probably not as honest as he might be, but I think he has a better grasp of the system than Ross Perot, who is indeed an exemplary man. But Gore is going to be the second-hand man, an ineffective position; and besides, it's too late anyway.

Zellner: You say that Perot is an exemplary man.

Saxon: I really don't think it matters who wins the presidency; the country is too far gone. But I do like what Perot has to say. I've recorded all his speeches. I do think he is an exemplary fellow. Nevertheless, he really rankles me when he talks about drugs. He said he wouldn't legalize drugs because "I have held these little crack babies in my arms." Well, I don't care if your child blows his mind with drugs. I would rather he do that than he come at me and blow my mind for a few dollars to buy them. I mean, he's your child. He's your problem. You take care of him. He's not my responsibility. If drugs were legalized—same kind of restrictions as on driving drunk—it would be a better system. In fact, I would go one step further. I would make drugs free to addicts. All they would have to do is go to the pharmacy, and show an ID card. On this card would be that person's certificate of sterilization. No crack babies, you see. Druggies and people with low IQs are not fit parents.

Zellner: What about George Bush?

Saxon: You remember that I said that people are becoming desensitized to people? Bush with his Desert Drizzle. He's got his oil friends, so he's got to make a statement against Saddam Hussein. He killed over 100,000 Iraqi civilians even though the fighting could have been confined to the ground in Kuwait. A couple of marine divisions could have mopped up all the Iraqi forces. They were totally ineffectual, and everybody knew it except Bush, [Norman] Schwarzkopf, and [Colin] Powell.

There was this absolutely unnecessary loss of life. Iraq had no air force to speak of. We shot down five or six of their planes and the rest of them fled. Bush has tried to take credit for the fall of the Soviet empire, which I think—as Perot said—is like giving the rooster credit for the sunrise.

But Bush probably had more do to with the fall of the Russian empire than he even knows himself. Because, you see, Bush is a very stupid man. When the Russians saw how ineffective their equipment was against modern technology, it probably took the heart out of them.

Zellner: I see our time is almost up, and I must know if you knew Gordon Kahl who was captured near here. I was also told that there was a network in Arkansas that was responsible for hiding him.

Saxon: I had no association with the man whatever. He was truly an evil and paranoid person. Well, maybe not evil—say just paranoid. And there was no network here in Arkansas. That was all media hype. I didn't know Kahl, but I met the guy who sheltered him—in his seventies. Nice enough old guy. Kahl should never have moved in with him. He should have given himself up.

I have the story from his side and the Feds' side, and these people [Posse Comitatus] are prone to shoot. It's not that they shouldn't have arms. It's just that they shouldn't take arms to their meetings. They get wound up, go off half-cocked, and they don't know their target. There were a couple of movies on the subject. The one with Rod Steiger was the best and most accurate.

Zellner: Let's close this interview with the same question I had for for Thom Robb. Any regrets? Are you happy with your life choices?

Saxon: Look, being a survivalist doesn't mean that you wear a name tag that says you're a survivalist. Have a garden, raise a few chickens. Alpena is a small town, but I can't say I know the last name of anyone in it, and I don't care to. Land here is cheap and there are hardly any taxes. That's because Clinton can't raise them. He would if he could. Wait until he gets to be president. Whoa—ho—ho—boy!*

When the present world system collapses, it'll be good people like you who will be shooting people in the streets to feed their families. Bad people like me won't have to.

Everyone here has a gun so when the urbanite invasion begins, they will be able to protect themselves. (Laughing) I'm probably the only person in town who won't need a gun. People here will protect me because they will come to know that I know how to survive, and they will want my help. Sure, like everyone else I would have done some things a little differently, but I am, for the most part, satisfied with the decisions I have made.

A Seditious Conspiracy to Violently Overthrow the U.S. Government?

On April 21, 1987, thirteen white supremacists were indicted by a federal grand jury in Ft. Smith, Arkansas on charges of conspiring to overthrow the government of the United States. Charges included alleged participation in a conspiracy to assassinate a federal judge and an FBI agent in Arkansas.

The trial stemmed from a 1983 meeting of white supremacists held at Richard Butler's encampment at Hayden Lake, Idaho. Prosecutors

---

*Arkansas has a law that mandates a balanced budget. Taxes cannot be raised without a popular vote.

claimed that "participants laid a plan to cripple the government by assassinations, destruction of utilities and poisoning a public water supply. The plot allegedly was to be financed by money that was either stolen or bogus. The goal of the plan was a separate white nation in the Northwest."[13]

Attorneys for the defendants argued that what their clients believed was not at issue; they were exercising their right to free speech and assembly. Among those charged were some of the nation's most notorious racists, including the four men described in the following sections.

Richard Girnt Butler   Butler is the leader of Aryan Nations and an Identity minister. Prior to becoming a full-time hate activist, Butler was an aerospace engineer. His activities include publishing a newsletter, *Calling Our Nation*, and carrying out an extensive "prison ministry." Each year at Hayden Lake, Butler hosts the annual Aryan Nations World Congress, which brings together racist leaders from around the country.

Journalist Bill Shaw, who interviewed Butler for the *Chicago Tribune*, characterizes the man:

> Butler slumps in his church office. He seems never to smile. The Bible and "Mein Kampf" sit on his desk. He is surrounded by stacks of hate literature and his computerized mailing list. He runs a board called Aryan Nations Liberty Net, which electronically spits out racist messages to anyone with a networked personal computer and the telephone number. He has the frustrated, weary look of someone who can't understand why others don't understand, why others don't readily grasp what seems so simple to him.
>
> "It's so obvious," he thunders, pounding the desk. He begins a long-winded, convoluted tirade against blacks, Jews, the post office, Catholics, Ted Kennedy, race traitors, homosexuals, Michael Jackson, the FBI, the government and anyone who doesn't understand him, which is many people.[14]

Glenn Miller, Jr.   During the 1970s, Miller was associated with the National Socialist Party. He later formed the Carolina Knights of the KKK. The group was renamed twice, first as the Confederate Knights and later, in 1985, as the White Patriot Party. During April 1980 the first "Hitlerfest" was held on land owned by Miller.

Louis Beam   A former Klansman, Louis Beam is a man who preaches violence. As grand titan of David Duke's Texas Klan, he once said, "I've

---

[13]Ray Roddy, "Jury Clears Separatists of Sedition," *Detroit Free Press*, April 8, 1988, pp. A1, A18.

[14]Bill Shaw, "Preaching a Gospel of Hate: Aryan Nations Bristles with Guns and Ex-Cons," *Chicago Tribune*, May 23, 1985.

got news for you, nigger. I'm not going to be in front of my television set, I'm gonna be out hunting you. I don't need any of the three Jewish-owned networks to tell me what I've got to do. I've got the Bible in one hand and a .38 in the other hand and I know what to do."[15]

Beam first came to national attention with the Klan in 1984 when he was identified as party to a plot to terrorize Vietnamese fishermen. According to journalist Paul Taylor, "the story of the Vietnamese take-over of shrimping in the Galveston, Texas area is in many ways the classic American immigrant saga. They came, they toiled, they sacri-ficed, they overcame hostility and violence, they prevailed."[16] Much of the hostility and violence directed at them was from Louis Beam, who purportedly said, "I promise them a lot better fight here than they got from the Viet Cong."[17]

Morris Dees of the Southern Poverty Law Center joined with the Vietnamese Fishermen's Association in a lawsuit against the Klan.* A permanent injunction was issued against the Klan, ordering them to cease their harassments.

Following the loss in court, Beam became a self-styled ambassador at large for Butler's Aryan Nations. In that capacity he developed a point system for qualification as an "Aryan Warrior." Killing a newsman or local politician was worth one-twelfth of a point, federal agents one-tenth, judges one-sixth, congressmen one-fifth. Anyone courageous enough to kill the president of the United States received a full point and instantly qualified as an Aryan Warrior.†

Robert Miles   Born and raised in New York City, Robert Miles moved to Cohoctah, Michigan, in 1953. He was appointed grand dragon for the United Klans of America in 1969. One year later he resigned his position as local manager of an insurance company, citing harassment stemming from his leadership position in the Klan.

During 1971, ten school buses intended for use in Pontiac, Michigan, in compliance with a court-issued desegregation order were destroyed by bombs. Miles and four others were convicted of the charges. In 1972 he founded the Mountain Church of Jesus Christ in Lansing, Michigan;

---

[15]Cited in Newton and Newton, *The Ku Klux Klan: An Encyclopedia*, pp. 41–42.

[16]Paul Taylor, "Vietnamese Shrimpers Alter Texas Gulf Towns: Natives' Economy and Pride Wounded," *Washington Post*, December 26, 1984, p. A6.

[17]Ibid., p. A1.

*Morris Dees is so despised by right-wing extremists that readers of the Klan publication *White Patriot* (issue no. 78, undated) were asked to pray for his death.

†Beam surfaced at the Branch Davidian compound in Waco, Texas, as a reporter for *Jubilee*, a conservative publication. He was charged with criminal trespass when he refused to leave an FBI meeting. According to the *Waco Tribune Herald*, the charges were eventually dropped.

but the church was without its pastor until 1979 when Miles was released from prison on parole. Miles died in late 1992. His obituary in the *White Patriot* notes that "he was one of the principle parties in the fraudulent sedition trials that took place in Ft. Smith, Arkansas, in January–April of 1987. The government lost its case after spending millions of dollars in an intensive yet fruitless investigation, attempting to connect the 'right wing' movement with illegal activity."[18] Because of his persistent courting of Klan and neo-Nazi groups, Miles had been indicted in the conspiracy case. Conspiracy is one of the most difficult charges to prove in a court of law. The Ft. Smith verdict, by an all-white jury of two women and ten men, ended the trial in favor of the defendants.

Solutions to the Problem

Tracking Hate Crimes   In 1990 President George Bush signed into law the federal Hate Crime Statistics Act, which directs the Department of Justice to gather data on crimes motivated by the victim's race, religion, ethnicity, or sexual orientation. Nevertheless, for several reasons it is impossible to know just how many hate crimes are committed each year, where such crimes occur, and who commits them.

The foremost difficulty apparently relates to reporting. When I called the Ada, Oklahoma (population 17,000), police department, the assistant chief was unaware that the law existed. I was referred to the Oklahoma State Bureau of Investigation. The Bureau's public relations officer said that when hate crimes are reported to them the data are stored in their computer, but that is the extent of it. Most of the information they had was from the Tulsa Police Department, which has a special hate crimes unit—the only one in the state. I then called FBI headquarters in Oklahoma City. Agent Dan Vogel stated that local law enforcement agencies have been instructed to report hate crimes to them, but he believes that only a fraction of such crimes are being reported. He, too, noted that the Tulsa Police Department was doing a better job of gathering statistics than most local law enforcement agencies.*

Another problem in gathering data involves defining victimization as hate-related. One police officer asked me, "How do you know if a gay was beaten up by a straight because of his sexual orientation or if other reasons motivated the perp's assault?"

Apart from the federal government, a number of other agencies are monitoring hate-crime activity. For example, the Anti-Defamation League of B'nai B'rith focuses on crimes against Jewish citizens. The National Gay

---

[18]Obituary appears in the *White Patriot*, issue no. 91 (undated) mailed January 1993.
*Telephone calls to all law enforcement agencies were made on April 2, 1993.

and Lesbian Task Force focuses on crimes against the gay and lesbian community. Klanwatch, a project of the Southern Poverty Law Center, monitors hate crimes by gathering data from police departments and media sources nationwide.

Of course, no group that monitors hate crimes has a complete list of such activities; despite some opinion to the contrary, a more effective national clearinghouse would be useful in tracking and controlling haters.

Litigation   In recent years, one of the most effective mechanisms employed in fighting hate crimes has been the civil law suit. As we saw in Chapter 2, the United Klans of America was bankrupted when the mother of a murder victim won a $7 million judgment against the organization. As we saw in Chapter 1, Morris Dees, acting on behalf of the Southern Poverty Law Center, won a $12.5 million award for the heirs of an Ethiopian man killed by skinheads in Portland, Oregon. The court found that Tom Metzger, his son John, and their hate organization WAR (White Aryan Resistance), had inspired the killing.

Klanwatch reports other court victories against hate groups: "in Greensboro, North Carolina, the survivors of five murdered anti-Klan demonstrators won a civil suit against the Klan even after two criminal trials failed to convict the Klansmen. Also, in Raleigh, North Carolina, the White Patriot Party was destroyed by a lawsuit that resulted in contempt of court convictions against its leader for violating a court order against paramilitary training."[19]

Police Training   Many who view themselves as survivalists are at war with the government. Law enforcement officers represent government at various levels: city, county, state, and federal. As such representatives, they are prime targets for violent attack. Klanwatch reports that "at an Aryan Nations training session in 1986, participants were instructed in how to kill police officers at routine car stops. Four law enforcement officers were killed and others were injured by members of the Order."[20]

The Order, Posse Comitatus, Branch Davidians (led by David Koresh), and a variety of Klan and neo-Nazi elements have killed law enforcement officers. In the past, officers have not taken haters seriously enough. For example, the Branch Davidian experience in Waco, Texas, is a sad lesson on how not to defuse a potentially volatile situation. Although Koresh and his followers were religious retreat-

---

[19]"Hate Violence and White Supremacy," in *Klanwatch: Intelligence Report* (Montgomery, AL: Southern Poverty Law Center, December 1989), p. 20.
[20]Ibid., p. 18.

ists, it was well known that they viewed government as an enemy. The ATF (Alcohol, Tobacco, and Firearms) regulatory agency should have proceeded cautiously with its search warrant for illegal firearms. There was no need to rush the Davidian compound. Four federal officers and five Davidians were killed in late February 1993 during the first assault on the compound. After the initial assault, the ATF agents backed off and waited nearly two months for the Davidians to surrender. It can be conjectured that they might have surrendered had they been facing illegal weapons charges rather than charges of killing federal officers. As it turned out, the government raided the compound, starting a fire that killed seventy-two Davidians, including a dozen children.

Despite some failures, intelligence gathering on survivalist groups has become more sophisticated in recent years. One mechanism for gathering data on potentially violent hate groups is the use of informants. Agent infiltration is sometimes used, but a more common method involves the use of an insider, someone trusted by organizational leaders. Perhaps the most effective informant to date has been Tom Martinez.

Education   Martinez is an odd name for a white supremacist, but that is exactly what Tom Martinez was. His father is of Hispanic-Swedish ancestry; his mother is Greek and Welsh. Neither parent is a racist. Martinez's prejudices began in junior high school in 1967 when black students were first bused into the Philadelphia neighborhood where he lived with his family. In his book, *Brotherhood of Murder*, Martinez writes:

> No one brought us into the auditorium and said new kids were coming in, and we'd have special programs. . . . No, they just came strolling in like they owned it.
>   From the first day of class, hatred became the first subject in the curriculum. . . . The boys (black and white) carried out the learning sessions in the hallways, in the gym . . . with insults and punching and shoving. We whites had our triumphant moment each day after school when the buses came to pick up the blacks. As they marched into them—most often under police protection—we had the sense that we had propelled them from our neighborhood.[21]

Martinez quit high school in the tenth grade after he was threatened by a black gang member the day after a white student had been killed. Later, married and trapped in a dead-end job, he heard a David Duke lecture on the radio. He liked the message so he joined the Knights of

[21]Quoted in Murray Dubin, "Army of Hate: Ex-Racist Risks Life to Warn Others," *Seattle Times*, January 12, 1989, p. B2.

the KKK. Young and full of frustrated energy, Martinez soon came to view the Klan as nothing more than a social club: all talk and no action.

Two years later Martinez joined the National Alliance. Journalist Murray Dubin describes how the change affected Martinez's view of the world:

> With the Klan, black people were the reason for the white man's woes, but the specter of Jews and Zionism was out there, hovering behind. The Alliance turned that around, dismissing black people as the lackeys of the Jews and accusing the Jews of destroying the white fabric of America. . . . Black people were inferior, and the Jews, those crafty Jews, controlled the government and the drug business and the media and the banking world. They ruled America.[22]

Because Martinez was an effective fund-raiser and speaker, William Pierce, head of the Alliance, took notice of him. But he wasn't the only one to notice. Robert Mathews, founder of the Order, was also interested in Martinez. In June 1984 Martinez began passing counterfeit bills in the Philadelphia area for the Order. He was soon picked up for having passed two phony ten-dollar bills.

While Martinez was in FBI custody, Mathews offered him the opportunity to go underground with him in Oregon. Learning of this, the FBI dealt. Martinez was to receive probation on the counterfeiting charge in exchange for flushing Mathews out, which he did. After Mathews was killed, a price was put on Martinez's head—more accurately, a price was set *for* his head. Elden "Bud" Cutler, leader of the Order after Mathew's death, offered a reward for Martinez's head, but only if it was severed from his body. He made a deal with a man named David Smith. Smith, an undercover FBI agent, later handed Cutler a cleverly doctored photograph of Martinez's head. When Cutler paid, he was arrested. When he was sentenced to twelve years in prison, the Order died.

Martinez testified against his former friends and allies at the Ft. Smith sedition trials. The FBI acknowledged that Martinez "had helped make a dent in the movement, but that nothing had really changed."[23]

Today, Martinez travels around the country and promotes his book, which describes his involvement with and subsequent rejection of hate groups. He also teaches people about hate groups and how they absorb the individual. He feels that education is the key to understanding minorities, and he expresses regret that he was cheated out of the kind of education that would have helped him understand minority problems at an earlier age.

[22]Ibid., p. B3.
[23]Ibid., p. B5.

Klanwatch reports some progress in education regarding hate crime, from grammar school to university systems. Following are just a few of the programs cited:

- A program in Montgomery County, Maryland, requires juvenile hate-crime offenders to attend a program called STOP wherein they discuss their offenses, learn about Jewish and black history, and perform community service.
- In Middlesex County, New Jersey, a program called Project Alliance has established a communications network between police and school officials to ensure the best response to hate incidents.
- Most entering students at the University of Wisconsin are required to fulfill an ethnic studies requirement.
- At Rutgers University in New Jersey, a new mini-course is being offered called "Race and Rutgers."
- Pennsylvania State University has a hotline for victims of racial harassment.[24]

Apart from education in the schools, education in the community is important. For example, in response to the Posse Comitatus and other such groups, "the Jewish community has tried to foster relations with communities affected by the farming crisis."[25] One group involved in this effort is "the Jewish Community Relations Bureau of Kansas City, which has assigned a 'crisis worker' to liaise with farming and religious groups and mobilize the local Jewish communities." [26]

All across the United States, citizens are banding together to learn about and fight hate groups. Klanwatch reports that in 1988,

> about 1,000 people attended a "Rock against Racism" concert. Funds raised at the benefit went to victim advocacy and to programs against bigotry in the schools.
>
> When white supremacist Daniel Johnson ran for House of Representatives in Wyoming in 1989, 2,000 people of both political parties turned out at a rally to oppose his candidacy.
>
> In Pulaski, Tennessee, the whole community demonstrated its opposition to an Aryan Nations march by agreeing to close downtown businesses that weekend.[27]

Klanwatch is certainly an important educational entity. Apart from issuing information to the general public on Klan, neo-Nazi, and survivalist activities, the organization publishes the *Intelligence Report*, "a bimonthly newsletter distributed nationally to more than 4,000 law en-

---

[24]"Hate Violence and White Supremacy," p. 21.
[25]"Radical Round Up," *Patterns of Prejudice* 22, no. 1 (1988) p. 33.
[26]Ibid.
[27]"Hate Violence and White Supremacy," p. 22.

forcement agencies."[28] The organization promises, too, that an even greater focus will be placed on education in the future. According to chief investigator Danny Welch, "litigation is still needed as a tool, but we realize that a major factor in hate crimes is the misunderstanding and ignorance a person has about people of a different race or different religion. Education is one way to change those attitudes and ultimately halt racial violence."[29]

[28]Ibid., p. 23.
[29]Ibid.

CHAPTER FOUR

SATANISM

The Salem, Massachusetts, witch scare of 1692 centered around chilling stories of black magic told by a female slave, Tituba, owned by a local minister, Samuel Parris. Thought to have been trained in the black arts in her native Barbados, Tituba's first audience was a group of girls from the pious Puritan community. Before long, two of the youngest girls began writhing on the ground, apparently in a state of convulsion. Soon thereafter, other girls in the community began emulating the behavior of Tituba's first listeners. Parents hastily drew the conclusion that their children were being bewitched and demanded an end to it.

Salem's powerful clergy, convinced of Tituba's guilt, instructed authorities to arrest her on charges of witchcraft. During her trial Tituba suggested that many people in Salem practiced the black arts. In the months that followed, the girls allegedly affected by Tituba were pressed to name others in the community who were in league with the devil. Soon the town's jail was overflowing. By summer's end 1692, twenty people had been tried and executed on charges of witchcraft.

It didn't take long before people in the community were in as much fear of being named a witch as they were of the purported witches themselves. But the witch hunt did not end until the girls attempted to extend the new-found power they held over the patriarchal Puritan community. In the zeal to ferret out Satan's allies, the girls named several of Salem's founding fathers, men with the power to resist the label. It was quickly decided that the girls had overreacted, and the witches departed Salem as quickly as they had arrived.

Definition of the Situation   Many years ago W. I. Thomas, one of the founding fathers of sociology, developed the concept of *definition of the situation*. Stated simply, a social situation is whatever it is defined to be by the participants. In Thomas's words, "What men define as real is real in its consequences." Thus, the people of Salem believed there were witches in their midst, and the consequences were very real—especially for those who were hanged.

Interest in Satan and the occult waned gradually in the United States following the tragedy at Salem. According to historian Jeffrey Russell, it "was virtually defunct by the end of World War II, possibly because there were so many more tangible evils."[1] But Satanism is making a comeback.

Satanism's Comeback

Fundamentalist Christianity   Satan has again become "real" in recent years in the sense that Thomas defined "real," and "real" consequences are observable. A recent poll conducted in Texas illustrates the level of public concern. The question was asked: "How serious a problem do you think Satanism is to our society, if at all?" Sixty-three percent responded, "very serious"; and another 23 percent said, "somewhat serious."[2]

A number of factors have rekindled public interest in Satanism, not the least of which is televangelism. Satan has always been real to fundamentalist Christians; and now that cable television reaches a vast audience, viewers are constantly reminded of the devil's evil works. They are also asked to contribute—and do contribute—large sums of money to fight his alleged destructive forces.

Sometimes unscrupulous individuals play on the public's renewed fear of Satan. Even the powerful are not immune from attempts to brand them Satanists.

The Procter & Gamble Saga   Studies indicate that actively religious people are more likely to view Satan as a threat than are the unchurched. Sociologist David Bromley observes that "Shelves in religious bookstores are filled with titles on Satanism. . . . People, including many who are only peripherally involved in fundamentalism, apparently accept the anti-Satanic message."[3]

I have in my files the June 1986 *Newsletter* of a rural Kansas church affiliated with a major Protestant denomination. The letter was approved and circulated by the church's board of directors on the assumption that information provided them about the Procter & Gamble corporation was accurate. The following is an exact reproduction of the letter, except for the church identification at the top:

[1]Jeffrey Russell, "The Historical Satan" in *The Satanism Scare*, eds. James T. Richardson, Joel Best, and David G. Bromley (New York: Aldine de Gruyter, 1991), p. 48.

[2]James T. Richardson, Joel Best, and David G. Bromley, "Satanism as a Social Problem" in *The Satanism Scare*, p. 3.

[3]Ibid., p. 7.

Subject: Support of the Church of Satan
Company Involved: Procter & Gamble
Person Interviewed: President of Procter & Gamble
Source of Information: Phil Donahue Show

The president of Procter & Gamble recently appeared on the Phil Donahue show. The subject of which he spoke was his company's support of the Church of Satan.

He stated that a large portion of Procter & Gamble's profit goes to the Church of Satan, also known as the Devil's Church.

When asked by Mr. Donahue if he felt that stating this on television would hurt his business, the president replied: *"There are not enough Christians in the United States to make a difference."*

The president of Procter & Gamble was contacted by the Church of Satan and notified that if he was going to support the Church of Satan, then Procter & Gamble would have to place the emblem/symbol of the church organization on the labels of each Procter & Gamble product. It is noted that since that time, the symbol of the Church of Satan has been placed on all of their labels.

Recently, on the Merv Griffin show a group of cultists were featured, among them the *owner* of Procter & Gamble. He said that as long as the gays and other cults have come out of the closet he was going to do the same. He said that he had told Satan that if he (Satan) would help him prosper then he would give his heart and soul to him when he died. He gave Satan all of the credit for his riches. Procter & Gamble manufactures the following products, among others:

Cake Mix: Duncan Hines products
Cleaning Aids and Detergents: Biz, Bold, Downy, Spic & Span, Cascade, Cheer, Comet, Dash, Tide, Top Job
Coffee: Folgers, High Point
Oils & Shortenings: Crisco, Fluffo, Puritan
Deodorants: Secret, Sure

Diapers: Pampers
Hair Care: Lilt
Mouthwash: Scope
Peanut Butter: Jiffy
Lotion: Wondra
Shampoos: Head and Shoulders, Pert, Prell
Soaps: Camay, Coast, Ivory, Safeguard, Zest
Toothpaste: Crest, Gleam

In doubt, watch for the Satanic symbol to be found on the front or back of all their products . . . . It is a tiny ram's horn with three sets of stars placed in such a way that if the stars of each set are joined they form the number 666 known as the devil's number.

Christians should always remember that if they buy any products with this symbol they will be taking part in the support of the Church of Satan

of devil worship. We suggest that you use what you have on hand, but make sure you don't buy any more!

Please feel free to make copies of this letter and pass them out to anyone who should be informed, so that as little business as possible will go to Procter & Gamble. Then we can easily prove to their president that there are more than enough Christians and other believers of God to put a large dent into his profits.

Similar letters published by other real and fictitious organizations have been circulating since the early 1980s, peaking in 1982, 1985, and again in 1990. The truth is that the president of Procter & Gamble has never been on either the Donahue or the Griffin show, and the corporate symbol has nothing to do with Satanic worship. The Kansas church published its newsletter in response to a perceived Satanic threat without checking what was reported as fact.

Procter & Gamble has filed a dozen or so lawsuits at enormous cost over the course of the last ten years to protect its reputation. In a court decision rendered in March 1991, the corporation was awarded a $75,000 judgment against a Kansas couple who were independent distributors of competing Amway products.

Remember, *if a situation is perceived as real, it is real in its consequences.* Officials at Procter & Gamble estimate losses in the millions of dollars, based on the spread of false rumors. The problem is so serious that the company has established a telephone hot line and invites calls. The number is 800-543-7270. Kelly Gillespie, public relations supervisor for the corporation, estimates that they have responded to more than 150,000 calls and letters.

Interested callers are mailed a packet of material explaining the corporate logo. Also included in the packet are letters from the producers of *60 Minutes, Donahue,* and *The Merv Griffin Show.** All state that no executive of Procter & Gamble has ever been a guest on any of these programs.

To assuage the fears of fundamentalists, the packet includes letters of support for Procter & Gamble signed by evangelists Billy Graham and Jerry Falwell, along with a letter from Jerry Vines, president of the Southern Baptist Convention.

The Media   Major newspapers such as the *New York Times* and the *Washington Post* have devoted little attention to the subject of Satanism. Less prestigious publications, such as tabloids found near supermarket

---

*Letters are inconsistent in identifying on which shows Procter & Gamble officials are purported to have been guests. For example, a good many of the mailing organizations said that Procter & Gamble's corporate president appeared on *60 Minutes.* My letter did not include this purported appearance.

checkout stations, often feature what are purported to be Satanic traves-
ties. Headlines such as "I Bore Satan's Baby" push the curious to purchase what is usually something less than "truth in journalism."

Hollywood producers have capitalized on the public's awakened interest in Satanism, and movies such as Ira Levin's *Rosemary's Baby* and
William Peter Blatty's *The Exorcist* have been big box office successes.
Low-budget horror films, replete with contrived Satanic rituals, are particularly popular with adolescent audiences.

Perhaps the greatest impetus promoting fear of Satanism comes from
secular television. The public is more likely to accept as plausible a
Satanic threat from what it believes is a legitimate news source than from
overtly religious programming. Popular talk show hosts such as Oprah
Winfrey, Geraldo Rivera, and Phil Donahue each do well over 200 shows
every year. "By the late 1980s, there were enough syndicated talk shows
with large appetites for fresh topics to ensure that almost any movement's claims could receive a hearing on national television."[4] One such
show, a two-hour Geraldo Rivera special entitled "Devil Worship,"
topped Nielsen talk show ratings in 1988. But who are the so-called
authorities who appear on such shows?

Who Says?

Occult Survivors   There are now hundreds of people who claim to
have escaped from Satanic cults. In fact, the numbers have become so
large that they have their own self-help group, Overcomers Victorious.
The typical member is female, in her thirties or forties, and has under-
gone extensive therapy. Philip Jenkins and Daniel Maier-Katkin state
that "At a minimum [her] reported experiences are likely to include cult
worship, blood drinking, and ritual sexual acts, often involving children
and pornography. Most [such] stories also involve ritual murder and
cannibalism."[5] Some of these women even claim to have been "breed-
ers" for Satanic cults, producing children for ritual sacrifices.

Apparently, media producers make very little effort to verify survivors
claims before such claims are aired on national television. For example,
one of the best-known claimants, Lauren Stratford, author of *Satan's
Underground*, aired a lurid story of Satanic involvement on both the
Geraldo special and Pat Robertson's *700 Club*. She told of an international conspiracy of Satanists sacrificing children and said that she her-

---

[4]Ibid., p. 12.
[5]Philip Jenkins and Daniel Maier-Katkin, "Occult Survivors: The Making of a Myth" in
The Satanism Scare, p. 127.

self was kept for two years in a "breeding warehouse," where she produced children for sacrificial purposes.

A team of researchers investigating Stratford for the Christian magazine *Cornerstone* reported many inconsistencies in her story, noting that she was given to "wild fantasies." For example, her Satanic "breeding" involvement is more than suspect. David Alexander reports:

> Stratford has told people that she is sterile; that she had two children who were killed in snuff films; that she had three children who were killed, two in snuff films and one in a satanic ritual; that she had children during her teens and twenties and that she lived in a "breeder" warehouse on Wilshire Boulevard in Los Angeles.
>
> Her ex-husband claims that she was a virgin when their marriage was consummated in 1966. Members of her family and friends who were around during Stratford's teens and early twenties never saw any signs of pregnancy. Finally, there is no unaccounted-for period of two years in her life when Stratford could have been held captive in a "breeder" warehouse.[6]

Stratford's story was so full of falsehoods that in 1990 her publisher withdrew *Satan's Underground* from the market.

When put to the test, stories of an international Satanic conspiracy either fall apart or are so vague as to make verification impossible. This does not mean that sick individuals do not conspire and commit horrendous acts in the name of Satan. They do. However, as I will show later in this chapter, such acts are relatively uncommon.

A Few Psychotherapists   The psychiatric community tends to be, for the most part, antireligious. However, often appearing with occult survivors on talk shows and at other forums are a few fundamentalist psychotherapists who are convinced of a Satanic conspiracy. These professionals can make even the most outlandish survivor claims credible. They argue that patient involvement with the occult is so horrible that it is repressed in the victim's memory. The memory, though sublimated, negatively affects the victim in her real world.

Treatment usually involves hypnosis to bring Satanic experiences from the subconscious to the conscious mind. The traumatic experiences are then relived in a controlled therapeutic environment. The purported goal of the therapy is to reintegrate the experiences into a unified conscious memory. Sigmund Freud used hypnosis as a treatment for hysteria, but he dropped the practice in favor of psychoanalysis after discovering that remembrances issued in a hypnoid state can be inaccurate. Nevertheless, hypnosis had a revival in the United States following

---

[6]David Alexander, "The Skeptical Eye," *Humanist*, May/June 1990, p. 41.

World War I, when therapists faced hoards of veterans suffering from battlefield trauma that required immediate treatment.

Studies indicate that from 5 to 10 percent of the population is highly susceptible to hypnosis. According to psychologist Herbert Spiegel, these subjects have "an intense, beguiling innocent expectation of support from others."[7] Moreover, the subjects are highly suggestible and generally "have unfailing confidence in the good will of their therapists, readily assimilating whatever is suggested by the therapist as being pertinent for them."[8]

Many so-called occult survivors had their first recollections of Satanic experiences while under hypnosis. There is a tendency for highly suggestible subjects to "fill in the blanks" with fantasy while in a hypnotic state, in the process unconsciously reproducing their therapists' expectations. Dr. Frank Putnam of the National Institute of Mental Health (NIMH) notes that "there is an enormous rumor mill out there. Patients pick up stories, and therapists trade stories."[9] Jenkins and Maier-Katkin suggest that "we may see . . . survivor stories as the product of the dynamic process between patient and therapist."[10]

It appears, too, that talk show producers are as lax in checking out the credentials of analysts who appear with occult survivors as they are the credentials of the survivors themselves. One frequent talk show guest is Dr. Rebecca Brown, a self-proclaimed "Satanic cult detoxifier" who lives in California. In an appearance on a Geraldo Rivera special, Brown claimed to have rescued over one thousand Satanists from mind-bending cults.

According to David Alexander,

> What Rivera . . . [did not tell his audience] . . .—or did not bother to find out—is that "Dr. Rebecca Brown" is the defrocked Indiana physician Ruth Bailey, who had her medical license removed by the Medical Licensing Board of Indiana for a number of reasons. Among the board's seventeen findings: Bailey knowingly misdiagnosed serious illnesses, including brain tumors and leukemia, as *caused by demons, devils and other evil spirits*; she told her patients that doctors at Ball Memorial Hospital and St. John's Medical Center were "demons, devils and other evil spirits themselves"; and she falsified patient charts and hospital records.[11]

The licensing board also concluded that Dr. Bailey had caused numerous patients to become addicted to drugs that required extensive with-

---

[7]Quoted in Sherill Mulhern, "Satanism and Psychotherapy" in *The Satanism Scare*, p. 148.
[8]Ibid.
[9]Quoted in Jenkins and Maier-Katkin, "Occult Survivors" in *The Satanism Scare*, p. 140.
[10]Ibid.
[11]David Alexander, "Giving the Devil More Than His Due," *Humanist*, March/April 1990, p. 7.

drawal, and that she had injected herself on an hourly basis with nontherapeutic doses of Demerol.

Cult Cops   During the mid-1980s, occult seminars taught by self-proclaimed police experts became popular fare. Continuing education is emphasized for professional educators, social workers, mental health personnel, victim advocates, probation officers, correction officials, and clergy. Because the occult is interesting, many professionals opted to participate in "cult cop" seminars rather than more mundane offerings.

Police expert Robert Hicks notes that "The instructors present the topic in terms of crime prevention and deterrence, . . . surrounding themselves with makeshift altars, candles, [and] . . . skulls."[12] He further states that presenting Satanism in this movie-set atmosphere "influences audiences by dissuading critical, analytical thinking, instead fostering mystery, implied causality, generalization, false analogies and spurious history. . . . The . . . success [of a presentation] depends on an audience's willingness to suspend critical analysis and accept the entire package without dissection or challenge."[13]

Cult cops tend to determine boundaries between what is moral and what is not, and they classify what is not as Satanic. Consider the following example. Halloween as a holiday has changed for the better since I was a preteen. Youngsters today are willing to accept a treat in lieu of a trick. My friends and I never made such an offer. In my youth, juvenile high jinks were the order of the day. One trick we never overlooked was toppling a tombstone or two in the local cemetery. Today, cult cops view such grave desecration as Satanic practice. In our case, it was not. It was vandalism, pure and simple. On thorough investigation, most such activity today is no more ideologically based than the behavior of my own band of country rogues some forty-five years ago.

It is difficult to know how many self-styled cult cops there are in the United States. *Newsweek* estimated in 1988 that that there were more than a thousand. Many of these officers share a born-again Christian experience. "Larry Jones of the Boise, Idaho, police department is head of the *Cult Crime Impact Network* (his newsletter reaches 1,500 readers); he thinks cops should investigate 'mockery of Christian sacraments,' and fears 'upper level' Satanists have infiltrated the criminal-justice system itself."[14]

How serious does the law enforcement community in the United States perceive the Satanic threat to be? The following paragraphs, ex-

[12]Robert D. Hicks, "The Police Model of Satanic Crime" in *The Satanism Scare*, p. 175.
[13]Ibid.
[14]"Networking to Beat the Devil: But Are the 'Satan Sleuths' Really on to Something?" *Newsweek*, December 5, 1988, p. 29.

cerpted from *Occult Crime Control: The Law Enforcement Manual of Investigation, Analysis, and Prevention** by William Edward Lee Dubois, indicate that the threat is perceived as very serious:

> Investigation of a satanic group suspected of criminal activity puts you on the ragged edge of violating citizens' rights. Be careful . . .
>
> If you think there is a problem with Self-styled Satanists in your community—and there almost certainly is; the situation is epidemic—start with the schools. Take samples of satanic symbols into the schools and see if administrators and teachers have seen them on clothing, as graffiti, as doodles, as art-class assignments, or on jewelry. Get the names of the juveniles associated with the symbols. Find out who they hang around with. Check their English-class essays to see what they write about.
>
> Don't limit yourself to the high schools. More and more, middle schoolers are becoming involved in Self-styled Satanism, and even second graders have drawn inverted pentagrams on their desks. Remember, however, the younger the children involved, the more likely they are to be victims, not practitioners. Check with school and public librarians to see which books from call number 133 (occult subjects) are missing or overdue. Get the name of the last person to check out the book. Also, many libraries still use cards that every borrower has to sign. A quick glance at this card in the back of the book will tell you who has checked out the book in the last year or so. Jot down the names; they could prove useful.
>
> Compile a list of all juveniles displaying the trappings of Self-styled Satanism. Acquire a copy of the school yearbook, which will provide you with mug shots of the juveniles on the list. When they violate criminal codes—and they will—prosecute rigorously to the fullest extent possible.
>
> This is not overreacting. Juveniles are traditionally given a break "the first time." You cannot do this with Self-styled Satanists. Letting them "off" proves to them what they believed all along: Satan will get them off the hook. The crime will be more serious, perhaps deadly, the next time around.
>
> If you are a street officer and you encounter juveniles who are displaying the trappings of Satanism and engaging in even minor breaches of the law, do not counsel and release. Take them downtown.
>
> If you are with the district attorney's office, prosecute. If you are with juvenile probation, recommend taking the case—no matter how minor— to court. If you are a judge, give the maximum sentence.
>
> This sounds harsh, but it is the only way. Most of these kids can be salvaged, but any sign of weakness on the part of the system will be disastrous. It will strengthen their religious convictions and their belief that the system is weak and Satan is Strong.
>
> You must teach them that this is not the case. When they feel the system is strong and Satan is weak, they often abandon their whole belief system. They feel it has been proven false. One incarcerated juvenile later told his

---

*The manual is the textbook for the National Association of Chiefs of Police home-study program for law enforcement officials on Satanic cult and ritualistic crime investigation.

friends that he prayed to Satan to get him out of jail and "the fucker wasn't there."

Early signs of future serious criminal activity can best be classified as terrorist activity in the form of threats and harassment—usually taking the form of notes, first aimed at fellow students, then at unpopular teachers.

Often each of the members of a Self-styled Satanist group will write a part of the threatening note. Get handwriting samples from all suspects and send the note and samples to your crime lab.

Follow up quickly and take action forcefully. What is normally considered harmless juvenile activity is not harmless when Self-styled Satanism is involved. Left unchecked, the level of Self-styled satanic criminal activity increases almost exponentially. Threatening notes in lockers can lead to dead bodies in less than six months.*[15]

At cult cop seminars, presenters employ a four-tier, progressive model to explain Satanism in society. Progressive in this sense means that some Satanic practitioners move from lower levels in the continuum to higher levels (see Table 1).

Social scientists find the police model difficult to accept. Cult cops lead seminar participants to believe that innocent children enter the model at Level I as dabblers by listening to heavy metal music and playing fantasy games such as Dungeons and Dragons. Some do not progress beyond that level; but others progress to Level IV, where they become part of an international Satanic conspiracy. Anthropologist Sherill Mulhern comments on the model: "By definition, a continuum is something in which no part can be distinguished from neighboring parts except by arbitrary division. The first thing remarkable about the alleged Satanic levels is that each level is a self-contained whole, defined by specific, real or imagined, exclusive parameters. The continuum is not in observable behavior, it exists only in [cult cops'] minds!"[16]

Promoted by the media, cult cop seminars, and a few psychotherapists, the police model has gained considerable public acceptance. It is

*Although Americans may not be able to recognize their own paranoia, the British have us pegged. The following is from the *New Statesman and Society*, September 21, 1990, p. 5: "Does your child make farting noises, laugh when other people fart, have nightmares, play aggressively or sing rude versions of nursery rhymes? These are some of the symptoms displayed by children subjected to satanic abuse, according to Pamela Klein, American expert on the phenomenon. If applied to [England's] children as a definitive test of satanism, our schools would be emptied, and they'd have to hold case conferences in Wembley stadium."

[15]"Witch-Hunting in High School," *Harper's*, December 1990, pp. 20, 22. Reprinted from "Investigation and Surveillance" in *Occult Crime Control: The Law Enforcement Manual of Investigation, Analysis, and Prevention*, by William Edward Lee Dubois (Las Vegas: San Miguel, 1989).

[16]Quoted in Ibid., p. 180.

Table 1. The Police Model of Satanic Crime[17]

Level	Visibility	Primary Attributes	Character Types	Criminal Associations	Primary Evidence Supporting Criminality
I	Semipublic	"Dabblers," or young adults who listen to rock music with occult themes; interest in occult or satanic imagery; interest in fantasy role-playing games, e.g., Dungeons & Dragons	Teens, young adults of diverse backgrounds	Suicide; narcotics use; violent crime; animal cruelty	Occasional narcotics use; juvenile delinquency
II	Semipublic	Self-styled killers, e.g., Charles Manson, Henry Lee Lucas	Psychopathic or sociopathic criminals	Violent crime; narcotics use	Violent crimes actually committed, prosecuted
III	Public	Organized churches or institutions, e.g., Church of Satan, Temple of Set	Unpredictable: intelligent, curious	None, except ideology might attract criminals	None
IV	Covert	Multigenerational family involvement; child abuse; human sacrifice; kidnapping; brain-washing; sexual violence; international network	High-level public officials; police; judges; lawyers	Violent crime such as homicide and kidnapping, assault, abuse; narcotics use	Cult survivors' tales; "ritual" child abuse allegations

[17]Hicks, "The Police Model of Satanic Crime" in *The Satanism Scare*, p. 179.

Important Notice for Personal Account Customers of Fleet Bank - Connecticut

Federal regulations require us to limit to a total of six the number of automatic, pre-authorized or telephone transfers that you may make from your savings or money market savings accounts during a monthly statement cycle. No more than three of the six transfers may be made by check. Please note that transfers such as wire transfers, mortgage payments to Fleet Mortgage Company, purchases made with your ATM or SELECT℠ Cash & Check Card and transfers from your savings or money market savings accounts by telephone, computer or instructions sent to us using a facsimile machine are also subject to these limits.

The Excessive Transaction Fee, noted in your Fee Schedule, will be assessed for each transaction in excess of these limits.

In addition, effective March 1, 1997, the Unavailable Funds Charge will increase to $25. To avoid this fee, we offer two convenient services - Cash Reserve, which is a line of credit, and Savings Overdraft Protection, which automatically transfers funds from your savings account to your checking account.

If you have any questions about how these pricing changes will affect your accounts, simply visit one of our conveniently located branch offices or call us at **1-800-833-6623**.

Thank you for banking with Fleet.

Important Notice for Personal Account Customers of Fleet Bank - Connecticut

The monthly fee, minimum balance requirement and transaction fees have been adjusted on certain checking and savings accounts. These changes will become effective with statement periods beginning on or after March 1, 1997. Please review the changes described below carefully in order to understand which changes may affect you. Fleet One® and Fleet Plus Accounts are **not** affected by these changes.

Please note that you will not be charged monthly or transaction fees when you maintain the minimum daily balances shown for your account.

Personal Checking Account Fees

Account	Monthly Fee	Transaction Fee	Minimum Balance to Avoid Monthly and Transaction Fees
Regular Checking	$6.00	$0.35	$1,000
Interest Checking	$7.00	$0.35	$1,500
Flat Fee Checking	$10.00	None	None

Personal Savings Account Fees

Account	Monthly Fee	Transaction Fee	Minimum Balance to Avoid Monthly and Transaction Fees
Regular Savings	$3.00	None	$500
Passbook Savings	$3.00	None	$500
Money Market Savings*	$6.00	None	$2,500

You may be able to eliminate or reduce your monthly fees by consolidating other banking relationships into a Fleet Relationship Account. A Fleet One or Fleet Plus Account lets you use your combined account balances to meet minimum balance requirements and avoid monthly checking and savings account fees.

And with most Fleet checking accounts, you save $2.00 on your monthly fee when you have your regular paycheck deposited directly into your account. Ask your employer or agency about signing up for this service.

*Includes Money Market Savings, Money Market Passbook, Check Access Money Market

therefore necessary to view the model level by level, to gain insight into its value.

Dabblers

Dabblers are defined in the police model as young adults who listen to rock music with occult themes, have an interest in Satanic imagery, and engage in fantasy role-playing games.

Rock Music   For more than forty years rock music has been an anathema to religious fundamentalists, as evidenced by the many record burnings conducted in church parking lots. Early antirockers denounced Elvis Presley for allowing his pelvis to gyrate with his music. The Beatles wore their hair long, a sure sign of depravity. Fundamentalists saw rock musicians as corrupting the nation's youth, moving them away from the traditional values of their parents. It was Satan's work, no doubt, but the full impact of Satan's powers was not recognized until the advent of heavy metal rock some years later.

Those who oppose rock music agree with Carl Raschke, author of *Painted Black*:

> . . . [T]he emblems of Satan and suggestions of so-called devil worship used in heavy metal performances are indeed, as the rockers themselves contend, stage props. The props, however, have a purpose. They are designed to "evangelize," not so much for some sort of organized and structured church of Satan, but for a summoning of the steely determination of "young America" to take charge, as the brownshirts did in the dusky streets of Weimar Germany.[18]

Those who defend rock music agree that "shocking symbolism" does exist in the music's lyrics; but they argue that it is simply a mechanism for attracting teenagers, not an organized plot to attract adherents to Satanic worship. Feelings of powerlessness affect many teens, and listening to music with shocking lyrics may be a way of striking back at their parents. Sociologist Marcello Truzzi suggests that even sex no longer shocks parents. "The only thing left is the devil."[19]

In recent years a number of litigants seeking damages have filed civil suits claiming that heavy metal musicians and record companies influenced listeners to commit deviant acts, including murder and suicide. The courts have routinely dismissed such cases in favor of the constitu-

---

[18]Carl Raschke, *Painted Black* (San Francisco: Harper & Row, 1990), p. 171.
[19]Quoted in Arthur L. Lyons, *Satan Wants You: The Cult of Devil Worship in America* (New York: Mysterious Press, 1988), p. 163.

tional guarantee of freedom of speech and expression. However, a suit involving the English rock band Judas Priest and CBS Records made national news.

On December 23, 1985, after a day of drinking beer, smoking pot, and listening to Judas Priest records, two Nevada teenagers entered into a suicide pact. The first teenager died instantly of self-inflicted shotgun wounds. The second was not so lucky and succeeded only in blowing his face off. He died three years later from an overdose of a prescription painkiller.

Some months after the suicide attempts, the families of the teenagers filed a lawsuit alleging that Judas Priest and CBS Records were responsible for the suicides. The case appeared to be just another litigation that would quickly culminate in a finding for the defendants based on freedom of speech and expression. However, lawyers for the plaintiffs added a new dimension to an old argument, insisting that subliminal messages "backmasked" in the music had caused the teenagers to form and carry out the suicide pact. Such messages, the attorneys argued, are not constitutionally protected because the listener cannot avoid them.

A subliminal message is one that is introduced below the level of consciousness, too slight to be perceived. The first use of such messages is attributed to the motion picture industry. Spliced between the frames of movie film were pictures of candy, hot dogs, soda, and other refreshments that are available at theater concession stands. Such pictures were not visible to the eye, but they collected in the subconscious of the viewer. It was thought that these hidden suggestions would emerge as the viewer's own idea and that improved concession sales would result.

In the suicide case, the plaintiffs' attorneys argued that Judas Priest and CBS Records had backmasked Satanic messages in the group's music, much as film producers hid suggestions to buy candy and soda. The phrase "do it" seemed to appear again and again in the music. Rob Halford, lead singer for Judas Priest, testified that the sound was merely his exhaling during the recording session.

Attorneys for the band argued that both teenagers had histories of drug and alcohol problems, did poorly in school, and were victims of child abuse. Judge Jerry Whitehead ruled for the defendants.

A Cardinal Speaks Out   Not all attacks on heavy metal music find their way into the courtroom. In March 1990 Cardinal John O'Connor, archbishop of New York, attacked rock music from the pulpit. Said O'Connor, "rock music can trap people, especially teenagers, into dabbling in disgraceful Satanist practices."[20] O'Connor particularly objected to the

[20]"No Sympathy for the Devil: A Cardinal Decries Satanic Influence," *Time*, March 19, 1990, p. 55.

lyrics of Ozzy Osbourne's "Suicide Solution." Osbourne, who first found fame with the group Black Sabbath, is noted for his bizarre stage performances in which shock techniques bring audiences to a frenzy. Once he even bit the head off a bat. In response to O'Connor's sermon, Osbourne wired the Cardinal that he had "insulted the intelligence" of rock music fans worldwide.[21]

Although it is possible to question the intelligence of Osbourne's fans, no evidence exists to suggest that rock music pushes juveniles to commit deviant acts. There is no question, however, that some delinquents are devotees of rock music.

Dungeons and Dragons   Cult cops hold that teens involved with many of the more than five hundred role-play fantasy games on the market are Satanic dabblers. A good many of these games are associated with science fiction characters. However, Dungeons and Dragons, the most popular of the games, derives from medieval European fantasy, from a time when demons were thought to share the earth and interact with humankind. Dungeons and Dragons is rife with monsters, dragons, and a variety of demons. Some fundamentalist Christians believe that demons attach themselves to the game's characters.

The producer of Dungeons and Dragons recommends the game for anyone eleven years of age or older. Similar fantasies are available to youngsters of every age on Saturday morning television. There appears to be an inconsistency of thought in our culture: imagination is encouraged in early childhood, but youngsters are expected to abandon imaginative thought by late childhood.

Many right-wing Christian organizations argue that fantasy games are precursors to full-fledged Satanism, but only one such organization was formed specifically to combat mind games. BADD (Bothered About Dungeons and Dragons), consciously modeled on MADD (Mothers Against Drunk Driving), was organized by Pat Pulling, a mother who blames the Dungeons and Dragons game for her son's suicide.

Mrs. Pulling claims that her son, Bink Pulling, gave no indications that he was suicidal before shooting himself in the driveway of their home. However, David Alexander made the following observation after reviewing the transcript of a cult cop seminar held in Fort Collins, Colorado:

> Pulling stated then—but not in any of her own publications or subsequent interviews—that several weeks before his death, her son had been displaying lycanthropic tendencies such as running around the backyard on all fours and barking. Pulling was also quoted as saying that within the month before her son's death, nineteen rabbits he had raised were inexpli-

[21]Ibid.

cably torn apart, although no loose dogs were seen, and a cat was found disemboweled with a knife. Other sources indicated that Bink was despondent over not "fitting in" at school and had written "Life Is a Joke" on the blackboard in one of his classes.[22]

Although there is little doubt that Bink Pulling was an angry youngster, his mother still says she had no warning that he was suicidal. Apart from what fundamentalist Christians perceive as "real," there is no corroborating evidence that fantasy games promote suicide. An in-depth review of 700 cases of attempted teen suicide conducted by the Albert Einstein College of Medicine in New York found no evidence that fantasy games were associated with any of the incidents. The Association of Gifted-Creative Children of California asked coroners in major cities across the nation to review psychological autopsies to determine the mind-set of adolescents who committed suicide. Fantasy games did not appear as a factor in even one case. The Centers for Disease Control in Atlanta and the American Association of Suicidology in Denver also find no evidence that Dungeons and Dragons, or any other fantasy game, is associated with teen suicide.*

There is no doubt that a few teenagers who commit suicide have played Dungeons and Dragons; however, there is no evidence that such games push young players to suicide or impel them toward any other form of deviance.

Animal Mutilation   As a preteen growing up in the foothills of the Pocono Mountains of Pennsylvania, I spent half a day with four friends looking for a cat. An older boy (we tried to avoid him, but that wasn't always possible) wanted to bury a cat up to its neck in his parents' yard and then mow the lawn. This youngster could whip us one at a time or as a lot, so we pretended to search. I don't know what would have happened had we found a cat. Turning over a tombstone on Halloween is one thing, but mutilating an animal belongs in an altogether different category.

The boy in question has paid very little rent in his lifetime. For most of his adult life, the Pennsylvania Department of Corrections has furnished him with room and board. Clearly he is a *sociopath*, a term sociologists use to define persons who do not develop a conscience. He grew to manhood with no more empathy for humankind than he had for animals. He was a sick child, but he was not a Satanist.

Cult cops are quick to believe that Satanists are responsible for most animal mutilations. There is no doubt that a small number of animals are

---

[22]Alexander, "Giving the Devil More Than His Due," p. 9.
*Similar discussion appears in Alexander's "Giving the Devil More Than His Due."

sacrificed every year in the name of Satan by a few mentally ill dabblers, acting alone or in concert with two or three others. Upon investigation, however, most suspected cases of Satanic animal mutilation turn out to be the work of predators. Alexander cites a rumor panic that began on Halloween 1989 in Tustin, California, after citizens found a number of mutilated cats:

> Orange County Animal Control concluded that increased construction in the nearby foothills had caused a loss of habitat for coyote prey. Coyotes were being forced to invade the urban setting and prey upon cats, the conditions of the cats' bodies clearly indicating predator attacks.
>
> A tiny group of "true believers" saw the mutilations . . . as evidence of ritual Satanic activity and refused to accept the initial conclusion of the animal control officers. The county was forced into an expensive, in-depth investigation expending hundreds of work hours and tens of thousands of taxpayers' dollars to make certain that no ritual Satanic cat mutilations were taking place. . . .
>
> This was, of course, ignored by the local extremists who exploited the situation by bringing in one or two outside "experts," forming an organization, instituting citizen patrols, and offering a reward for information leading to the arrest of "Satanists" who were perpetrating this atrocity.[23]

An occasional dead cat is still found in Orange County, but despite all the efforts of extremists, no evidence of Satanic activity has been discovered.

Killers

Level II of the model suggests that "dabbling" leads to committing violent, Satanic crimes. There is no doubt that some sociopaths are self-styled Satanists. Richard Ramirez, the Los Angeles "Night-Stalker," painted Satanic symbols on his victims' walls. Charles Manson apparently perceives himself to be in league with the devil. Henry Lee Lucas, who has confessed to committing from 50 to 360 murders (depending on the day he is asked), claims he is a Satanist. Some writers—most notably the journalist Maury Terry—have tried to tie David Berkowitz, the "Son of Sam" murderer, to a Satanic conspiracy. (There is little support for this theory.)

Although some sociopaths relate their antisocial behavior to Satanic imagery and trappings, most do not. For example, the Milwaukee slayer Jeffrey Dahmer tortured his victims before killing them and cannibalized their bodies afterward; but he is not a Satanist. Ted Bundy, who was put to death in the Florida electric chair in 1989, had brutally killed thirty women; but he was not a Satanist. Yet fundamentalist Christians tend to

[23]Ibid., p. 14.

believe that all heinous acts of violence are induced by Satan, whether the perpetrator admits to it or not. What other explanation could there be for such outrageous actions?

Satan, by cultural definition, represents all that is evil, the antithesis of Christ, the spirit of all that is good. The demonology of Satanism is a Christian phenomenon. Few religions in the world have a comparable myth, an evil spirit with the power to interact with and affect the lives of humans. But one obscure religion with a similar myth, Palo Mayombe, brought headlines in 1989.

Murders at Matamoros   In March 1989, Mark Kilroy, a premed student at the University of Texas–Austin, and three friends decided to cross the Rio Grande at Brownsville, Texas, and spend part of their spring break in Matamoros, Mexico. Separated from his buddies, Kilroy was abducted and his whereabouts were unknown for almost a month.

At this time the Mexican Federal Police (Federales), conducting a drug seizure operation in conjunction with U.S. drug enforcement agencies, searched a ranch about twenty miles west of Matamoros for contraband. During the raid the Federales seized seventy-five pounds of marijuana, but the officers were totally unprepared for what they discovered in a corral and in a tin-and-tar-paper shack located near the ranch house. Guy Garcia described the scene for *Rolling Stone* magazine:

> As the lawmen approached the corral, they were engulfed by the sickening stench of decaying flesh. Buried in several shallow graves in the immediate area were the remains of twelve males, including the mutilated body of Mark Kilroy. Some of the victims had been slashed with knives, others shot. At least one had been burned, another hanged. Many had been savagely disfigured, their hearts ripped out, their ears, eyes and testicles removed.
>
>   . . . On the blood-smeared floor [of the shack], amid a battery of still-glowing candles, stood an iron kettle filled with iron and wooden spikes, a charred human brain and a roasted turtle. Other urns contained a grisly stew of congealed blood, human hair and animal parts. . . .
>
>   . . . When . . . police found Kilroy's body in one of the graves . . . his legs had been severed at the knee and his brain and spine had been removed.[24]

Participants, members of a non-Christian cult, testified that the victims had been ritually slain in the belief that "human sacrifices would make the gang invincible and protect their drug business from the police."[25]

The leader of the cult was identified as Adolfo de Jesus Constanzo, age twenty-six, a self-proclaimed Palo Mayombe priest. A Caribbean religion

[24]Guy Garcia, "The Believers," *Rolling Stone*, June 29, 1989, pp. 48–49.
[25]Ibid., p. 49.

that originated in the Congo, Palo Mayombe is an admixture of African gods and voodoo. It is believed that Constanzo was "dedicated to a specific spirit of the Palo Mayombe cult known as Oggun, the patron god of criminals and and criminal activity."[26]

Oggun high priests (*mayombreros*) are perceived by practitioners to be spirit-possessed. Before making a human sacrifice, the *mayombrero* must blow cigar smoke and spit liquor in his victim's face. When Constanzo was killed in a shoot-out with police in Mexico City two weeks after the grisly discoveries at Matamoros, police discovered that he possessed all the trappings of a black magic priest, for example, "a horseshoe, a chain, railroad spikes, things of metal."[27]

Before Matamoros, the last known human sacrifice attributed to practitioners of Palo Mayombe occurred in the Caribbean region around the turn of the century. Animal sacrifice and the exhumation of human bones is common practice in Palo Mayombe; human sacrifice is not.

In checking Constanzo's background, investigators learned that both his mother and grandmother were Santeras priestesses who worshipped spirits at altars constructed in their homes.* Neighbors recall that as a child Adolfo Constanzo would sometimes leave dead animals on their doorsteps, an indication that his socialization in the black arts began early.

Through *socialization*, the process of teaching culture to each new generation, Adolfo Constanzo, a dangerous, sadistic sociopath, learned of Oggun, the black spirit of his Caribbean culture. Sociopaths in Christian communities learn of the devil in much the same way that Constanzo learned of Oggun. Thus, it appears that sociopaths are not impelled by evil spirits to commit deviant acts, but that some sociopaths choose to associate their deviant activities with the demonology accepted in their culture.

This does not mean that law enforcement officers should overlook Satanic trappings in their investigations. Obviously, some sociopaths are prone to couch their deviant activities in cultural fantasy. Nevertheless, not all so-called Satanic imagery can be tied to sociopaths. The following discussion of organized Satanic churches gives evidence of that.

Organized Satanic Churches

Even ardent supporters of the police model of Satanic crime admit that organized churches of Satan (Level III) rank low in priority as a law

[26]Ibid.
[27]Ibid., p. 63.
*Santeria is an underground Caribbean religion in which African gods are identified with Roman Catholic saints.

enforcement problem. Only a few such churches exist, and combined membership does not exceed two thousand—in a country of more than a quarter billion. The two largest organized churches are the Church of Satan and a spin-off church, the Temple of Set. Anton LaVey, founder and self-labeled "Black Pope" of the Church of Satan, is the best-known Satanist in the United States. Some of the ideology and much of the Satanic imagery adopted by self-styled Satanists is the product of the fertile mind of LaVey. Hence, a discussion of LaVey and the Church of Satan is appropriate.

Anton Szandor LaVey   An accomplished musician, Anton LaVey became second oboist in the San Francisco Ballet Symphony Orchestra while he was in high school. Interested in art and music but bored by academia generally, he left high school in his junior year to join the circus.

One of the most popular circus acts of the 1940s was Clyde Beatty's animal act, featuring ferocious lions and tigers forced to obedience by the snap of a trainer's whip. Beatty put LaVey to work feeding and watering the animals. As his trust in LaVey grew, Beatty occasionally allowed him to work in the ring. LaVey claims he liked the big cats but that his first love was still music.

One evening the circus calliopist was too drunk to perform, so LaVey volunteered to fill in. The story goes that he performed so well that Beatty fired the drunken calliopist and gave LaVey the job permanently. At age eighteen he quit the circus to become a magician's assistant in a carnival show. There he learned hypnotism and began studying the occult.

On Sundays he played the organ for tent evangelists. The same men he saw ogling show-girls on the strip on Saturday nights would come to the meetings with their wives and children and pray for forgiveness on Sunday. The next Saturday night he would see them back on the strip ogling show-girls. LaVey concluded that Christianity was an exercise in hypocrisy, so in 1966 he formed the Church of Satan in direct opposition to it.

Always the showman, LaVey dresses the part. There is no doubt about it, he looks like the devil—or better said, Christianity's stereotype of the devil. He shaves his head, has a pointed goatee, and dresses in black.

In 1969 LaVey authored the *The Satanic Bible*. The Church of Satan claims sales exceed a half-million copies, but don't try to get a copy at your local library. I asked a librarian why there was no copy in our university library. I was told that such items were stolen almost as soon as they were shelved—not by Satanic dabblers, but by religious fundamentalists. Calls to other area libraries confirmed what our school librarian had told me. Some fundamentalists apparently condone theft in the name of Jesus, if it saves the weak from succumbing to Satanism.

The Satanic Bible   LaVey's bible is a spoof of Christianity, its beliefs and rituals. In the book he equates what is normally considered the "Christian ethic" to weakness. The book includes passages on human sacrifice, the black mass, Satanic symbols, lewd sexuality—in short, all things abhorred by most Christians. His "Invocation to Satan," for example, was probably written to provoke Christians and sell bibles:

> In the name of Satan, the Ruler of the earth, the King of the world, I command the forces of Darkness to bestow their Infernal power upon me!
> Open wide the gates of Hell and come forth from the abyss to greet me as your brother (sister) and friend!
> Grant me the indulgences of which I speak! I have taken thy name as a part of myself! I live as the beasts of the field, rejoicing in the fleshly life! I favor the just and curse the rotten!
> By all the Gods of the Pit, I command that these things of which I speak shall come to pass!
> Come forth and answer to your names by manifesting my desires![28]

The Satanic Bible has four books: Book of Satan, Book of Lucifer, Book of Belial, and Book of Leviathan. The book of Leviathan is a book of prayers written in both English and Enochian. LaVey explains that Enochian is a language "thought to be older than Sanskrit."[29] Edward Kelly, a sixteenth-century occultist, was the first to rediscover the ancient language in his crystal ball.

A single line of Enochian should be enough to satisfy the average reader: "Otahil elasadi babaje, od dorepaho gohol: gi-cahisaje auauago coremepe peda, dasonuf vi-vau-di-vau?"[30] The punctuation is apparently not the same in Enochian as it is in English. LaVey translates as follows: "I have set my feet in the South, and have looked about me, saying: Are not the thunders of increase those which reign in the second angle?"[31]

The Satanic Bible runs to 272 pages. The Book of Leviathan is 120 pages long, and half of it is Enochian babble. There are many pages with fewer than five words to the page; some pages are blank. A skeptic might argue that the paperback is puffed so that purchasers will think they got their $5.95 worth.

In defense of the Church of Satan, the Book of Lucifer clearly states that "Under no circumstances would a Satanist sacrifice any animal or

---

[28]Anton Szandor LaVey, *The Satanic Bible* (New York: Avon Books, 1969) p. 144.
[29]Ibid., p. 155.
[30]Ibid., p. 179.
[31]Ibid., p. 180.

baby."[32] However, this does not mean that Satanists are completely opposed to human sacrifice. LaVey further writes that "The only time a Satanist would perform a human sacrifice would be if it were to serve a two-fold purpose; that being to release the magician's wrath in the throwing of a curse, and more important, to dispose of a totally obnoxious and deserving individual."[33] Only hexes and curses may be used to dispose of "obnoxious and deserving" individuals—violence, never!

Some of the ritual spelled out in *The Satanic Bible* dates to the Middle Ages, but much of it is simply the invention of LaVey. The "black mass," for example, appears in *The Satanic Bible* as a spoof, a parody of the Catholic mass. LaVey argues that the Christian concept of the "black mass" is absurd. Christians believe, he writes, that the "black mass" is conducted by "a defrocked priest standing before an altar consisting of a nude woman, her legs spread-eagled and vagina thrust open, each of her outstretched fists grasping a black candle made from the fat of unbaptized babies, and a chalice containing the urine (or blood) of a prostitute."[34] But by promoting such a myth, ministers keep decent people in their Christian churches.

The Church of Satan and similarly organized churches forbid murder, denounce child abuse, and do not condone the ritual killing of animals. Although the Church of Satan is offensive to most Christians, there is no question that it is a legitimate minority religion protected by the Constitution. This is as it should be. The guarantee of religious freedom must be extended to any religious organization that does not violate secular law. This is the very essence of freedom.

The police model is correct in its assessment. Such churches do not constitute a threat to society. But is there a diabolical, international Satanic underground that is a threat to society?

Covert Satanists

Level IV of the model appears to be the most absurd, yet it is the most difficult to refute. Those who believe there is an international Satanic conspiracy do not accept the argument that there is no evidence to support the theory. They counter that covert Satanists are so clever that they are able to conceal their deviant activities, which include kidnapping, making human sacrifices, and committing crimes against children.

Kidnapping   In the early 1980s much attention was focused on missing children. Some anti-Satanist groups reported that as many as 50,000

[32]Ibid., p. 89.
[33]Ibid., p. 88.
[34]Ibid., p. 99.

children per year were being kidnapped by strangers. One California cult cop suggested that as many as 95 percent of such kidnappings were occult-related. Because government responds to panic, the Office of Juvenile Justice and Delinquency Prevention was mandated to conduct a study of the problem.*

In 1990 officials reported that no more than 300 children per year are abducted by strangers. Of course, one missing child every year is one too many. The point is, however, that the numbers claimed by anti-Satanists are wildly exaggerated. Furthermore, there is not a shred of evidence to suggest that any kidnapped children have been taken by Satanic conspirators.

Nevertheless, some fundamentalist preachers continue to claim that kidnapping and ritual child killing is an everyday occurrence. For example, Mike Warnke, who claims to be "a former" everything evil (e.g., drug user, Satanist), is now a born-again preacher who travels the country convincing fundamentalists that most everything wrong in the world is the work of Satanists.†

Fictive allegations of massive Satanic conspiracies too often go unchallenged and sometimes end up being presented as fact at cult cop seminars and in the media. Ultimately, public officials, police officers, social workers, teachers, and other professionals are sensitized to look for occult answers to troubling problems. As in the case of the Orange County cats, time, money, and effort are often wasted.

Human Sacrifice   In his book *The Edge of Evil: The Rise of Satanism in North America*, Jerry Johnston quoted a Utah State Prison official as saying that "between forty and sixty thousand human beings are killed through ritual homicides in the United States each year."[35] If such is the case, where are the bodies?

Some occult survivors say that corpses are cremated in portable ovens, or that bodies are buried in graves underneath legitimately buried bodies. Still others insist that cult members eat the bodies. A common explanation is that the power of Satan is so great that he simply makes the bodies disappear. All this is wild speculation—nothing more.

---

*Much of the information in this and subsequent paragraphs was drawn from the following chapters from Richardson, Best, and Bromley, eds., *The Satanism Scare:* David G. Bromley, "The New Cult Scare," pp. 49–72; Debbie Nathan, "Satanism and Child Molestation," pp. 75–94; Joel Best, "Endangered Children in Anti-Satanist Rhetoric," pp. 95–123.

†For additional discussion of Warnke, see Terry Mattingly, "Readers Protest Story on Comic," *Daily Oklahoman* (Oklahoma City), August 29, 1991.

[35]Jerry Johnston, *The Edge of Evil: The Rise of Satanism in North America* (Dallas: Word Publishing, 1989), p. 4.

Again, Christian fundamentalists argue that Satanic conspirators prone to human sacrifice are so powerful and clever that they have the ability to conceal their deviance. The police model "character types" likely to be Level IV Satanists are public officials, police, judges, and lawyers. But read the daily newspaper: these character types seem unable to cover up other forms of deviant involvements. For example, some judges take bribes, some police officers take payoffs, some lawyers steal from their clients, and some politicians are guilty of graft. How often do we read that these professionals are guilty of human sacrifice?

Child Abuse   Of great public concern is child abuse, and well it should be. Without evidence, however, anti-Satanists have linked the vilest forms of child abuse, kidnapping, kiddie porn, and other threats to children to a Satanic conspiracy.

Cult expert Sandi Gallant of the San Francisco police department states that there were fewer than 100 credible ritual abuse cases filed nationally over the past five years. According to David Alexander, "None of those accused were members of any Satanic church or identified devil-worshipping cult. Only a fraction of those reports resulted in convictions. Of those cases that did result in conviction, the majority occurred in day care centers and involved a single pedophile or pornographer, who, working alone, used ritualistic trappings to frighten children into keeping silent."[36]

Most child abuse involves one or both of the child's own parents. A few of these sick parents associate Satanic trappings with their deviance. Devotion to Satan is a symptom of their sickness, not the cause of it.

A Gathering of Evil Forces

In the fall of 1990 rumors spread in the fundamentalist community that a meeting of Satanists was being held in Washington, D.C. From Europe and the Americas, thousands of devil worshippers were allegedly gathering to plot the destruction of Christianity and unleash the power of Satan upon the world. *Christianity Today* reported that "Word of the Satanic convention circulated widely . . . prompting 'prayer alerts' and fund-raising calls of alarm. Reports even included a day-to-day schedule of events for the meeting, complete with Satanic baptisms and weddings.[37]

The entire farce began persuant to the reports of one man, Hezekiah ben Aaron, a self-labeled Messianic Christian and former Satanist. His story of

[36]Alexander, "Giving the Devil More Than His Due," p. 13.
[37]Ken Sidey, "Bedeviled in D.C.?: Satanist Convention," *Christianity Today*, December 17, 1990, December 17, 1990, p. 40.

a Satanic convention quietly taking place in the nation's capital was first told to Richard Shannon, pastor of "Grace of His Presence Church" in Fairfax, Virginia. Impressed by ben Aaron's sincerity, Shannon sent letters to approximately twenty religious leaders in the Fairfax area, asking them to evaluate what he had been told. Unfortunately, the letters were passed on and some of the pastors preached ben Aaron's message as fact. *Christianity Today* reported the snowball effect of the Satanic scare:

> Driven by photocopiers and fax machines, news of the Satanic convention spread quickly. It was repeated as a "prayer alert" sent to all 50 states by Women's Aglow Fellowship, which was planning a national convention for November 4–6 in Washington, D.C. MasterMedia International, a Redlands, California-based ministry to media professionals, used the story in a September fund-raising letter. Pat Robertson mentioned news of the Satanic convention on his "700 Club" broadcast on October 31. And eventually, *USA Today* reported the rumors of the Satanist gathering and the Christian countermeasures.[38]

Prior to turning up in Fairfax, Virginia, Hezekiah ben Aaron had a ministry in Cleveland, Ohio. Formerly second in command of the Church of Satan (we have only his word for that), ben Aaron sold literature and cassettes revealing the alleged truth about the Church of Satan as well as his personal conversion to Christianity.

Among fundamentalists, conversion stories sell well. It follows that if Christ can enter the lives of the likes of Satanist Mike Warnke, Black Panther Eldridge Cleaver, and Watergate conspirator Chuck Colson, then salvation must surely be possible for anyone. The conversion experience is never questioned. Confession of sin by a wrongdoer coupled with a plea for forgiveness can give the worst sinner credibility. In fact, the reputations of the men just named were so shattered that they probably could never have achieved credibility, except as born-agains. It is quite possible that ben Aaron's incredible story was accepted because of his self-proclaimed conversion experience.

Those who believe that Satan is active in the world are hard to convince otherwise. Many Christians still believe that thousands of Satanists met in the nation's capital in the fall of 1990 to plot the downfall of Christianity—despite the fact that not a shred of evidence exists to justify the claim.

The Future of Satanism

Finding source material for this chapter was not difficult. Had I chosen to research Satanism in the United States from 1700 to 1980, my task

[38]Ibid.

would have been much more difficult. But with the advent of cable television, religious fundamentalism has become a powerful force—and for fundamentalists, Christ's second advent is imminent and Satan is mustering his dark forces against Christ's return. Learn more about Satan and his plan! For a book, cassette, or videotape, send a check to your favorite televangelist.

An even more powerful force promoting Satanic myth is irresponsible telejournalism. Secular programming featuring so-called occult experts and occult survivors plays to large audiences. Rarely is the credibility of such guests investigated before their stories are aired on national television. Upon investigation, most occult survivor stories either cannot be proven, are fraudulent, or are found to be the products of a sick mind. It appears, too, that survivor tales are often enhanced through the interaction of survivor and therapist, the survivor echoing what the therapist suggests.

Cult cops and fundamentalist preachers promoting a Satanic conspiracy have convinced some mental health professionals, teachers, and Christian leaders to take seriously all bizarre stories of widespread ritual child abuse, cannibalism, animal and human sacrifice, and kidnappings. Such professionals are now looking to Satan as a cause of social problems rather than viewing the Satanic trappings used by some sociopaths as symptomatic of their illness.

Look for Satanism to be a growth phenomenon in the 1990s. As more sick people learn about Satanic trappings, an increased number of sociopaths and psychopaths will associate their activities with Satanic ritual. As dabblers and street gangs learn Satanic symbolism, they will include it in their graffiti. The more parents, preachers, and teachers cry out against heavy metal music and fantasy games, the more likely rebellious youths will incorporate such themes into their life-styles. Mental health professionals, cult cops, and fundamentalists who already view Satan as the cause of social problems will note increases in so-called Satanic activity. It is quite probable that a domino effect will occur as professionals, giving the devil more than his due, enlist others in their war against Satan.

CHAPTER FIVE

THE CHURCH
OF SCIENTOLOGY

White-collar criminality is frequently expressed in forms of misrepresen-tation, manipulation, and exploitation, in what Al Capone called "the legitimate rackets." Some Scientologists, guilty of all of these, have effec-tively hidden behind the First Amendment's protection of religious free-dom. Without this constitutional guarantee, they would have been ex-posed as racketeers years ago and dealt with appropriately. In a 1991 special report on Scientology, *Time* magazine concluded, "Scientology poses as a religion but is really a ruthless global scam."[1] However, in October 1993 the Internal Revenue Service (IRS) granted the Church of Scientology a tax exemption as a religious institution. What exactly is the institution? Let me introduce it by describing my own introduction to it.

In the fall of 1981, I was living in Minneapolis, Minnesota, and teach-ing at a two-year college in a nearby community. One evening after class, a student handed me a flyer advertising a special meeting scheduled at the downtown Church of Scientology. One of the Scientologists had discovered a past life (incarnation), and he was going to share his experi-ence with the public, free of charge.

The storefront church, located on Hennepin Avenue, was just a few blocks from the city's busiest office buildings, quality department stores, an exclusive hotel, the theater district, and plush restaurants. But a few blocks downtown can make a lot of difference. Business districts go from posh to seedy with little transition. Near the church are two infamous bars, several porno shops, and buildings that have bouncers instead of doormen.

I arrived at the church about twenty minutes before the meeting was scheduled to begin. Members were sitting behind desks and around the room in chairs, the kind you find in dentists' waiting rooms. Others were standing, chatting amiably, and drinking coffee from styrofoam cups. The church had the appearance of a large, fairly busy office complex.

---

[1]Richard Behar, "The Thriving Cult of Greed and Power," *Time,* May 6, 1991, p. 50.

It was an interesting evening. Before the lecture I talked with a young man wearing black shoes, green trousers, a hat like bus drivers wear, and a white cotton shirt with a braided green cord looped over the shoulder. Had the cord been blue, it would have looked exactly like the cords army infantrymen wear.

Never having seen a uniform quite like his, I asked, "Are you in a band?" He smiled, tilted his head to one side, and proudly waited for a friend to explain the significance of his dress. "No, Jeff is a 'clear,' " his colleague said. I looked at her quizzically. She added, "That means he has reached a high level in our church." Before I could delve into what she meant, we were joined by another Scientologist.

Wearing a black graduation gown and a Scientology cross (not symbolically associated with the Christian cross), he introduced himself as Delbert Cory, chaplain of the Minnesota Church of Scientology. After a handshake he handed me a single-page document, "The Scientology Church Service." On the back was a one-paragraph biography of Chaplain Cory. It noted that he was a graduate of the Oberlin Graduate School of Theology and that he had completed several Scientology courses, including the Scientology minister's course. Six years of his life had been spent as a navy chaplain, representing the Reorganized Church of Jesus Christ of Latter-Day Saints. The handout said he was still a practicing Mormon priest.

The purpose of the handout was to assure visitors that whatever they believed in before discovering Scientology was OK. Scientology, the paper said, is a distinct religion but one that is compatible with all other religions. I didn't know much about Scientology before that evening, but I did know something about the Reorganized Church of Latter-Day Saints (RLDS). I doubted that RLDS was as accepting of Scientology as Scientology appeared to be of it. I wondered what Cory's status really was in the Mormon church.

Cory said he hoped I would enjoy the lecture, and I must admit that I did. The audience was small but enthusiastic. Of the dozen or so people in attendance, I was the only one who wasn't a Scientologist. The speaker told his rapt audience that in a previous life he had been a common soldier during the first part of the seventeenth century in Oliver Cromwell's army. He told of the cruelty of King Charles, of the bravery of his peers, of privations suffered in the field, of food shortages and primitive medical care.

I couldn't help but wonder if the speaker—a balding, rather round man, thirty-something—had a body better suited for combat in his previous life. "At first," he said enthusiastically, "I wasn't sure I could find a past life, but with Scientology, anything is possible."

Discovering previous incarnations is not unusual for Scientologists. Lafayette Ronald Hubbard, founder of the Church of Scientology, discovered a number of his own before his death in 1986. In one life he had been the British-born South African diamond magnate, Cecil Rhodes. In another he had been a marshal in Joan of Arc's service. A church publication issued after his death described him as the first musician, a muse named Arpen Polo. His first song, the article stated, was written "a bit after the first tick of time."[2]

I attended a half dozen or so Scientology meetings a few months after discovering the group before moving from Minnesota to Oklahoma. Although the period of interaction in Minnesota was brief, I drew a number of conclusions about Scientology:

1. Scientology is a harmless religion; most members seem to be science fiction buffs.
2. Most Scientologists have difficulty coping with the so-called real world. For example, most of the Scientologists I interacted with had problems before joining the group: drug abuse, alcohol abuse, problems in the workplace, marital problems, or a combination of these. Most claimed that with the help of Scientology they had overcome their difficulties.
3. Because of past problems and new religious beliefs, most converts were alienated from their families, their workplace, and their former friends. Scientology provides converts a peer group of like-minded people.

I lost contact with Scientology until late 1989 when one of its front organizations, Narconon, hawked as a drug treatment program, moved amid protest into Oklahoma. My experience with Scientology in Oklahoma has given me a better understanding of the group's leadership. I will elaborate on this later in the chapter.

In Minnesota I knew only rank-and-file members, and for them, Scientology is a religion. They were, in the truest sense of the word, "believers"—as I think most Scientologists are. But I no longer consider Scientology a harmless religion. It is a hard-sell, money-gouging, high-stakes enterprise shielded by the constitution's First Amendment protection of religious freedom. And what are rank-and-file Scientologists to the leadership?—shills. Hooked themselves, their energies are utilized by the top echelon to hook others.

To understand Scientology, it is necessary to look back from the present and attempt to understand the mind and character of its founder, L. Ron Hubbard. Arrogant, a proven liar, an alleged paranoid-schizophrenic, Hubbard earned his living writing science fiction for pulp magazines before founding Scientology. On one occasion he declared, "Writing for a penny a word is ridiculous. If a man really wants to make a million dollars,

---

[2]Quoted in Joel Sappell and Robert W. Welkos, "Defining the Theology," *Los Angeles Times*, June 24, 1990.

the best way would be to start his own religion."[3] He did start his own religion, and his first million stretched into hundreds of millions.

L. Ron Hubbard (1911–1986):
Man of Controversy

Compiling an accurate biography of L. Ron Hubbard is difficult. Hubbard's personal recollections presented in approved biographies vary greatly from researchers' reports based on interviews and official documents.

In 1984 the Church of Scientology sued former member Gerald Armstrong in the Superior Court of Los Angeles for stealing personal papers belonging to Hubbard. Attorneys for Armstrong argued that he took the documents to protect himself from possible harassment by the church. Judge Paul B. Breckenridge, Jr., found for the defendant, stating from the bench that "the evidence portrays [Hubbard] a man who has been a pathological liar when it comes to his history, background and achievements." Judge Breckenridge further noted, "Hubbard is a very complex person. It appears that he is charismatic and capable of motivating, manipulating and inspiring his adherents."[4]

Son of the Wild West?   A church-approved biography states that Hubbard was born in Tilden, Nebraska, in 1911 and that his family moved to Montana, where he grew up on a large ranch. The book says that during his childhood, "Long days were spent riding, breaking broncos, hunting coyote and taking his first steps as an explorer."[5] When a *Los Angeles Times* reporter phoned Hubbard's aunt, Margaret Roberts, who still lives in Montana, she laughed and said, "We didn't have a ranch, just several acres with a barn on it. . . . We had one cow [and] four or five horses."[6]

Nuclear Physicist?   Hubbard claimed to have developed Scientology from his understanding of the sciences. On many occasions, both public and private, he said he was a trained nuclear physicist. Records show that he was enrolled in a molecular and atomic physics class at George Washington University while unsuccessfully pursuing a degree in civil engineering. He flunked the course.

---

[3]Eugene H. Methvin, "Scientology: Anatomy of a Frightening Cult," *Reader's Digest*, May 1980.

[4]Quoted in Joel Sappell and Robert W. Welkos, "Creating the Mystique," *Los Angeles Times*, June 26, 1990.

[5]Ibid.

[6]Ibid.

Hubbard bragged of having a doctorate. Records show it was a mail-order degree from Sequoia University.

Naval Hero?   Hubbard's most outrageous claims center around his military career. He often bragged that he had commanded a squadron of fighting ships during World War II, that he had been wounded in battle and had won twenty-one medals. Navy records indicate that he had four decorations: the American Defense Service Medal, the American Campaign Medal, the Asiatic-Pacific Campaign Medal, and the World War II Victory Medal, which were awarded to all Pacific-theater servicemen.

Hubbard did see combat, if only in his mind's eye. One of his two commands was a submarine chaser, the PC 815, docked along the Willamette River in Oregon. According to navy records, Hubbard took the PC 815 on a test cruise. Within two hours of departure he alleged an encounter with two Japanese submarines. During the fifty-five consecutive hours the PC 815 monitored the subs, Hubbard radioed for additional ships and aircraft. His craft dropped thirty-seven depth charges on the alleged intruders.

In his report to the Admiralty, Hubbard claimed there was nothing left of the submarines but an oil slick on top of the water. "This vessel wishes no credit for itself," Hubbard wrote in his report. "It was built to hunt submarines. Its people were trained to hunt submarines."[7] And Hubbard and his shipmates got no credit. Following an investigation, the commander of the Northwest Sea Frontier wrote, "an analysis of all reports convinces me that there was no submarine in the area."[8] Church officials argue that Hubbard was probably reprimanded for disclosing his encounter with an enemy off the Pacific coast at a time when the navy was claiming no hostile activity in the region.

Hubbard's next great sea battle took place in Mexican coastal waters off the Coronado Islands near San Diego. To test fire his ship's guns, he ordered rounds shot at the uninhabited islands. Mexico, a neutral nation during World War II, complained to the U.S. government. Hubbard was admonished for anchoring in Mexican waters and ordering gunnery practice in violation of standing orders. A letter of reprimand was placed in his personnel file. Other navy records describe him as "garrulous," an officer who "tries to give impressions of importance," as being "not temperamentally fitted for independent command" and "lacking in the essential qualities of judgment, leadership and cooperation. He acts without forethought to probable results."[9]

[7]Ibid.
[8]Ibid.
[9]Ibid.

Wounded in Action?   Church biographies extol Hubbard as a hero, the first U.S. casualty to be returned from the Far East. Blinded and crippled in action in 1942, he was reportedly flown home in the secretary of the navy's private plane. Hubbard claimed that he was awarded the Purple Heart for his efforts.

Navy records, however, tell a different story. In his application for a disability pension, Hubbard claimed a chronic hip infection, the result of being transferred from a tropical climate to a navy school on the East coast. His eye problems stemmed from conjunctivitis—caused, he said, by too much tropical sunlight. Hubbard spent the last seven months of his service in a military hospital, where he was treated for a duodenal ulcer. He was awarded a 40 percent disability pension.

Dianetics: The Modern Science of Mental Health

Hubbard told his followers that, in 1947, he had cured himself of all mental and physical problems by the power of his mind and by using techniques that were to become a part of Scientology. But that is not what he told officials. Later that year, he wrote to the government claiming "long periods of moroseness" and "suicidal inclinations." The following year, in a letter to the chief of naval operations he described himself as an "invalid."

Hubbard's book, *Dianetics: The Modern Science of Mental Health* (Bridge Publications, 1950), was an instant success. Dubbed a poor man's psychotherapy, the book claimed that mental health could be achieved without the assistance of expensive professionals, which only the wealthy could afford. The book offered cures for what Hubbard defined as psychosomatic illnesses: migraine headaches, the common cold, ulcers, allergies, arthritis, and poor eyesight. All the reader had to do was discover "engrams" (traumatic experiences) hidden away in the recesses of the "reactive mind" and confront them.

It is interesting that during a medical examination at a V.A. hospital in 1951 Hubbard still complained of eye problems and stomach pains, particularly when he was under "nervous pressure." The examination took place after the publication of *Dianetics*.

From Science to Religion   In the introduction to *Dianetics*, Hubbard stated he had invented a new science of mental health, a feat possibly more important than "the invention of the wheel, the control of fire, the development of mathematics."[10] But not everyone was impressed. For

---

[10]Quoted in Joel Sappell and Robert W. Welkos. "The Mind behind the Religion," *Los Angeles Times*, June 24, 1990.

example, noted psychoanalyst Rollo May wrote in the *New York Times* that "books like this do harm by their grandiose promises to troubled persons and by their oversimplification of human psychological problems."[11]

Critics accused Hubbard of brainwashing, bilking the gullible, and practicing quackery. *Dianetics* soon fell from the *New York Times* best-seller list, and Dianetics counseling centers, which had been established at the height of the book's success, fell into financial ruin. Adding to Hubbard's difficulties was an IRS investigation of his tax returns.

With interest in Dianetics ebbing and tax collectors at his door, Hubbard turned to religion—albeit of his own making. With the discovery that engrams could be accumulated from previous incarnations, Hubbard moved Dianetics out of the realm of psychology and into the realm of religion.

The change from secular to sacred was too much for many who had cast their lot with Dianetics in the early 1950s, and for a while Hubbard lost followers. But others, perhaps a more zealous lot, took their place. After all, a religious leader is less likely to be questioned than a pop psychologist. And Hubbard, revered by his new followers, was able to sell the incredible theology of Scientology.

Theology of Scientology

Hubbard wrote that as a youth he had traveled extensively in China, where he studied at the feet of holy men. The experience, according to Church of Scientology approved biographies, "kindled in him a burning desire to learn all there was to know of the spirit of man."[12] After a year as a neophyte, Hubbard wrote in his diary that he was ordained a Lamaist priest. Hubbard did in fact tour China when his father, also a navy man, was stationed in Guam. But a diary reveals that Hubbard was insensitive to the culture. He characterized the "yellow races" as simplistic and said that the problem with China was the presence of "too many chinks."[13]

Hubbard went on to say that the Great Wall of China could be highly profitable if it were to be used as a "rolly [sic] coaster."[14] He described the Lamaist temples as "very odd and heathenish"[15]—certainly a strange comment for a Lamaist priest. There appears to be no Chinese influence in Scientology, despite Hubbard's experiences in China.

[11]Ibid.
[12]Quoted in Welkos and Sappell, "Creating the Mystique."
[13]Ibid.
[14]Ibid.
[15]Ibid.

Sci-Fi   After his discharge from the navy, Hubbard had a modicum of success as a science fiction writer. His theology of Scientology bears that mark. Intergalactic warfare, tyrants that roam the universe, interplanetary civilizations, and out-of-body travel are all part of Hubbard's ruminations.

Xenu   According to Hubbard, 75 million years ago the earth, then called Teegeeack, was part of a 76-planet galactic confederation ruled by a tyrant called Xenu (pronounced *Zeenew*). To solidify his power and control the population, Xenu gathered his officers and told them to capture beings of all shapes and sizes living within the confederation and freeze them in an alcohol and glycol compound. Billions of these frozen creatures were then transported to earth in aircraft that resembled DC-8s and were thrown into volcanos.

To add to the woes of these creatures, hydrogen bombs were dropped on them. Their souls (called thetans) were then captured by Xenu's forces and implanted with religion, sexual perversions, and other weaknesses to remove the memory of what Xenu had done to them. An example of a false implant, according to Hubbard, is the idea of a Christian heaven. It was implanted to make thetans believe they have only one life and that reincarnation is impossible. As a consequence, it directs thetan activity toward a goal that does not exist.

Overthrown soon after the mission was accomplished, Xenu was taken to a mountain and put into a wire cage, where he remains today. His mischief, however, was not without lasting consequences. According to Scientology, each human has a main thetan. Unfortunately, the implanted thetans (called body thetans) attach themselves by the thousands to the operating thetan in each of us, causing emotional distress, confusion, and internal conflict.

In order to "clear" the operating thetan, Scientologists with advanced levels of training are told to feel their bodies for "pressure points," a sure sign of body thetans. The trick is to develop telepathic communication with the body thetans and remind them of Xenu's treachery. Once reminded, body thetans detach themselves.

Auditing

Scientology-trained ministers, called auditors, use an E-meter (two tin cans hooked to what looks like a bathroom scale) to discover implants. The E-meter, a battery-powered galvanometer, measures electrical impulses in the skin and functions in the fashion of a crude lie detector. The subject grips the cans and is questioned. When the needle jumps, the subject is told that an engram (implant) has been discovered. Engrams are defined for the novitiate as recollections of unpleasant experiences, either in this life or in past incarnations. Only when these engrams are confronted can the client become clear.

Scientology's salespeople, called registrars, claim that "clears" become "superbeings." Their health improves and their IQs increase 1 point for each hour spent in auditing. As an added benefit, some clears are able to "exteriorize," or benefit from out-of-body experiences.

L. Ron Hubbard, for example, after seventy-four years on this planet, exteriorized permanently on January 24, 1986, at his ranch near San Luis Obispo, California. Doctors attributed his exteriorization to a stroke. But thousands of cheering Scientologists were told at a meeting held in the Los Angeles Palladium that Hubbard's body had "become an impediment to the work he must now do outside of its confines . . . on a planet a galaxy away."[16]

Clear—for a Price   Doubt exists as to whether the clearing process benefits the client's thetan, but there is no doubt that it does clear his or her wallet.

"Raw meat," Hubbard's term for those newly recruited to Scientology, are charged as much as $1,000 an hour for auditing. But bargains are available. Joel Sappell and Robert Welkos, reporters for the *Los Angeles Times*, noted that the church recently offered "a limited time only deal" on a select package of Hubbard courses that represent a small portion of "the Bridge."* If bought individually, those courses would cost $55,455. The sale price: $33,399.50. A promotional flyer for the discount observed, "You save $22,055.50."[17]

Newcomers to Scientology are warned that having a clear thetan is not enough. The "Supreme Answer" is still a step away. To this end, Scientology continues to create new courses. "To complete Hubbard's progression of courses, a Scientologist could conceivably spend a lifetime and more than $400,000. . . . The Scientology Bridge is always under construction . . . a potent sales strategy devised by Hubbard to keep the money flowing, critics contend."[18]

The process works for Scientology if not for the client. Senior editor Eugene Methvin wrote for *Reader's Digest:*

> Hubbard's moneymaking machine succeeds phenomenally. One French Scientologist spent $200,000 for a few weeks' "services" at the [Clearwater] Florida center. A son of a former U.S. ambassador to London poured in

---

[16]Sappell and Welkos, "The Mind behind the Religion."
*"The Bridge" is a Scientology argot. It must be crossed before one is a clear.
[17]Joel Sappell and Robert Welkos, "Scientology Markets Its Gospel with High-Pressure Sales Pitch," *Los Angeles Times*, June 25, 1990.
[18]Ibid.

$123,000. A German couple took out a $125,000 mortgage to pay for "advanced enlightenment" in Copenhagen.

And at the end of this galactic fantasyland of salvation? Once [Scientology] is firmly in control of mind and money, it reduces converts to emotional serfs . . . fervidly proselytizing and delivering more recruits and more money to "help . . . clear this planet" of insanity, crime and evil.[19]

As previously noted, most rank-and-file Scientologists are religious believers. Unfortunately, the negative aspects of Scientology are institutionalized through their efforts. Made to believe they are world-savers, church members work for a few dollars a week to promote Scientology's cause—making money. In a policy statement, Hubbard once wrote: "Make money, make more money, make others produce so as to make money." During his lifetime, hundreds of millions of dollars were siphoned from the organization and deposited in foreign bank accounts.

Differential Association   Criminologist Edwin H. Sutherland published a paper in 1940 entitled "White Collar Criminality." In it he set forth an interactionist theory of crime and deviance:

White collar criminality, just as other systemic criminality . . . is learned in direct association with those who already practice the behavior; and . . . those who learn this criminal behavior are segregated from frequent and intimate contacts with law-abiding behavior. Whether a person becomes a criminal or not is determined largely by the comparative frequency and intimacy of his contacts with the two types of behavior. This may be called the process of differential association.[20]

Not everything that Scientologists do is criminal. In fact, many Scientologists never commit crimes. Nevertheless, some Scientologists do violate laws and many others do not adhere to the same ethical standards as most citizens. Scientology provides a *culture of deviance*, a source of alternative ethical norms, for its members, particularly for those assigned to the Sea Organization. For this "elite" group, twelve to sixteen hours a day are spent in the service of the church.

The Sea Organization

At least 3,000 Scientologists belong to the Sea Organization. Members are given room, board, and a small stipend in exchange for a contract

---

[19]Eugene H. Methvin, "Scientology: The Sickness Spreads," *Reader's Digest*, May 1980, pp. 3–4.

[20]Edwin H. Sutherland, "White Collar Criminality," *American Sociological Review*, May 1940, pp. 11–12.

that binds them to full service in this life and future lifetimes—for a billion years. Their motto: "We come back."

The Sea Organization is paramilitary in structure. Men and women alike dress in uniforms similar to navy issue. Both sexes are addressed as "Sir." They are assigned navy rank: ensign, lieutenant, commander, and so forth. In his lifetime, Hubbard was affectionately called the Commodore. Sea members are taught to obey orders in a military fashion and to sell. In their zeal to sell they sometimes overstep good judgment.

One example of overzealous salesmanship attributed to the Sea Organization involved the widow of Larry Wheaton, pilot of the Air Florida jet that plunged into the Potomac River shortly after takeoff from National Airport in Washington, D.C., in 1982. The Wheatons were long-time church members.

> Joanne Wheaton gave nearly $150,000 to the church and almost as much to a private business controlled by Scientologists. But the deal was blocked when a lawsuit was brought by an attorney appointed by the court to protect the children's interests.
>
> The suit claimed that the Scientologists had disregarded the future welfare and financial security of the Wheaton family by taking money that was supposed to be used solely for the support of the children and their mother.[21]

The money was returned to the Wheaton family after lengthy arbitration. The Scientologists who had negotiated the deal were expelled from the church.

Methvin notes that policy "directs . . . [Scientology] 'ministers' to watch newspapers for stories of accident, illness or death." Ministers are expected to "as speedily as possible, make a personal call on the bereaved or injured person. . . . Unless you have bodies in the shop, you get no income."[22]

One such body was that of Alan Wilson of Vancouver, Washington. "Recovering from a mangled hip suffered in an auto accident, [he] met a Scientology field-staff member working on a 10 percent commission. Promised a cure, he took some courses and soon [lost] his $7,000 accident insurance settlement."[23]

A Scientology sales and recruiting practice in Minneapolis involved running ads in the help wanted sections of local newspapers: "Counselors Wanted. No Experience Necessary." Of course, most of the respondents were out of work, looking for a job. Applicants were told they

[21]Sappell and Welkos, "Church Markets Its Gospel with High-Pressure Sales Pitch."
[22]Methvin, "Scientology: The Sickness Spreads."
[23]Ibid.

would have to take courses before they could be given a position. The courses could be purchased or taken free in exchange for a billion-year contract.

According to W. I. Thomas, one of the founding fathers of sociology, a social situation is whatever it is defined to be by the participants: "What men define as real is real in its consequences." Scientologists have defined the world as hostile. If you are not for Scientology, you are against it. You are, in Hubbard's words, "fair game."

Rehabilitation Project Force   Sea Organization Scientologists who violate church policies risk being assigned to the Rehabilitation Project Force and confined.

> Prisoners are guarded constantly, never left alone or allowed to speak to any outsider without permission. They eat leftovers, sleep on the floor, and fill their days with strenuous physical and menial labor, classroom study of Ron's works and grueling auditing to detect "crimes against Ron" in "this or past lives."
>
> As defectors have attested, subjects become hysterical and psychotic in their auditing. Then they are locked in isolation. Not surprisingly, suicides occur. . . . For example, a Scientology member hurled herself in the Bay [at Clearwater, Florida] and drowned.[24]

L. Ron Hubbard wrote Scientology's one-page creed. It states the following:

> All men have inalienable rights to their own lives . . .
> All men have inalienable rights to their own sanity . . .
> All men have inalienable rights to their own defence [sic] . . .
> All men have inalienable rights to think freely, to talk freely, to write freely their own opinions and to counter or utter or write about the opinions of others . . .

In reality, it appears that some Scientologists trade their inalienable rights for group acceptance. During his lifetime, Hubbard was the unquestioned leader of the group. The gospel according to Ron went unchallenged. Since his death it has been business as usual for Scientology—except, perhaps, for a bit of sophistication brought to the organization by its new leader, David Miscavige.

Miscavige, a high school dropout, is much like L. Ron Hubbard. Irascible, given to fits of temper, he rules Scientology with an iron hand. A second-generation Scientologist, he began as one of Hubbard's personal messengers at age fourteen. To understand Miscavige and his rise to power, it is first necessary to continue the saga of L. Ron Hubbard.

---

[24]Methvin. "Scientology: Anatomy of a Frightening Cult."

The Commodore's Family

Born of Wedlock   Married three times and divorced twice, Hubbard had seven children. Insiders say he was never close to any of them. His first child, L. Ron, Jr., feuded with his father for more than two decades. In 1959 he left the church because he claimed he wasn't making enough money to support his family. So deep was the rift between father and son that he changed his name to Ronald DeWolfe.

Another son, Quentin, who was hooked on drugs and confused about his sexual orientation, committed suicide at age twenty-two. According to Laurel Sullivan, Hubbard's public relations officer at the time, "Hubbard shed no tears. His first reaction was to express concern over the possibility of publicity that could be used to discredit Scientology."[25]

Hubbard's only daughter, Alexis, born to Sara Northrup Hubbard, his second wife, was a pawn in a bitter divorce dispute. When she was one year old, Hubbard spirited her off to Cuba in an attempt to retain custody of the child. In her divorce suit, Sara charged that "Hubbard had deprived her of sleep, beaten her and suggested that she kill herself, 'as divorce would hurt his reputation.' "[26] She submitted into evidence a letter received from his first wife that described Ron as "not normal." The letter said that she had been forced to endure beatings and threats on her life for twelve years.

Sara was awarded custody of Alexis; Hubbard, bitter and vindictive, told her the child would be cut from his will. Never given to empty threats, he denied parentage and never saw Alexis again. Hubbard's family of procreation is not influential in Scientology today, but he was to adopt a family that is.

Hubbard Hides at Sea   The Church of Scientology experienced phenomenal growth during the 1960s. Hubbard's ploy, the switch from secular to sacred, slowed the IRS for a time. After all, it is more difficult to proceed against a church than against a business. But government, though slow, is doggedly persistent. In 1967 the IRS revoked the tax-exempt status of the Church of Scientology of California. That same year, Hubbard bought three ships and took to the high seas with several hundred followers. From aboard the command ship *Apollo* (a converted cattle ferry), the commodore controlled Scientology from a distance.

Interestingly, many governments along the Caribbean and Mediterranean coasts thought Hubbard and his clean-cut crew were CIA operatives. One crew member recalled an incident while anchored at the

[25]Quoted in Joel Sappell and Robert W. Welkos, "Life with L. Ron Hubbard," *Los Angeles Times*, June 25, 1990.
[26]Sappell and Welkos, "The Mind behind the Religion."

Portuguese island of Madeira. "We were stoned by townsfolk carrying torches and chanting anti-CIA slogans. They [were] throwing Molotov cocktails onto the boat but they weren't lit. Fortunately this was not an experienced mob."[27]

It was during his years at sea that Hubbard developed Scientology's paramilitary chain of command with its emphasis on strict obedience. It was also at sea that he began to develop his "adopted family," those who now control Scientology.

Hubbard Hides on Land   Hubbard was not often seen after he took to the seas. When he did return to the mainland, he surrounded himself with teenage followers. All were second-generation Scientologists, some the children of those who sailed with him.

Followers considered it an honor to have a child selected to serve Ron. And he did demand service. Called the Commodore's Messengers, they carried his cigarettes, held his ashtray, and made sure that the room temperature was never more nor less than 72 degrees. One of the most difficult jobs required of a messenger was the laundry. Hubbard had an aversion to detergent, and a trace scent of soap would throw him into a rage. To avoid his wrath, messengers rinsed his clothing in thirteen separate buckets of water.

Life for a messenger wasn't always easy. Hubbard issued stinging, sometimes screaming rebukes for slight transgressions. But there were rewards. Those he trusted were put into positions of responsibility, and the reward for work well done was more responsibility and a measure of power. As the teenagers grew to young adulthood, they were given authority over even the highest-level church officials.

Deep Hiding   Almost all negative biographies of L. Ron Hubbard describe him as paranoid. Characteristic of this malady is an unjustified fear that people are "watching," intent on doing the sufferer harm. In Hubbard's case, people were watching, intent on breaking him and Scientology. Among the groups monitoring his activities were the FBI, the federal Food and Drug Administration, various psychiatric associations, and foremost, the Internal Revenue Service. Hubbard's assessment of the situation was more real than imagined. In February 1980 he withdrew from public life forever.

Following his disappearance, church officials advised that Hubbard had retired to do research and continue his writing career. Aides have since testified that he fled to avoid anticipated prosecution for skimming hundreds of millions of dollars in church funds.

Only two people knew Hubbard's whereabouts during the last five

[27]Ibid.

years of his life: Pat Broeker, then his "personal messenger," and Broeker's wife, Anne. For the first two years in deep hiding, Hubbard and the couple drove up and down the Pacific coast, using aliases and living in a motor home. For short periods they stopped traveling and lived in rented apartments near Los Angeles. Hubbard would sometimes color his hair and wear makeup to disguise his appearance. Pat Broeker was nicknamed Agent 007 by fellow messengers because of his love for cloak-and-dagger activities.

The Broekers, using the cover names Mike and Lisa Mitchell (with Hubbard posing as her father, Jack), bought a $700,000 ranch at Creston, California, population 270. Thirty cashier's checks drawn on various California banks were used to complete the transaction.

Townspeople in Creston viewed "Jack" as a crusty, somewhat eccentric old man, given to fits of temper, who lived in a motor home while his ranchstead was being remodeled—over, and over, and over again. Local workmen just couldn't finish projects to suit the capricious Hubbard. For example, the interior of the house had to be repainted several times because the white paint wasn't white enough. During the final three years of his life, Hubbard pumped an estimated $3 million into the small town's economy.

Hubbard was out of sight but not out of touch with his empire. His directives, sent via Pat Broeker, were delivered to David Miscavige, another member of Hubbard's adopted family.

David Miscavige   Selected to serve as one of Ron's messengers at age fourteen, David Miscavige heads what is now a huge labyrinth of Scientology enterprises. While Hubbard was in hiding, two messengers—Broeker and Miscavige—controlled the communications lines between Hubbard and his church. Sappell and Welkos reported in the *Los Angeles Times*, "When messengers spoke, they did so with Hubbard's authority. Bad-mouthing a messenger, Hubbard said, was tantamount to personally challenging him. . . . It was Miscavige's job to ensure that Hubbard's orders, secretly relayed to him, were followed by church executives. In effect, Miscavige became the sole link between church leaders and Hubbard."[28]

For a short time following Hubbard's death, there was confusion as to who was in charge of the Church of Scientology. Pat and Anne Broeker, as well as David Miscavige, laid claim to the top spot. The Broekers staked their claim on having been Hubbard's trusted confidants, natural heirs to the leadership position. But Miscavige had a power base beyond the ranch.

[28]Joel Sappell and Robert Welkos, "The New Man in Control," *Los Angeles Times*, June 27, 1990.

While Miscavige was still in his teens, Hubbard had appointed him head of Author Services Inc., created in 1981 to handle Hubbard's financial and literary affairs. Miscavige wasted no time in making his presence felt. Within months of his appointment, he spearheaded a purge of the church's executives accused of "plotting to seize control of the organization."[29]

Scientology franchises, also called missions, did not escape Miscavige's watchful eye. All were required to pay 10 percent of their gross income to the "mother church," and Miscavige warned them not to cheat. If they fell under suspicion, "finance police" would conduct audits. The audits, franchise-holders were told, would cost $15,000 per day.

Trained at Hubbard's knee like a son, Miscavige is much like his role model. He is described as a tireless worker with a volatile temper; some say he uses street language filled with invective to emphasize a point. Sappell and Welkos reported the following: "One former [Scientologist] recalled the time that Miscavige became enraged with the performances of Scientology staffers on a church record album. He propped its cover up against an embankment outside his Riverside, California office and shot it repeatedly with a .45-caliber pistol."[30]

Like Hubbard, Miscavige maintains a low profile and refuses interviews. His official title, chairman of the board of the Religious Technology Center, puts him in control of the trademarks "Scientology" and "Dianetics," which are necessary to operate franchises. All suborganizations operate at his pleasure.

Apparently Miscavige is content with his backstage role in giving direction to Scientology. Nominally, Rev. Heber Jentsch is president of the church. His position, however, is president without power. A skilled public relations man, Jentsch appears frequently on talk shows and issues press statements. But it is Miscavige who controls the many church fronts that lure the unwary to Scientology.

Church Fronts

Sterling Management Systems   One of Scientology's most lucrative fronts is Sterling Management Systems, a consulting firm founded in 1983. Sterling offers management advice to professionals. For a fee of $10,000, dentists, podiatrists, and chiropractors can purchase courses that purportedly will increase their profits. But the fee isn't enough. High-pressure sales techniques are used to impel the clients toward Scientology. The following excerpt from *Time* magazine concerning the

[29]Ibid.
[30]Ibid.

plight of Robert Geary, a dentist from Ohio, illustrates the tie between Sterling Management and Scientology:

> Sterling officials told Geary . . . that their firm was not linked to Scientology. [Geary says] they eventually convinced him that he and his wife had personal problems that required auditing. Over five months, the Gearys say, they spent $130,000 for services, plus $50,000 for "gold-embossed, investment grade books" signed by Hubbard. Geary contends that Scientologists not only called his bank to increase his credit card limit but also forged his signature on a $20,000 loan application. . . . At one point, the Gearys claim, Scientologists held Dorothy hostage for two weeks in a mountain cabin, after which she was hospitalized for a nervous breakdown.[31]

Celebrity Centre International   In a mansion overlooking the Hollywood freeway, Sea Organization Scientologists operate Celebrity Centre International, a special branch for the "stars." One of Hubbard's early edicts was to encourage notables to endorse Scientology, thus lending credibility to the movement.

Those endorsing Scientology today include movie stars John Travolta and Tom Cruise. Kirstie Alley, star of the popular TV sitcom *Cheers*, is also a spokesperson. The ranks of lesser-known celebrity Scientologists include singer Al Jarreau, jazz pianist Chick Corea, actress Karen Black, Priscilla and Lisa Marie Presley, opera star Julia Migenes, Olympic gymnast Charles Lakes, and Nancy Cartwright, the voice behind cartoon character Bart Simpson.

The stated purpose of Celebrity Centre International is to direct and promote the careers of celebrity members. What stars pay, if anything, for Scientology's guidance is not known. But the advantage of catering to "star" members is known. Kirstie Alley, for example, a former cocaine addict, claims that in 1979 Hubbard's Narconon program "salvaged my life and began my acting career."[32] Today, Alley travels the nation hawking the value of Scientology's dubious drug treatment program, Narconon.

Narconon   Life in the community of Newkirk, Oklahoma (population 2,400), is slow-paced, the way most of its citizens like it. The *Newkirk Herald Journal*, published every Thursday, reports what everybody already knows. Until recently some subscribers bought the paper for the classified ads, others for obituary and wedding announcements, but few bought the paper for the news.

---

[31]Behar, "The Cult of Greed and Power."

[32]Quoted in Joel Sappell and Robert Welkos, "The Courting of Celebrities," *Los Angeles Times*, June 28, 1990.

Near Newkirk is what was for ninety-six years the Chilocco Indian school. After the school closed in 1980, the federal government declared the 200-acre, 80-building campus surplus and turned it over to five Indian tribes: the Ponca, Kaw, Pawnee, Otoe-Missouria, and Tonkawa. In 1988 tribal members signed a twenty-five-year lease with Narconon, for which they were to receive $16 million in return. The Indian nations were not told of a tie between Narconon and Scientology. Robert Lobsinger, publisher of the Newkirk newspaper, did discover the tie— and people have been buying his newspaper for the news ever since. Following are excerpts from one of his editorials:

> Whoa, now! Maybe it's time for us backwater Cowboys and Indians to slow down our wagons and ponies a bit, before we git stampeded into thunderation by a bunch of slick talkin' riverboat shysters toutin' some new fangled snake oil cure for the fire-water frazzles. . . .
>
> We need to wake up quick and smell the horse apples. This Narconon outfit appears to be a front for [the Church of Scientology]. . . . It looks like a religious cult. . . .
>
> Conanon . . . I mean Narconon is settin' up shop at Chilocco with some "generous" assistance from a philanthropic outfit called the Association for Better Living and Education (ABLE), which says it has been impressed with Narconon's worldwide record. Just like it was a separate outfit looking for a good cause. And the Narconon guy profusely thanks the ABLE lady for the "donation" [$200,000] that will insure the success of the Chilocco project! How wonderful it all is. The melodrama is tear-jerking.
>
> ABLE and the Narconon International Association share the same building in Los Angeles. In fact, they share the same floor of the same building. In fact, *they share the exact same office suite* of the same floor of the same building. Why did they bother to come here to [publicly] "donate" the money from their left hand to their right? Unless it was a hokum-pokum show for us dummies out here in the gulch.
>
> They ain't selling snake oil . . . or nickel bingo. What they're selling is hope, vitamin pills, and steam baths. Packaged in blarney, their own propaganda says their treatments "cannot be construed as a recommendation of medical treatment or medication and it is undertaken or delivered by anyone on his own responsibility." In other words, if it don't work, tough cookies.[33]

Lobsinger correctly assessed Narconon's goal, to sell Scientology. The price for rehabilitation varies. One youth from California who was institutionalized at Chilocco said his family paid a $15,000 treatment fee. A New Yorker said his fee was $10,000. Neither found the treatment helpful.

One of the men, who was infected with the HIV virus, was concerned that no one on the Chilocco staff knew anything about AIDS. He left via a back road. Chased by security guards carrying walkie-talkies and

[33]*Newkirk Herald Journal,* April, 27, 1989.

armed with clubs, he was forcibly detained until a Scientology staffer could arrive on the scene. Eventually, after persuasion failed, he was dropped off at a convenience store in Newkirk.

Asked about Narconon's treatment program, he said he was given large doses of vitamins and "Cal-Mag," a mixture of oil, vinegar, calcium, and magnesium. Staffers call the vitamins "drug bombs"; patients call the magnesium drink "Cal-Gag." To sweat out drug residues, five hours each day are spent in a sauna. The rest of the day is spent in therapy, taking courses and being audited, doing exactly what an individual would do if he or she walked through the front door of a Scientology church.

Narconon does not just have ordinary individuals as clients. Even some government officials, unaware of the Scientology connection, have attempted the treatment program. Narconon officials claim a cure rate of 86 percent. An ad hoc study done in West Berlin, after city officials wasted more than $700,000 on the treatment program, found the cure rate to be about 10 percent. The Michigan Department of Corrections was also a victim. It laid out $100,000 to rehabilitate its prisoners. A follow-up study indicated that after six months in the community, Narconon subjects fared worse than other parolees.

To date Narconon has not been able to produce a single scientific study attesting to the value of its treatment program, except for glowing reports issued by the Foundation for Advancements in Science and Education—yet another Scientology front organization.

Concerned Businessmen's Association of America   Scientology is being promoted in America's schools by a front organization called Concerned Businessmen's Association of America. Millions of copies of a 96-page booklet (*The Way to Happiness*, compiled by Hubbard in 1981) have been distributed nationwide. The text stresses widely held moral values. For example, the booklet admonishes students to "take care of yourself," "honor and help your parents," "do not murder," and "be worthy of trust." Apart from distribution in this country, 28 million copies have been translated into "at least 14 languages and distributed throughout the world."[34]

The group sponsors an annual contest with a "stay off drugs" theme. Each year students are encouraged to write an essay using Hubbard's precepts for submission in the Set a Good Example contest. To encourage educators to participate, the organization awards $5,000 to each winning elementary, junior, and senior high school. By focusing on the drug problem, the organization has won the backing of many educators and politicians who are unaware of the group's connection to Scientology.

---

[34]Joel Sappell and Robert W. Welkos, "Church Seeks Influence in Schools, Business, Science," *Los Angeles Times*, June 27, 1990.

Critics argue that the contest is used to enlist new church members, who "may be so inspired by *The Way to Happiness* that they will reach for Hubbard's other writings. They argue that the booklet's distribution in public schools violates constitutional mandates separating church and state."[35] The Concerned Businessmen's Association, however, denies that its purpose is to proselytize.

Another church-affiliated organization, Applied Scholastics, is attempting to sell a Hubbard tutorial program to school systems. Derived from a training program for Scientologists, the program is based (according to the *Los Angeles Times*) on the simplistic premise that "learning difficulties arise when students read past words they do not understand." [36] Hubbard wrote in 1967 that "The misunderstood word in a subject produces a vast panorama of mental effects and is the prime factor involved in stupidity. . . . This is a sweepingly fantastic discovery in the field of education."[37] Hubbard's solution? Have students use a dictionary when they see a word they do not understand!

Applied Scholastics has made claims in promotional literature of success relative to the effectiveness of the program. However, the acting superintendent in one district where the tutorial has been tried reports that only limited data are available and that Scientology's claims are unsubstantiated. Nevertheless, Applied Scholastics has plans to construct a 1,000-acre campus that will be used as a training site for educators who will teach Hubbard's program. One promotional piece states that the center will be a "model of real education for the world" and will "create overwhelming public popularity for Hubbard."[38]

Health Med Clinic   Target groups for Health Med Clinic, yet another Scientology front, are workers who have been exposed to toxins or carcinogens. The purification treatment is the same as the regimen employed by Narconon: vitamins and saunas.

Officials for Health Med regularly write articles that appear in trade magazines and union journals, preying on the fears of those who have been exposed to hazardous materials. The articles are little more than advertisements for Hubbard's purification program. Backing Health Med claims are endorsements from the Foundation for Advancements in Science and Education, the same front organization that endorses Narconon.

Health Med has been particularly aggressive in trying to recruit firefighters into its program. The following example typifies Scientology's approach to generating business. In 1987, more than a dozen

[35]Ibid.
[36]Ibid.
[37]Ibid.
[38]Ibid.

firefighters in Shreveport, Louisiana, were exposed to PCBs while fighting a transformer fire at the Louisiana State University Medical Center. Afterward, a number of the firemen complained of headaches, dizziness, skin rashes, and other symptoms. Blood tests conducted at the medical center did not show abnormally high levels of PCBs in the firemen's blood, but some of the firemen thought the university might not be telling the truth in an attempt to protect itself from liability. Seeking an alternative, one of the firemen read an article in *Fire Engineering* magazine written by Gerald T. Lionelli entitled "Chemical Exposure in Firefighting: The Enemy Within." The author was billed as "a senior research assistant for the Foundation for Advancements in Science and Education."

Lionelli discussed the horrors of exposure to toxins and then got to the point. His foundation endorsed a treatment offered by an organization called Health Med, which was using a detoxification technique developed by an American researcher, L. Ron Hubbard. The article made no mention of Scientology.

City officials in Shreveport contacted an official at Health Med. To reassure the city's medical claims officer, Health Med gave as a reference William Marcus, a toxicologist employed by the Environmental Protection Agency (EPA). Marcus, a non-Scientologist (like Lionelli), is listed as a senior advisor to the foundation.* He told the city that in his opinion, "L. Ron Hubbard is a bona fide genius." Although Marcus told Shreveport officials that he wasn't speaking for the EPA, they took the recommendation as an endorsement from the regulatory agency.

Approximately twenty firemen were sent to Los Angeles, where they were told they had high levels of PCBs and fatty tissues in their blood. After treatment, most of the firemen said they felt better. The city paid $80,000 to Health Med and was ready to spend more when a private insurance carrier suggested they hire a consultant to check the effectiveness of the treatment. The Health Med program was dropped after Shreveport officials read the bottom line of the report prepared by the National Medical Advisory Service Inc. of Bethesda, Maryland: "The treatment in California preyed upon the fears of concerned workers, but served no rational medical function. . . . Moreover, the program itself, developed not by physicians or scientists, but by the founder of the Church of Scientology, has no recognized value in the established medical and scientific community. It is quackery."[39]

Citizens Commission on Human Rights   Among L. Ron Hubbard's earliest critics were members of the psychiatric community. In the early

---

*Marcus does not receive a salary from the foundation.
[39]Ibid.

1950s a number of psychiatrists deemed Dianetics a worthless, potentially dangerous treatment for mental illness. Psychiatrists and their professional organizations roundly panned Hubbard and his program. In turn, Hubbard said that if "psychiatrists had the power to torture and kill everyone . . . they would do so. Recognize them for what they are; psychotic criminals—and handle them accordingly."[40]

In 1969 the Church of Scientology established the CCHR (Citizens Commission on Human Rights). According to the *Los Angeles Times*, the purpose of the organization was to "investigate mental health abuses."

The commission's record of effectiveness is undeniable. The CCHR attacks the use of drugs as a mechanism for controlling human behavior. Ritalin, often prescribed by psychiatrists and pediatricians to control hyperactivity in children, is a stimulant that paradoxically produces a calming effect. Almost single-handedly, the CCHR wages war against the use of Ritalin by staging protests at psychiatric conventions. "Airplanes trailing banners that read 'Psychs, Stop Drugging Our Kids,' and children on the ground carrying placards that plead 'Love Me Don't Drug Me' effectively warn parents of the drug's danger."[41] But is there a danger?

Food and Drug Administration statistics indicate that the drug, which has been used for more than three decades, is both safe and effective when used appropriately. Physicians are concerned that there has been some increase in the use of Ritalin over the past two decades, but the excesses of a few physicians are not the fault of the drug.

Scientologist Dennis Clarke, president of CCHR, is not a doctor; nevertheless, he has positioned himself as the nation's leading authority on Ritalin and its effects. Often appearing on talk shows and at public forums, Clarke uses an impressive array of unsubstantiated statistics to prove his case against the drug. For example, he claims that 20 percent of the students under age ten in the Minneapolis, Minnesota, school system are on Ritalin, and that the figure is at least double that for children in predominantly black schools. The effect, he says, is that children wear a "chemical straight-jacket" that leads to violence and, sometimes, suicide.

School officials in Minneapolis disagree. According to their records, in 1987 (the year cited in the Church of Scientology's alleged study) fewer than 1 percent of the 39,000 students in the district were on Ritalin or any other behavior control drug.

Prozac, the leading antidepressant manufactured by Eli Lilly, is also

---

[40]Quoted in Joel Sappell and Robert W. Welkos, "Suits, Protests Fuel a Campaign against Psychiatry," *Los Angeles Times*, June 29, 1990.
[41]Ibid.

under attack. Spokespersons for CCHR claim that Prozac can lead to suicide and murder. "Through mass mailings, appearances on talk shows and heavy lobbying, CCHR has hurt drug sales and helped spark dozens of lawsuits against Lilly."[42] As of April 1994, none of the lawsuits had been decided against Lilly.

Bridge Publications Inc.   L. Ron Hubbard authored a plethora of books, short stories, screenplays, and many of the self-improvement courses sold by the Church of Scientology. It is interesting that since late 1985 at least twenty of his books have become best-sellers. Two years after Hubbard's death, in March 1988 *Dianetics* was again number one on the *New York Times* best-seller list. How was this publishing miracle accomplished?

In an effort to refurbish Hubbard's tarnished image, Bridge Publications Inc., founded and controlled by Scientologists, used a mass-media blitz to push *Dianetics* and other Hubbard books to the forefront. Credibility for Hubbard equates with credibility for Scientology. Billboards, TV commercials, and full-page ads in *Publishers Weekly*, an important trade magazine, are all part of the campaign strategy. But Bridge Publications apparently gets a little help from its friends.

Welkos and Sappell interviewed a number of booksellers in the Los Angeles area. Sheldon McArthur, former manager of a B. Dalton bookstore, reported, "Whenever the sales seem to slacken and a [Hubbard] book goes off the best-sellers list, give it a week and we'll get these people coming in buying 50 to 100 to 200 copies at a crack—cash only."[43] McArthur also reported that after *Buckskin Brigades*, Hubbard's first novel, was re-released, the Western adventure "just sat there. . . . Then in one week it was gone. . . . We started getting calls asking, 'You got *Buckskin Brigades*?' I said, 'Sure we got them.' 'You got a hundred of them?' 'Sure,' I said, 'here's a case.' "[44]

Another former B. Dalton manager, Gary Hamel, reported that shipments arrived from the publisher with B. Dalton price stickers already on them. "We would order more books and . . . they'd come back with our sticker as if they were bought by the publisher."[45]

There is little doubt that Scientologists have been priming the pump. There is no better advertising for a book than sustained stays on best-seller lists. And mass consumption lends credibility to the book's author.

[42]Behar, "The Cult of Greed and Power."

[43]Quoted in Joel Sappell and Robert Welkos, "Costly Strategy Continues to Turn Out Bestsellers," *Los Angeles Times*, June 28, 1990.

[44]Ibid.

[45]Ibid.

The Guardian Office

L. Ron Hubbard was well aware of the fact that he and his church have powerful enemies. But it was not in his nature to capitulate. Hubbard made that clear when he said that all of Scientology's enemies are "fair game" and may be "tricked, sued or lied to or destroyed."[46] To protect the church from perceived threats, the Guardian Office was formed in the early 1970s as a legal and investigative branch of the church. Mary Sue, Hubbard's third wife, took charge of the operation. An "enemies list" was developed and those on it were given special attention.

Paulette Cooper, who authored *The Scandal of Scientology* in 1970, was near the top of the enemies list. In an attempt to discredit her as well as her book, the Guardian Office obtained stationery with her fingerprints on it. Then they sent a bomb threat to themselves that read in part, "You're like the Nazis or the Arabs—I'll kill you!"[47] Scientologists turned the letter over to the FBI and suggested that Cooper might be its author. After finding her fingerprints on the document, a grand jury indicted her not only for making bomb threats but for lying under oath about her innocence. Two years later the charges were dropped, but the episode cost Cooper $20,000 in legal fees and $6,000 for psychiatric services. Cooper filed a lawsuit against the church seeking $25 million in damages. The suit was later settled.

Civil litigation is sometimes used to discredit, harass, and bankrupt enemies of the church. Hubbard put this warning in writing for his followers: "beware of attorneys who tell you not to sue . . . the purpose of the suit is to harass and discourage rather than to win."[48] To that end, *Time* magazine estimates that more than 100 lawyers are paid more than $20 million annually to handle church litigation.

During 1973 Hubbard initiated project Snow White in an attempt to purge government files of all documents that he felt contained lies about himself and the church. To acquire documents not available through the Freedom of Information Act, the Guardian Office recruited spies to penetrate such high-security agencies as the Department of Justice and the Internal Revenue Service. Working at night, they photocopied mountains of documents pertaining to the church. One such "mole" took a job as a clerk-typist for the Internal Revenue Service. Another spy found employment as personal secretary to an assistant attorney in the U.S.

[46]Quoted in Joel Sappell and Robert Welkos, "On the Offensive against an Array of Suspected Foes," *Los Angeles Times*, June 29, 1990.

[47]Joel Sappell and Robert W. Welkos, "Burglaries and Lies Paved a Path to Prison," *Los Angeles Times*, June 24, 1990.

[48]Behar, "The Cult of Greed and Power."

Department of Justice who was handling Freedom of Information Act lawsuits filed by the church.

The lid came off the operation after two Scientologists, using fake identification, gained access to government agencies and photocopied documents relating to the church. After eleven months on the run, one of the suspects contacted authorities and confessed to his part in the conspiracy. The confession triggered a massive raid involving 134 FBI agents at three Scientology locations in Washington, D.C., and Los Angeles.

Along with eavesdropping equipment and burglars' tools, agents found 48,000 documents detailing operations against "enemies" in both the public and private sector. Mary Sue Hubbard and ten other top-level Scientologists were indicted. L. Ron Hubbard was listed as an unindicted co-conspirator. None of the seized documents linked Hubbard to the Guardian Office, and he claimed no knowledge of the group's activities.

Federal prosecutors sought stiff sentences and wrote in a memorandum, "The crime committed by these defendants is of a breadth and scope previously unheard of. No building, office, desk or file was safe from their snooping and prying. No individual or organization was free from their despicable conspiratorial minds. The tools of their trade were miniature transmitters, lock picks, secret codes, forged credentials and any other device they found necessary to carry out their conspiratorial schemes."[49]

All eleven Scientologists were convicted and sentenced to five years in a federal prison. All eleven are now free. After the scandal the Guardian Office was disbanded, but a new branch was established called the Office of Special Affairs.

Church Detectives   In recent years, in place of church members the Office of Special Affairs has hired private detectives to harass and intimidate perceived enemies. The detectives provide the church with plausible deniability when odious activities are brought to the public's attention.

Working from the premise that everyone has something to hide, detectives hired by the Church of Scientology plot to intimidate adversaries. A U.S. district judge in Washington, D.C., had his sex life investigated. In running down a "squirrel" (Hubbard's term for former members who teach Dianetics, usually at a lower price than the church charges), one of the detectives passed out business cards that read "Special Agent, Task Force on White Collar Crime."[50] In talking to the squirrel's neighbors and banker, the detective suggested that the subject of his inquiry was implicated in drug smuggling and terrorism, which were totally false accusations. On another occasion, detectives told the neighbors of an antagonistic former Scientologist that she had pinworms.

[49]Sappell and Welkos, "Burglaries and Lies Paved a Path to Prison."
[50]Sappell and Welkos, "On the Offensive against an Array of Suspected Foes."

Such abuses are not isolated incidents, but not enough pages are available in this chapter to recount all the excesses of the Church of Scientology's detectives. Nevertheless, church efforts to discredit civic leaders in Newkirk, Oklahoma, to pave the way for Narconon must be retold, if only to add humor to what has been to this point a rather bleak narrative.

After Bob Lobsinger exposed Narconon in his paper as a Scientology front, Scientologists spread the rumor that anyone who opposed the drug treatment center at Chilocco must be an advocate for drugs. The same accusation was leveled at Newkirk pastors who spoke from the pulpit against Scientology. This kind of attack might work in a big city where people don't know their neighbors, but it did not work in Newkirk where everybody knows everyone else and everything about them—including whether they have pinworms. The effort only served to further alienate the community from the Scientologists.

I asked Lobsinger if he was afraid that the Church of Scientology would sue him. "Look around you," he said. "All I've got is this old building and a couple of old computers that half the time don't work. And apart from that, I heard that they are way behind on paying their attorneys' bills. Let them sue! I haven't written anything that isn't true."

Lobsinger also said that the church's attorneys had sent an open letter to many of Newkirk's citizens advising them that "a few local individuals have sought to create intolerance by broadsiding the Churches of Scientology in stridently uncomplimentary terms." The letter further informed readers that Eugene Ingram, a private detective, had been hired to investigate the matter.

Ingram's first contact in Newkirk was with Mayor Garry Bilger's twelve-year-old son, whom he found browsing in the local public library. He handed the youngster a business card and told him to have his father call him. Lobsinger called it a bit of "subtle intimidation. It really unnerved his mother."

Also according to Lobsinger, "Investigators . . . camped out at the local courthouse, where they searched public records for 'dirt' on prominent local citizens. They were checking on the banker, the president of the school board, the president of the Chamber of Commerce, and, of course, the mayor and his family, and me."

Rambo tactics do not work in Newkirk. The more the detectives dug, the angrier the citizens' response became. Finally, Kirstie Alley came to Oklahoma in an attempt to defuse the negative response to the Church of Scientology. Lobsinger reported in the *Herald Journal*:

> Scientology is not an organization we need in our midst, no matter how many TV barmaids they parade before the governor.
>   It was just another desperation dog and pony show to generate a little free publicity and impress folks who don't know any better yet.

Hollywood, long the neurotic center of the universe, and its equally strange population of overpaid shiny people, fails to impress most Oklahomans, who tend to laugh at them instead of with them. There's a big difference; it just doesn't show up in the Nielsen ratings.[51]

A state certificate of need for a drug treatment center was issued to Narconon in 1988, before anyone knew of its Scientology connection. Narconon began operation the following year, pending certification by the Oklahoma Department of Mental Health. Certification was denied in June 1990. The Chilocco school, however, is on Indian land, and Scientologists argued that the state did not have jurisdiction in the matter. In October 1992, after inspecting the buildings and food and sanitary services to verify that fire-safety and health codes were being met, the Department of Mental Health capitulated, granting a license to Narconon.

Combating Scientology

The IRS, FBI, and Foreign Governments   Scientology is a religion. Why? Because L. Ron Hubbard said it was. That is all the Constitution of the United States requires, no matter how unconventional the religion. But being classified as a religion does not mean that a religious organization is exempt from taxation. The IRS has codified exceptions to acceptable religious practice to the extent that a church must not operate primarily for business purposes, commit crimes, engage in partisan politics, or enrich private individuals.

In its war against the Church of Scientology, the IRS has focused on set fee schedules associated with Hubbard's self-fulfillment courses and auditing. The IRS argues that Scientology is a business.

In 1967 the IRS stripped the Church of Scientology of California of its tax-exempt status. The church disagreed with the decision and ignored it. In response the IRS conducted a massive audit of church records and demanded back taxes of more than $1 million for the years 1970–1972. The church appealed to the U.S. Tax Court; and in 1984 the court denied relief, noting that "[Scientology] made a business out of selling religion" and "had conspired for almost a decade to defraud the United States government by impeding the IRS."[52] The blistering decision further stated that Hubbard had diverted millions of dollars of church funds for his personal enrichment.

The church sought to reverse the decision in the 9th Circuit Court of Appeals in San Francisco and lost again. The U.S. Supreme Court al-

[51]*Newkirk Herald Journal* October 12, 1992.
[52]Joel Sappell and Robert Welkos, "Shoring Up Its Religious Profile," *Los Angeles Times,* June 25, 1990.

lowed the lower court decision to stand, but not without objections. Among the voices in favor of reversal were the National Council of Churches and the American Civil Liberties Union (ACLU). Each argued that it is unconstitutional for an entity of the government to define religion or place restraints on church fund-raising activities. Neither the ACLU nor the National Council of Churches endorses Scientology; each fears the courts are tampering with First Amendment guarantees.

As evidenced throughout this chapter, the Church of Scientology aggressively attempts to stifle critics. As of 1991, the church had seventy-one lawsuits pending against the IRS. One suit, *Miscavige* v. *Internal Revenue Service*, required the government to produce 52,000 pages of documents. Finally, in 1993, the IRS and the Church of Scientology settled their disputes, with the IRS awarding tax exemptions to the church and more than 150 related corporations. A Scientology spokesman compared the settlement to "the Palestinians and the Israelis shaking hands."[53]

Time magazine reported in May 1991 that the FBI had been debriefing Scientology defectors for the past several years, hoping to build a major racketeering case against church officials. Government insiders report, however, that the effort has stalled because the Justice Department is unwilling to fund an all-out war with the church and fears the added cost of fending off Scientology's "notorious jihads against individual agents."[54] According to Ted Gunderson, former head of the FBI's Los Angeles office, "In my opinion, the church has one of the most effective intelligence operations in the U.S., rivaling even that of the FBI's Los Angeles office."[55]

It appears that foreign governments are moving more aggressively against the Church of Scientology. For example, the Church of Scientology in Toronto, Canada, was fined $250,000 in 1992 for creating a ring that spied on agencies such as "the Royal Canadian Mounted Police, Ontario Provincial Police, Toronto Police, the attorney-general's office, Revenue Canada, two law firms and medical associations in the mid-1970s."[56] The agencies were infiltrated "to find out how much authorities knew about Scientology's activities."[57]

According to *Time* magazine, "Since 1986 authorities in France, Spain and Italy have raided more than fifty Scientology centers."[58] Eleven

[53]Stephen Labaton, "Scientologists Granted Tax Exemption by the U.S.," *New York Times*, October 14, 1993, p. A1.

[54]Behar, "The Cult of Greed and Power."

[55]Ibid.

[56]"Church of Scientology Fined $250,000 for Spying," *Edmonton Journal* (Edmonton, Alberta, Canada), September 12, 1992.

[57]Ibid.

[58]Richard Behar, "Pushing beyond the U.S.," *Time*, May 6, 1991.

Scientologists were arrested in Spain and accused of falsification of records, coercion, and capital flight. Magistrate Jose Maria Vasquez Honrubia said, "The real god of [Scientology] is money."[59] In 1989 Spain's Ministry of Health concluded that the sect is "totalitarian" and "pure and simple 'charlatanism.' "[60]*

Civil Suits   Courts have been generous in finding for Scientology's victims, in some cases awarding plaintiffs in suits against the church unusually large damages. However, the church settles a number of these cases out of court—perhaps to avoid negative publicity, perhaps out of fear that a court judgment will far exceed an offer of compromise. With such settlements, the church sometimes insists on a gag order barring the plaintiff from ever criticizing the church in the future. Such was the case in *Wakefield* v. *Church of Scientology of California* (1982).

Margery Wakefield had been a church member for twelve years before filing suit in 1982. She alleged that Scientologists had held her captive, committed fraud, and failed to cure her of mental illness as promised. Wakefield, who joined the church in 1970, says she began suffering from bouts of depression while she was a student at the University of Michigan. Scientologists, she says, promised her she would be cured of the problem.

Fearing that Wakefield was suicidal, church members held her captive on two occasions for several weeks. Her attorneys argued that she was deprived of adequate psychiatric care at a time when she desperately needed it. Since leaving the Church of Scientology, she has been institutionalized for mental instability at least fourteen times.

In 1986 Wakefield agreed to a $200,000 settlement in exchange for her silence. The gag order was sanctioned by a federal judge, but it hasn't stopped Wakefield from talking. Her goal, she says, is to make the public aware of Scientology so others won't suffer as she did. The church sought a criminal contempt hearing in the case.

The case of *Titchbourne* v. *Church of Scientology* exemplifies the difficulties associated with suing a religious organization. A member for only a few months in 1975–1976, Julie Christofferson Titchbourne paid the Church of Scientology $3,200 for courses that promised to improve her communications skills, vision, and academic abilities. Instead, her attorneys argued, she was left with a warped personality and an inability to cope with stressful situations.

[59]Ibid.
[60]Ibid.
*Telephone conversation with Cynthia Kisser, executive director, Cult Awareness Network, July 1993. Ms. Kisser said she had recently appeared on a television program with Mr. Jentsch, who said that Scientology had resolved its problems in Spain. It had all been a mistake.

In 1979 Titchbourne was awarded a judgment of $2,067,000 in an Oregon court. The judgment was set aside in 1982 by the Oregon Court of Appeals on the basis that the trial judge had erred "in allowing too much scope in considering fraud because the truth of religious beliefs could not be determined by courts."[61]

In 1985 the case was retried in Portland, Oregon, before Circuit Judge Donald H. Londer. To avoid the error committed in the previous trial, he instructed jurors that Scientology, under the law, is a church. He also informed the jury that "if a religion made promises on matters wholly secular and failed to keep them, it might be liable for claims of fraud."[62]

The second set of jurors demonstrated an even greater willingness to punish the Church of Scientology than the first set of jurors, awarding Titchbourne $39 million in punitive damages. The church's attorneys asked Judge Londer for a mistrial, noting in a memorandum that "the size of the award will have a [chilling] effect on the free exercise of all religions."[63] Attorneys also warned that "To permit the punitive damage award to stand would be tantamount to declaring open season on all minority religions."[64]

Two months later, in a ruling that criticized his own actions, Judge Londer granted the mistrial. In his written opinion he stated, "The case had gone astray from the fraud accusations leveled by Julie Christofferson Titchbourne. . . . It became an attack on the church."[65] Had Hubbard not moved Dianetics from the secular to the sacred, the judgment would have stood.

In a California case, *Wollersheim* v. *Church of Scientology of California* (1986), a jury awarded former Scientologist Larry Wollersheim $30 million for harassment, being driven to the brink of mental collapse, and bankruptcy. The Court of Appeals reduced the judgment to $2.5 million but did not overturn the decision. In his written opinion, Justice Earl Johnson, Jr., wrote, "Scientology leaders made the deliberate decision to ruin Wollersheim economically and possibly psychologically. . . . Such conduct is too outrageous to be protected under the Constitution and too unworthy to be privileged under the law of torts."[66]

In an unusual ruling, a special court master in a Los Angeles district court ordered in 1993 that "Scientology must pay $2.9 million in attor-

[61]Wallace Turner. "Scientologists Scale Back Protests over Portland Jury Verdict," *New York Times*, June 13, 1985.
[62]Ibid.
[63]Ibid.
[64]Ibid.
[65]Ibid.
[66]Ibid.

neys' fees for using the federal courts to destroy [a] small church."[67] The ruling stated in part that the Church of Scientology used the federal courts " 'to destroy their opponents rather than to resolve an actual dispute.' "[68] The church had alleged that "the infant church stole Scientology literature and used it for counseling programs to gain a commercial edge over the Scientology church."[69] The charge was dismissed for lack of evidence.

In 1992, the *Toronto Star* reported that "the highest libel award in Canadian history . . . got sweeter for a top Crown attorney. . . . [A] judge rejected the Church of Scientology's bid to slash the record $1.6 million damage award for libelling Crown attorney Casey Hill."[70] Instead, the judge added another $500,000 interest to the judgment awarded in 1985 against the church and a codefendant, lawyer Morris Manning.

Finally, ties to Scientology front organizations can be costly. Applied Scholastics, the consulting firm that bases its work on the writings of L. Ron Hubbard, has a client list that includes IBM, Hewlett-Packard, and Memorex. A former client was Applied Materials, which makes equipment used in the manufacture of computer chips. It retained Applied Scholastics to run a training program. Dyan Machan, writing for *Forbes* magazine, states that "three employees . . . sued Applied Materials, claiming that they were driven out of the company after they complained about the courses. Applied Materials settled out of court with the three former employees for an estimated $600,000 or more."[71]

The Media   It is also possible to combat Scientology through the media. Making the public aware of the church and its front organizations will certainly affect its growth and ability to function. In the past, publishers have been hesitant to print articles casting the church in a negative light. After all, Scientology's propensity for using the courts to harass critics is well known. Defending lawsuits is expensive and time-consuming. Even when you win, you lose.

In recent years, however, courageous publishers have extensively examined the church's activities. The series of articles by Sappell and Welkos published by the *Los Angeles Times* are examples of quality investigative reporting. Both authors knew the church would attempt to punish them after the articles hit the newsstands. They were right. Scien-

[67]"Scientology Church Must Pay $2.9 Million," *Santa Barbara News-Press* (Santa Barbara, California), January 23, 1993.
[68]Ibid.
[69]Ibid.
[70]Tracey Tyler, "Judge Adds $500,000 to Record Libel Award," *Toronto Star*, Mar 12, 1992, p. D26.
[71]Dyan Machan, "Scientologizing," *Forbes*, September 14, 1992.

tologists purchased space on hundreds of billboards and bus placards in the Los Angeles area at an estimated cost of $1 million. Above the reporters' names were statements taken out of context that portrayed the church in a positive light.

The excesses of Church of Scientology members can be curbed. Federal, state, and local law enforcement agencies must continue to monitor the organization's activities and must crack down if crimes are committed. Those who have been wronged by the church should not be intimidated but should seek their day in court. And the media must continue to expose Scientology. Combating Scientology will not be easy. Scientologists will fight back—they always do.

CHAPTER SIX

THE UNIFICATION CHURCH (MOONIES)

American sociologists have lost the querulous spirit of C. Wright Mills, who was at odds with American society and harshly challenged many of its institutions. In fact, Mills's criticisms were so harsh that the Soviet Union perceived him as an ally. Yet after he had been invited to Moscow as an honored guest, he promptly criticized the Soviets for censoring the press. Mills was never concerned with being "politically correct." He simply "did" sociology.

In his book *The Power Elite* (1956), Mills argued that America was dominated by a small group of businessmen, politicians, and military leaders. He maintained that policy was shaped in back rooms where the advantaged met to protect their interests. There, deals were struck that lined the pockets of the rich—deals that were explained to the masses as being in their interests. During the 1950s, through his exposés Mills created an interest in America for *critical theory*, a subdiscipline of sociology that developed in Frankfurt, Germany, in the early 1920s.

The *critical school* views modern society as rife with irrationality, despite the fact that society appears to be the embodiment of the rational. Herbert Marcuse, who achieved prominence within the critical school, viewed technology as one means of dominating the public. He saw on the horizon a one-dimensional society in which people lose the ability to think critically or negatively about their world. He saw, among other factors, the media as promoting a mind-set destructive of individuality.

The mass media, which includes newspapers, magazines, television, and radio, shapes public opinion. In the United States, exposure to media is so extensive that much of our attitudes and behaviors are reflections of media influence. What we see and hear, however, is often limited to thirty-second sound bites or a few inches of editorial assessment; news for busy Americans is reduced to the lowest common denominator. Unfortunately, incomplete news often evokes an emotional response from the masses rather than a thinking response.

Without favorable public opinion, elites are sometimes unable to act when they think that action on their part is necessary. Ever since the first

Nixon administration, the public has been hearing much about pressures from the so-called liberal media. Reactionaries believe that the media is so "bent to the left" that a conservative president cannot function constructively in the face of its bias. To combat this perceived liberal bias there is an ever-growing conservative media, much of it created by Korean evangelist Sun Myung Moon, the founder of the Unification Church. The purpose of Moon's media is to generate public opinion in support of conservative ideology. All the technological tools that Marcuse feared—television, radio, the press—are used effectively by Moon's church to generate public support for conservative political agendas.

For more than a decade I have been an observer of Moon and his church. I have attended Unification Church services, participated in church-sponsored seminars, accepted Unificationist hospitality, and benefited from their favors. I have traveled to many parts of the United States and have visited South Korea, mostly at church expense. The so-called Moonies have spent upwards of $7,000 on me. Tens of thousands of other professionals have also been recipients of what appears to be Moon's largess.

Early Research on the Unification Church

The Unification Church has a long history in the United States. Through the efforts of missionaries, there was already a small but vibrant church here before Sun Myung Moon's arrival thirty years ago.

Social scientists have written much about the church. Few, however, have tried to look at the church as a whole. For example, there has been a plethora of scholarly work on brainwashing: it was alleged that potential converts were induced to accept church doctrine by being subjected to mind-control techniques.

Another facet of the church that drew the attention of researchers was Moon's practice of arranged marriages. Through what the church called divine inspiration, Moon often matched youngsters from different cultures; some had never seen each other before, and many did not share a common language. Following pen-pal engagements that lasted several years for most couples, Moon held mass "blessings," often marrying several thousand couples at one time. Researchers were interested in if, and how, such marriages worked.*

Still other researchers focused on Moon's businesses in the United States. How could wage-paying businesses compete with Moon's enter-

*According to Joy Garratt, a church spokesperson, "about 10 to 15 percent of the missionaries reject [Moon's] suggestions as to whom they should marry." See Richard Severo, "Unification Church Acceptance Gains," *New York Times*, July 21, 1984.

prises, which were staffed by unpaid missionaries? Unification theology and the political activities of Moon's organizations also came under the scrutiny of social scientists.

My first interest in the church centered on how Unificationists were able to attract converts to a religious perspective that the majority of Americans in the early 1980s considered beyond the pale. Most converts sacrificed family and friends and severed other social ties once they joined the church. In interacting with the Moonies, it became apparent to me that most of Moon's followers were alienated youngsters with a need for "answers." They wanted to know how to survive in a complex world, and most were willing to participate in changing the world for the better—as Moon defined better. Moon's microcosm provided converts with a plan for living and a safe haven from the outside world. In return, Unificationists worked without pay at whatever tasks they were assigned.

Studying a single aspect of Moon's complex church, the conversion process, left me with a limited and simplistic understanding of Unificationism. I tried to build a better understanding by fusing my research findings with those of researchers who had explored other aspects of the church. I was not satisfied with the results, and this prodded me to accept every possible opportunity to continue study of the church.

It wasn't until after I had participated extensively in church activities over a long period of time that I was able to develop a sense of the whole. From this broadened perspective, I have come to the conclusion that Moon and his allies pose a threat to the free functioning of our political system. Moon heads a large and effective group of political organizations that are engaging in political machinations at the highest level.

C. Wright Mills saw society as governed by a military, industrial, and political elite. Time has not altered that. What *has* been altered is public acceptance of the elite's activities, through perceptions shaped by Moon's media.

To understand the Moon organization as I now do, it is necessary for the reader to develop a sense of the whole. This requires a return to my first experiences with the Unification Church.

In the Woods with the Moonies

During the 1970s and early 1980s, much was written about Sun Myung Moon and his followers. Most accounts were negative. The media focused on charges of brainwashing: it was alleged that potential church defectors were fed high-carbohydrate diets to weaken them and then were kept in a sleepless, zombielike state to make mind control easier.

Early in 1981 I met Andy Compton, center director of the Unification Church in Minneapolis, Minnesota. Andy often complained that the Unification Church was being treated unfairly in the press. He said that his group built membership in the same ways that other new churches build membership: missionaries living in his center went door-to-door and issued invitations to meetings, spoke before groups, and passed out literature on the streets.

Those who believed that the Unificationists were guilty of mind control argued that seminars held at remote campsites were used to facilitate the brainwashing of unsuspecting participants. To prove this untrue, Andy invited me to attend a regional workshop held in the spring of 1981 near DeKalb, Illinois. The campsite, owned by a retired dentist, had at one time been a Christmas tree farm. Trees that had not been cut for sale towered majestically over the isolated retreat. When our contingent arrived, there was a game in progress. The Moonies were taking a "faith walk."

There were two columns with eight or nine youngsters in each column. Participants were required to keep their eyes shut, except for the column leaders. Locked hand-in-hand, the leaders (senior Moonies) carefully led their followers over rocks, stumps, and through briar patches, being careful to tell each person in the column when to step up, over, or around to avoid obstacles. Critics suggest that such follow-the-leader games create a sense of dependence on group leaders. The boys and girls in the columns were giggling and having a good time. If this was brainwashing, then it appeared that having one's brain washed could indeed be fun.

Unification Theology   Following the faith walk, everyone attended a lecture entitled "The Fall of Man." The Unificationist conducting the lecture explained that God had put Adam and Eve on earth to form a perfect family, which would be a blessing to Him. God would love Adam and his offspring, and they would return His love. But before Adam and Eve could have children, they would have to be in a perfected state. Enter the snake!

Jealous of the affection that God had for Adam and Eve, Satan plotted to discredit them. Shedding his snakely disguise, he confronted Eve in human form and seduced her. She in turn seduced Adam. Satan's plan worked: Adam and Eve fell from God's grace, and as punishment they were denied eternal life. The lecturer went on to say that eating an apple had nothing to do with the Fall. To prove that the fruit actually symbolized forbidden sex, the instructor reminded us that after the Fall Adam and Eve covered their sexual parts, not their mouths.

Despite His anger, God promised redemption for Adam's offspring. To keep His word, God sent Christ (whom Unificationists often refer to as the second Adam) to complete the first Adam's mission—to marry, have children, and form the perfect family. Christ failed, but it was not his fault.

Now, for the Unification Church to gain converts in American culture, it would be foolhardy to discredit Christ. In the last chapter of the Old Testament, Malachi, it is stated that Elijah will return and pave the way for the Messiah. Unificationists believe that John the Baptist was Elijah incarnate. Our lecturer pointed out that John wavered in proclaiming Jesus the Messiah, thereby dooming Christ's mission to failure. Instead of being able to marry and form the perfect family, Jesus had to contend with a political situation that led to his execution.

Because John failed, God decreed that humankind should endure an additional 2,000 years of trial and tribulation. "But," our speaker announced triumphantly, "the dispensation is over! The third Adam is here—the Reverend Sun Myung Moon. And I am here to tell you that you can be adopted into his perfect family."

Although Unification theology has changed somewhat over the years (this happens frequently when there is a living leader), one aspect of Unificationism has remained constant. Followers consider Reverend Moon the messiah. He is not Christ returned but a different man, God-sent to establish a God-centered earthly kingdom. Columnist Tim Folzenlogen, writing for the *Unification News* fully a decade after my week in the woods with the Moonies, expressed the way Unificationists feel about their church and leader: "In my book the name of the game is 'to win.' You know? I mean, I didn't join this movement to lose. Father [Moon] is the Messiah, Divine Principle [the Unification holy book] is the Completed Testament, our mission is to build the Kingdom of Heaven on Earth. I believe that. I intend to accomplish that."[1]

Zellner Wins at Volleyball   After lunch on our first day in camp we played a strange game of volleyball. The Moonies and their guests (other than myself) were between the ages of twenty and thirty. I was forty-six. After a few minutes of play, it was apparent that I was dominating the game. I took a short ego trip, but I knew it shouldn't have been happening that way. The Moonies delicately tapped the ball over the net, and I spiked it back at them as hard as I could.

After the game a Moonie from St. Louis stopped me and said, "You are really aggressive and competitive." The Moonies play volleyball cooperatively. They try to hit the ball over the net in such a way that the other team can return it. It's like playing tennis with your mother: you hit the ball softly into an area you hope she can cover.

---

[1]Tim Folzenlogen, "Homeboy Three," *Unification News*, October 1991, p. 22.

Perhaps I am overly competitive. There were times during the volley-ball game when I wanted to shout with frustration. It was not uncommon for the teams to stop play, even with the score tied. The server would swing an arm at the ball without hitting it and chant:

Um, Umgawa
We Got The Spiritual Powa
Um, Umgawa
We Got The Spiritual Powa

The chants seemed infective. Players on both sides of the net got involved; they spun and danced and chanted. The game soon turned into a religious experience. There were no Moonie volleyball stars. And no one was keeping score—except me.

The Love Bomb   After the volleyball game we listened to another lecture. Then it was time for dinner. A tray was prepared for each state represented at the workshop. This kept invited guests with those who had brought them. Newcomers, including myself, never went anywhere without a senior Moonie tagging along.

Whatever a guest said was elevated in importance, which had a profound net effect. The message was simple: we love you and you are important. To the youngster who has never felt important and has never been listened to, the effect is overwhelming. The Moonies tend to attract dropouts and, by giving them a sense of importance, keep them in the organization.

Brainwashing?   Was an attempt at mind control evident at the workshop? For the most part, the experience as I perceived it was tame; not much different happened in DeKalb than what happens at other church retreats. Without question, some who attended such retreats did come to accept Sun Myung Moon as the messiah. If this acceptance is proof of brainwashing, then indeed brainwashing does occur. I have yet to meet a Moonie who does not believe that Moon was God-sent to save the world.

As previously noted, critics of the Unification Church during the 1970s and early 1980s argued that converts were kept in a sleepless state, becoming like zombies. In truth, we didn't get much sleep. But most of the Moonie leaders in camp were young and their charges even younger. When I was their age, sleep was not very important to me either. Moreover, considering the number of students who sleep through my daytime lectures, it appears that sleeping at night is still not very important—even to young adults who have never heard of the Unification Church.

I'm Not Very Hungry—Thank You Very Much!   A decade ago, Unification Church detractors argued that converts were kept on a high-carbohydrate diet to induce a state of lethargy. I am not a nutritionist, so I cannot comment from that standpoint. We were given three meals a day. The food, although inexpensive, seemed nutritious enough. However, the preparation was awful!

For example, our first evening meal consisted of chicken—red and raw in the middle   and two bowls of mixed vegetables. One bowl was a mixture of carrots, potatoes, and onions, steamed only enough to barely warm them. The potatoes and carrots were still crunchy. The other vegetable dish consisted of half-cooked Brussels sprouts and something unidentifiable, perhaps hominy.

Cooking and housekeeping arrangements typified the church stratification system. Because many of the Oriental missionaries spoke very little English, they were assigned the cooking and cleaning chores. This freed the European and American youngsters to perform evangelistic duties.* Our Korean and Japanese cooks had to prepare typically American food, with which they had little experience. To compound their problems, they had only a wood stove and the water supply was a well some distance from the kitchen. I was not at all surprised that the food was not particularly tasty. Sometimes it was easier to politely decline food rather than participate in mealtime events.

More Games   We played a lot of games in camp. Team arrangements were much like meal arrangements: guests were expected to stay with the leaders who had brought them to the workshop. Because each of the states represented at the workshop had only one center, we participated as states. For example, we (Minnesota) were champion charaders, having beaten Michigan in the Charade-Off.

Cultural relativist that I am, I left the workshop thinking that all the fuss about the Unification Church was much ado about nothing. The Moonies were few in number, and prospects for group growth seemed limited. Also, they seemed a poor lot. Their centers, located in working-class neighborhoods, were old buildings that were usually mortgaged to the hilt. Even the necessities of life were an everyday struggle for them. I remember an occasion when the state director in Minnesota took his missionaries as a group to a Salvation Army resale shop to refurbish their wardrobes. Early on, Moon ordered that his followers must be clean, have a good haircut, and dress neatly, but he never said their clothing had to be new. Food in the centers was much like food at the workshop: adequate but inexpensive.

---

*In my interaction with the Unificationists, I have found that European converts to the movement usually have better English skills than youngsters from other parts of the world.

In the early 1980s, Moon was messiah to a small group of believers. The average American viewed him as a religious crackpot. Established churches tended to view him as an anathema, a religious megalomaniac, perhaps a criminal. I was not convinced that any of these assessments was accurate.

Moon Jailed

On October 22, 1981, Moon addressed a gathering in Foley Square Park, New York. It was his first public appearance in five years. A week earlier he had been indicted in a federal court for tax evasion. The indictment charged that he had failed to report more than $150,000 of his income from 1973 to 1975. Moon accused the federal government of bigotry, telling his audience in the park, "I would not be standing here today if my skin were white and my religion Presbyterian."[2]

At the end of summer 1982, I accepted a teaching position at Doane College in Crete, Nebraska. In Lincoln, twenty-five miles northeast, the Unificationists maintained a church center. I visited on a number of occasions, just to stay in touch with the movement. During my first year in Nebraska, while Moon awaited trial, the church seemed on the verge of dissolution.

At the trial, attorneys argued that Moon, being unfamiliar with U.S. banking laws, held church money in his name but had not personally benefited from it. In May 1982 Moon was convicted of the charges. Two months later he was sentenced to eighteen months in prison and fined $25,000.[3]

In the months prior to Moon's conviction, the church abandoned vigorous recruitment efforts in an apparent effort to avoid negative publicity. During the 1970s church leadership positions at state and local levels were dominated by American-born males. By the early 1980s the church was appointing foreign-born missionaries, including young women, to lead state organizations. With the publicity accompanying Moon's imprisonment and anticult charges of brainwashing, Unificationists were unable to recruit effectively in this country.

In truth, the Unification Church in America has never attracted a large following. Membership estimates of up to 45,000 have appeared in the press, but such numbers were a reflection of what reporters were told by

[2]Charles Austin, "Bigotry Charge Raised at Rally for Reverend Moon," *New York Times*, October 23, 1981, p. B4.

[3]"Moon Asks Courts to Reverse His Tax-Evasion Conviction," *New York Times*, December 5, 1982. See also "High Court Bars Moon's Appeal of Tax Verdict," *New York Times*, May 15, 1984.

church spokespersons. After all, size portends respectability. According to church records, at its acme in the early 1970s the church's core membership never exceeded 2,000.[4] By the late 1970s the church had already suffered shrinkage. American youth were returning to conservative values, the anticult movement was having an effect, and simple demographics were affecting the organization—there were fewer young people from whom to recruit. By the time Moon was jailed in 1984, the Unification Church in America probably numbered fewer than 1,000. Consequently, many observers (including myself) were ready to lay a wreath on a strange but interesting epoch in American religious history. But the Unification Church was anything but dead![5]

CAUSA

With Moon in jail, the church launched a massive educational blitz. Fully 300,000 clergy across the United States received five-pound gift boxes from church headquarters in New York City. In each box were two books, six hours of doctrinal lectures on video cassettes, and a picture of Reverend Moon standing next to his prison bunk. An estimate published in *Christian Century* placed the cost of the public relations campaign at $10 million.[6]

The mailing was followed by personal visits to pastors who had received the gift boxes. In Nebraska, local Moonies were assisted in this work by a team of mobile evangelists in an expensive new motorhome. Team members said that Moon had purchased 100 such vans to invite the nation to an understanding of the Unification Church.

Pastors who showed an interest were invited to attend a four-day, all-expenses-paid, CAUSA seminar. By the time I accepted an invitation in April 1985, more than 7,000 had already attended similar conferences. Because the seminars were held around the world, usually at vacation meccas, the Moonies had little trouble finding willing participants.

The seminar I attended was held at Marina Del Rey, a community developed as a yacht parking lot for the rich and famous in the Los Angeles area. There were 320 others in attendance at the conference, some from as far away as Alaska, Hawaii, Florida, and New York. Except for 33 legislators from the state of Idaho, it was a typical Unification

---

[4]Anson Shupe, "Sun Myung Moon's Mission in Retreat," *Wall Street Journal*, November 1, 1989. See also George Bryjak and Gary Macy, "The Fall of Sun Myung Moon and the Unification Church in America," *U.S.A. Today*, November 1985, pp. 62–65.

[5]Bryjak and Macy, "The Fall of Sun Myung Moon and the Unification Church in America."

[6]"High Priced PR," *Christian Century*, April 17, 1985, p. 376. See also "Sun Myung Moon's Goodwill Blitz," *Time*, April 22, 1985, p. 60. The *Time* article put the cost of the media campaign at $4.5 million.

Church assembly. Apart from a large number of Mormons (who were heavily recruited because of their conservative values),* most of the pastors at the meeting represented Protestant evangelical churches. I was one of only a few who was not a minister.

Dr. Phillip Sanchez   Keynote speaker at the convention was Dr. Phillip Sanchez, president of CAUSA USA. A biography distributed by the Unificationists noted that in 1968 Ronald Reagan, then governor of California, had appointed him to the governing board of California community colleges. A few years later, Reagan appointed Sanchez to the board of trustees of California state colleges and universities.

During 1972 Richard Nixon appointed Sanchez head of the Office of Economic Opportunity, the highest cabinet post ever held by a Hispanic. In 1973 Sanchez was named ambassador to Honduras. Solidly tied to Republican administrations, in 1975 he was appointed ambassador to Colombia by Gerald Ford. Also in that year, the American Association of State Colleges and Universities named him Man of the Year. The handout further noted that "In 1980 Ambassador Sanchez declined to serve in the cabinet of Ronald Reagan in order to devote more time to family and business."

During his presentation, Sanchez explained that CAUSA was an acronym for the Confederation of Associations for the Unity of the Societies of the Americas. The organization's goal, he said, "is to fight communism by providing Latin American leaders with a God-centered ideology that explains and refutes Marxism."

It is interesting that very little was said about religion during the conference. The focus was on the war against communism, particularly in Nicaragua. Although Latin America received the most attention, other communist insurgencies were also discussed.

Dr. Mohamed Omar   While the conference participants enjoyed the comforts of a posh hotel, war raged in Afghanistan. Dr. Mohamed Omar, former secretary of commerce for Afghanistan, urged the pastors to support the mujahidin (Afghan resistance) by supporting President Reagan's policies. Much of his presentation was emotional; for example, he accused the Soviets of boobytrapping children's toys. True or not, his claims had enormous impact on the gathering of ministers.

In 1987 articles appeared in the newspaper announcing the death of Tulsa, Oklahoma, native Lee Shapiro. Shapiro, purported to be an independent filmmaker, and his cameraman, Jim Lindelhof, were killed by machine gun and rocket fire from Soviet helicopters while making a

---

*Utah senator Orrin Hatch once praised Moon for providing "a religious alternative to communism." See Eric Alterman, "In Moon's Orbit," *New Republic,* October 27, 1986, p. 13.

documentary in northern Afghanistan.[7] What the articles did not reveal was that Shapiro and Lindelhof claimed they were Moonies. Prior to filming in Afghanistan, Shapiro won a commendation from President Reagan for depicting the brutal treatment of the Mesquite Indians in Nicaragua at the hands of the Sandinistas. Before joining Shapiro, Lindelhof was active in establishing emergency medical facilities in Afghanistan. As an early witness to the Afghan struggle, Lindelhof had testified before Congress that Soviet soldiers were, as Dr. Omar reported, "boobytrapping children's toys."[8]

Dr. Donald Sills   The only collection taken at the CAUSA convention was for Dr. Donald Sills, a Baptist minister with a radio ministry headquartered in Alexandria, Virginia. Sills's concern was freedom of religion. In his presentation, Sills elevated Moon to a position of martyrdom in a war against undefined elements of "the system" that were out to destroy freedom of religious expression. In the process of discussing this war, Sills attributed Moon's income tax conviction to religious bigotry.*

Introduced as president of the Coalition for Religious Freedom, Sills stated that one of the main objectives of the coalition was "kicking the CAN" (Cult Awareness Network), an Illinois-based organization devoted to deprogramming cult members. To that end, Sills published the bulletin *Religious Freedom Alert*. The magazine focused on alleged violations of religious freedom, highlighting deprogrammer activities and perceived prejudice toward fundamentalist churches.

Between March 1991 and July 1991 I received five unsolicited issues of *Alert* magazine. The Church of Scientology, Hare Krishna, the Unification Church, or a combination of these groups is presented as persecuted in each issue, along with fundamentalist Christian churches. The magazine provides common ground (perceived religious persecution) for binding together Christian fundamentalists and groups usually defined as cults by fundamentalist preachers.

To enhance the credibility of the coalition, the executive committee of the organization, chaired by Dr. Robert C. Grant, reads like a *Who's Who* of evangelicals: Dr. Ben Armstrong, Dr. E. V. Hill, Rev. Rex Humbard, Dr. Jess Moody, Dr. Joseph Paige, James Robison, and Dr. W. Cleon Skousen.†

Some months after receiving my first copy of *Alert*, I began receiving literature from Friends of Freedom based in Cockeyville, Maryland. The first mailing was a slick magazine attacking CAN, entitled *A Criminal*

---

[7]Ed Godfrey, "Filmmaker Murdered, Widow Says," *Daily Oklahoman*, January 6, 1988, p. 29.
[8]Ibid.
*For a full account of Moon's problems with the IRS, see Michael Isikoff, "New Moon," *New Republic*, August 26, 1985, pp. 14–16. For Moon's arguments, see "High Court Bars Moon's Appeal of Tax Verdict," *New York Times*, May 15, 1984.
†Names of executive committee members appear on the organization's letterhead.

Assault on Religious Freedom: The Anti-Religious Movement. Featured was an article by Donald Sills. It is interesting that readers were asked "to report . . . abuses by CAN or its officials"[9] to local police departments and to the attorney general in the state where the offense occurred. The booklet went on to say that the FBI, IRS, and Church of Scientology should also be informed.

In April 1992 I called Sills's office in Virginia to ascertain the current status of the coalition. The phone had been disconnected. I then called George Robertson, executive vice president of Friends of Freedom in Maryland. He said that all money intended for Sills should be channeled through Friends of Freedom. According to Robertson, "Most of Sills's funding in the beginning came from the Unification Church. But it dried up, and he has had to scale back his operation."

Sills, like Sanchez, had a connection to former president Reagan. A CAUSA handout noted that he had served under "Reagan in California as director of the American Drug Abuse Foundation."

Eldridge Cleaver   Former Black Panther leader Eldridge Cleaver was introduced to the CAUSA audience as a born-again Christian. His message addressed the need for the United States to unite against communist expansionism.

Apparently Cleaver was also a born-again capitalist. In 1968 he fled the United States to avoid prosecution for his part in a shoot-out between the Panthers and the Oakland, California, police. For the next seven years Cleaver spoke out against the evils of capitalism, first as the guest of Fidel Castro and later as an honored visitor in Algeria, China, and North Korea. Finally, in Paris, with his welcome worn thin in communist countries, Cleaver repented and requested permission to return to the United States. With the assistance of CARP,* a Unificationist student organization, Cleaver was allowed to return and the charges were dropped.[10] When I met Cleaver he told me he was working full-time as a lecturer for the Unification Church, although he was not a member. He further stated that he was impressed with the Mormon people he had met and that he now shared many views with the Mormon church.

Thomas Ward and William Lay   There was no free time allocated for tourism during the CAUSA convention. The schedule was full; lectures

---

[9]*A Criminal Assault on Religious Freedom: The Anti-Religious Movement* (Cockeyville, MD: Friends of Freedom, undated), p. 23.

*CARP is the acronym for the Collegiate Association for the Research of Principles.

[10]Cf. Wallace Turner, "Cleaver Returns to Coast Campus," *New York Times*, May 20, 1982; Wallace Turner, "Cleaver an Anachronism to New Panther Leaders," *New York Times*, November 19, 1975.

began with breakfast and lasted well into the night. Nevertheless, most of us did visit the famed "marina of the stars" at the expense of skipping some of what Thomas Ward and William Lay had to say. Both CAUSA lecturers followed the script set out in the 264-page *Introduction to the CAUSA Worldview* given us when we arrived in Los Angeles. We could read what they had to say at our leisure.

Reading the CAUSA manual was in some ways like reading alarmist literature distributed by the John Birch Society in the 1950s. The following is typical:

> Communists are already working to build a Hispanic separatist movement calling for the secession of Texas, Utah, California, Nevada, Arizona, and Colorado from the United States.
>
> The Soviets are also backing a "New Afrika" movement which calls for the secession from the United States of Mississippi, Louisiana, Alabama, Georgia, and South Carolina. Communists proclaim that through the secession of "Occupied Mexico," New Afrika, and the Native American Nations, they will "defeat U.S. imperialism."[11]

Lay and Ward concentrated on a history of Marxism, highlighting the atrocities committed in the name of Marx and the purported 150 million people slaughtered to establish Marxist governments. Liberation theology was attacked and emphasis was placed on support for the Nicaraguan Contras. Pictures of torture victims were used to generate an emotional response from the audience.

We were told that we would have to organize to help President Reagan fight the communist dupes and sympathizers in Congress so that aid could be sent to the Contra freedom fighters. This meant that we should explain to our congregations exactly what was going on behind their backs in Washington, D.C. Finally, and most important, we were urged to encourage members of our churches to write letters to the editors of their local newspapers and get in touch with their representatives in Congress.

At the end of the conference the CAUSA people said they would be in touch. But for now, we were told, all we had to do was sign a pledge: "We solemnly resolve to put an end to God-denying communism throughout the world, to defend and advance the God-centered values and tradition of our civilization, and to work together toward the creation of a free, moral world. In the name of God we commit our lives and our sacred honor to the accomplishment of this noble imperative."

---

[11]*Introduction to the CAUSA Worldview*, CAUSA Institute Publication 101 (New York: CAUSA International, 1985), pp. 20–21.

A Wealthy Japanese Industrialist   The seminar ended and I was certain that I had missed something. What was the bottom line? The conference had cost a small fortune, probably in the neighborhood of $250,000. At that time, seminars were being conducted at the rate of one every third week.

   During the conference I asked every Moonie that I could buttonhole, "Who is paying the bill?" All responsed that it was a wealthy Japanese industrialist—a member of the church. None said "I don't know" or "Reverend Moon is paying for it." It was always an enigmatic, nameless, wealthy Japanese industrialist, helping Reverend Moon fight communism. I am certain that rank-and-file Moonies were told that the question would be asked and that because financing is difficult to explain, it would be better to give a simple answer.

   In a *Frontline* report entitled "The Resurrection of Reverend Moon," which aired on PBS in January 1992, reporters attempted to confirm a report that Moon's Japanese friend is billionaire boat builder and legalized gambling czar Ryoichi Sasakawa. In an interview, Sasakawa told *Frontline* that he had met Moon about twenty-five years ago but that he has never supported him financially or politically.

Why?   My flight wasn't scheduled to leave Los Angeles until four hours after I had to check out of my room. To kill time, I sat around the hotel lobby and visited with pastors who, like myself, had poor luck scheduling an early flight out. I asked them what they had thought of the seminar. Most described the meetings as positive and said they had learned something about communism. They thought, too, that they could work with the Unificationists on that problem. A fair number of the ministers had come to agree that Moon was, indeed, a martyr to the cause of religious freedom. However, all said that his theology was bunk.

   I asked the ministers, "Why is Moon spending all this money? He isn't converting anybody." Most of the pastors thought he was trying to build a positive image for his church while he was in prison.

   I left the conference with an uneasy feeling. Why would Phillip Sanchez use his credentials to lend credibility to the Unification Church? Why was the church on a spending spree when its leader was in prison? Surely not for religious credibility! At the local level, the vigorous proselytizing efforts of the 1970s had been abandoned. Work at the centers was geared to recruiting seminar participants, not converts.*

---

*James W. White describes similar experiences at a CAUSA conference. See "Unification Church's Anticommunist Drive," *Christian Century*, August 28–September 4, 1985, pp. 771–72. See also "Sun Myung Moon's Followers Recruit Christians to Assist in Battle against Communism," *Christianity Today*, June 14, 1985, pp. 55, 57.

An Easy Move

A few weeks after returning from Los Angeles I began receiving bulletins from CAUSA, updates on what the communists were up to around the world. Such mailings were expected. The bulletins encouraged seminar alumni to organize and fight communism, but little else. What an incredible waste of money, I thought.

Four months after the CAUSA convention, in the fall of 1985, I moved from Crete, Nebraska, to Ada, Oklahoma. My new place of employment, East Central University, was 90 miles southeast of Oklahoma City, 500 miles directly south of Lincoln, Nebraska. Near the time of the move, I complained to Moonie friends about the high cost of renting a truck. Heidi, who had recently arrived from Germany, was now director of the center in Lincoln. "Don't worry," she said. "I will see to your move."

During the previous week Moon had purchased a fleet of box vans with rear-end lifts—Heidi thought there were a hundred of them. There was at least one truck in every state. Heidi said she wasn't quite sure what she was supposed to do with the truck; she had only vague instructions. It was her understanding, however, that the truck was to be used to help pastors and other friends of the Unification Church.

On moving day four Asians and a German couple showed up at our house. After loading the van, the Oriental youngsters returned to Lincoln while the German couple followed us to Oklahoma in the truck. They stayed the night with us in our empty apartment and helped unload our furniture in the morning. I gave them a check made out to the church, which they were reluctant to take. It was clear that the church was out to "make friends," price notwithstanding.

New Friends in Oklahoma   I did not lose touch with the Unificationists after the move. Eric Bobrycki, head of the church center in Oklahoma City, came to Ada on several occasions to lecture to my students on Unification principles. A graduate of the Unification Theological Seminary at Barrytown, New York, Eric was an engaging speaker.

On one of these trips he brought the members of his congregation with him—six or seven youngsters. All were foreign nationals. When I left Nebraska, there were no American-born Moonies in the Lincoln center. Eric was the only American-born Unificationist in the Oklahoma City center. As previously noted, the church was simply unable to recruit new members in this country during that period.

While Eric lectured, his congregation stood in the parking lot of a local shopping center and asked people to sign pledges supporting President Reagan's position on Nicaragua. I was unaware that they were doing this until I went shopping later in the day. Nothing on the pledge forms indicated that the signature drive was being sponsored by a Moon organization. A number of my students signed pledges, and within a few weeks they began receiving literature from Unification Church fronts. Eric later told me that the Oklahoma effort was part of a nationwide campaign to compile a mailing list of Reagan supporters.

During the mid-1980s, a concerned media was asking a myriad of questions about the Unification Church. Was the church a cult? Were church leaders brainwashing potential converts? Was Moon a megalomaniac? Did he really believe he was the messiah?

I felt as though I had entered a theater in the middle of a movie. By this time I knew a great deal about the Unification Church, but there was still much I did not know. I was beginning to believe that the questions asked by the media were only peripheral to what the church was really about. I began to read.

Brief History of Korea

Throughout most of its history, Korea has been fought over, influenced, or controlled by its larger Asian neighbors. During the first part of the twentieth century, Japan held military dominance over both China and Russia; and in 1910 it annexed Korea. Near the end of World War II, Roosevelt, Churchill, and Stalin met at Yalta to partition the Allied conquests. It was agreed that Japan would surrender the Korean peninsula north of the 38th parallel to the Soviet Union and that all land south of the parallel would be surrendered to the United States. This division was intended as a temporary administrative measure, with the Soviet Union and the United States to meet later with a reunification plan. Relations between the superpowers deteriorated, however, and no mutually agreeable plan could be found.

On August 15, 1948, the Republic of Korea was established in the south and Syngman Rhee was elected president. A month later the Soviet Union established a government in North Korea, and Kim Il Sung, a former major in the Soviet army, claimed authority over the entire peninsula. In 1949 the United States withdrew its occupation forces from South Korea.

In June 1950 the North Koreans launched a massive invasion, crossing the 38th parallel into South Korea. With the assent of the United Nations, the United States joined forces with fifteen other member states and drove the North Koreans to near the Yalu River, the border between China and North Korea. The war seemed near an end when, in November 1950, Chinese forces crossed the Manchurian border and joined forces with the North Koreans. War was waged up and down the peninsula until the spring of 1951, when battle lines stabilized north of Seoul near the 38th parallel.

Armistice negotiations began in July 1951, but hostilities continued for another two years until July 1953, when an armistice agreement was reached between the United Nations Command, the Chinese, and the North Korean forces. Neither the Republic of Korea (ROK) nor the United States is signatory to the agreement.

Prior to the war, Korea was one of the poorest nations in the world. About the size of Indiana, South Korea has 40 million people with a population density much greater than that of India or Japan. The peninsula has few natural resources; there is no oil and only limited supplies of coal. For the most part, Korea is energy-dependent.

Following the war, with massive infusions of U.S. aid, South Korea was rebuilt. Today it is on the threshold of becoming a major economic power.

Chung Hee Park

Postwar South Korea is a shining success economically, but it has not been a success as a democracy. In 1961 an army coup led by General Chung Hee Park deposed Syngman Rhee's successor, Myong Chang. Within weeks following the coup, the junta increased the size of the Korean Central Intelligence Agency (KCIA) and broadened its powers. Park ruled by military fiat for two years, then retired from the army and was elected president in 1963.

In 1972 the Korean Constitution was altered to give the executive branch almost unlimited power. Important provisions of the new constitution included indirect election of the president, presidential appointment of one-third of the National Assembly, and presidential authority to limit the rights of citizens during times of emergency. Park issued several such decrees—including EM-9, which banned political demonstrations by students, discussion of false rumors, and criticism of the constitution.

Park built an economically progressive, modern Korea from the rubble of war by emphasizing the need for U.S. financial aid and a continuing U.S. military presence on the peninsula. By the mid-1960s, when the United States was heavily involved in Vietnam, support for continued aid to South Korea began to ebb in the U.S. Congress.

During 1965 and 1966, however, Park strengthened ties to the United States by sending 45,000 ROK troops into Vietnam. In the truest sense of the word, the ROK forces were paid mercenaries: the American taxpayer footed the bill. Despite this show of support, costs of the war in Vietnam forced Washington to reduce the number of U.S. troops in Korea from 64,000 to 44,000. This decision, along with rumblings of still further cuts, triggered a series of mind-boggling events.

Moon Comes to America

Sun Myung Moon arrived in America in 1972 and began what he called his "Day of Hope" tour. He took a message to all fifty states that was not out of sync with messages being sent to Washington from the Chung Hee Park government. Communists were expanding their influence worldwide, and the United States and Korea had to band together to put an end to God-denying communism.[12]

Giant rallies were held at Madison Square Garden, Yankee Stadium, and the Washington Monument. Millions of dollars were spent on the crusade. Because the events were free to the public and included entertainment, and because people were curious about Moon, the meetings drew large though unenthusiastic audiences.[13]

Unification theology—an admixture of Korean shamanism, numerology, scientism, and evangelical Christianity—proclaims that a new messiah from the East (Korea) will establish a God-centered family and moral order in which "Godism" can prevail.[14] As noted earlier, Moon's followers believe him to be that sinless messiah. According to church members, when Moon is asked if he is the messiah, he responds, "Am I? You be the judge. Observe the way I live." Against that backdrop, it was difficult for most Americans to grant Moon religious credibility. Nevertheless, many Americans found his political message credible.[15]

Watergate

By 1973 the Nixon administration was completely hamstrung by the Watergate affair. Support for the Vietnam War and military spending in general was ebbing. Richard Nixon was being pressured to resign. The Korean government feared that a less friendly U.S. president would withdraw more troops and make further cuts in aid to South Korea. In response to that threat, Moon placed full-page ads costing a total of $73,000 in leading U.S. newspapers. The following is excerpted from the *New York Times*, November 30, 1973: "I have prayed to God earnestly, asking him to reveal His message. The answer came. The First word God

---

[12]Cf. Ann Crittenden, "Moon's Sect Pushes Pro-Seoul Activities," *New York Times*, May 25, 1976; Eleanor Blau, "Moon Rally Draws 25,000, Half of Stadium Capacity," *New York Times*, June 2, 1976; "Sun Myung Moon Ends Ministry in the U.S. with Anti-Communist Speech in Capital," *New York Times*, September 20, 1976.

[13]Crittenden, "Moon's Sect Pushes Pro-Seoul Activities." Crittenden reported in her account that in an interview Pak said the church had spent more than $1 million preparing for the "God Bless America" rally at Yankee Stadium.

[14]Bryjak and Macy, "The Fall of Sun Myung Moon and the Unification Church in America."

[15]Ibid.

spoke was 'Forgive.' . . . I asked God, 'What shall we do with the person of Richard Nixon?' . . . The second word that God spoke to me was 'Love. It is your duty to love him.' Jesus Christ loved even his enemies. Must you not love your president?"

On December 29, 1973, fourteen leaders of the Unification Church met in Washington to plan strategy in an attempt to block the impeachment of Richard Nixon. According to the minutes of the meeting, Nixon was referred to as the "Archangel Nixon." Neil Salonen, then president of the Unification Church in America, told the assembly that Moon felt he was on the verge of making an impact in America and that he wanted to address a joint session of Congress. Salonen further told the group that the church had to "impact the media, impact Congressmen, and impact community leaders to approach Congressmen themselves."[16]

Following Salonen's remarks, Daniel Pfefferman, national projects director for the church, emphasized the need for demonstrations involving groups like the Young Republicans and the Young Americans for Freedom; patriotic organizations like the Veterans of Foreign Wars and American Legion; ethnic groups with an anticommunist bent; and conservative churches like the Mormons.[17]

The Moonies rallied, prayed, and fasted for two months. A final rally was held on January 31, 1974, in Lafayette Square across the street from the White House. Patricia Nixon-Cox, the daughter of the president, and her husband, Edward, visited the rally and thanked the Moonies for their support. The following day, Reverend Moon met with Nixon in the White House and is reported to have told the president: "Don't knuckle under to pressure. Stand up for your convictions."[18]

On August 9, 1974, with impeachment imminent, Richard Nixon did knuckle under and resigned the presidency. Following his resignation, Moon retreated from overt political involvement and concentrated on building his church in America. This did not, however, keep him out of the news; he remained a media figure. Charges of brainwashing of young converts continued, and the actions of deprogrammers moved the Unification Church to litigate against members' parents.[19]

In addition, both the media and the public were interested in the same aspects of the church that early researchers found interesting: Moon's matchmaking, church-run businesses, theology, and political activities.

[16]Richard Halloran, "'73 Record Tells of Plan by Sun Myung Moon Aides for Drive against Nixon Impeachment," *New York Times*, September 19, 1977.

[17]Ibid.

[18]Ibid.

[19]Cf. Marcia Chambers, "Moon, on Stand, Tells of His Religious Beliefs," *New York Times*, May 28, 1982. See also Bryjak and Macy, "The Fall of Sun Myung Moon and the Unification Church in America."

Koreagate

By mid-1975 rumors of Korean influence peddling emerged in the press. The key agency involved was the KCIA; the key figure was a Korean businessman, Tongsun Park.* More than $500,000 (usually $100 bills stuffed in plain white envelopes) was passed to U.S. legislators by Park or other operatives. KCIA code names for the bribery operation were "white snow" and "ice mountain." KCIA chief of operations in the United States was the "Catholic Father"; South Korean president Park was the "Patriarch"; and "six units of cloth" was the code for $600,000 in bribe money.[20]

It was learned that more than one hundred legislators took money or gifts from the Koreans. Many reported the transactions, albeit in a variety of ways. For example, John Brademas of Indiana, then House Majority Whip, accepted a campaign contribution of $5,000. Former House Whip John McFall put $4,000 into his office account. Contributions from foreign nationals were not illegal at the time, unless the giver was acting as an agent of a foreign government.[21]

The bribery operations involved more than cash. An exile in the United States, Wook Hyung Kim, who headed the KCIA from 1963 to 1969, told federal investigators that he gave Tongsun Park "$3 million in South Korean funds in 1967 to help finance the fashionable Georgetown Club, which Park founded in 1966 to get cozy with top U.S. officials. The posh club's 1976 roster of 400 members included six Supreme Court

---

*Tongsun Park was not a relative of Korean president Chung Hee Park. In fact, *Newsweek* reported on November 8, 1976, that he was allegedly arrested by the KCIA in the 1960s for "describing himself as a relative of the South Korean president" (p. 20). The report went on to say that he traded sensitive intelligence reports for his freedom.

[20]"The Patriarch's Blessing," *Newsweek*, October 31, 1977, p. 38.

[21]The Koreagate scandal was well covered in the popular press. Information is drawn from the following sources: Richard Halloran, "South Korean CIA Extends U.S. Activities, Seeking to Infuence Government Policies," *New York Times*, October 1, 1976; Richard Halloran, "Inquiries May Force Koreans to Quit U.S.," *New York Times*, October 25, 1976; Richard Halloran, "Inquiry Raises Possibility That U.S. Citizens Work Illegally for Seoul," *New York Times*, October 30, 1976. "Lid About to Blow on New Congress Scandal," *U.S. News and World Report*, November 8, 1976, pp. 27–28; "The Korean Connection," *Newsweek*, November 8, 1976, pp. 29–32; "Koreagate on Capitol Hill?" *Time*, November 29, 1976, pp. 14, 19; "Seoul's School for Scandal," *Time*, December 13, 1976, pp. 16, 21; Richard Halloran, "Former KCIA Head Says Park Tong Sun Was Korean Agent," *New York Times*, June 5, 1977; "The Swindler from Seoul," *Time*, July 4, 1977, pp. 8, 11; "New Scandal in Congress," *U.S. News and World Report*, August 1, 1977, pp. 9–10; "Fresh Stirrings on Koreagate: Jaworski Is the Catalyst, But He Faces Some Stone Walls," *Time*, September 5, 1977, pp. 19–20; "Lid Finally Blows Off Korean Bribery Scandal," *U.S. News and World Report*, September 19, 1977, pp. 28–29; "Talking with Tongsun Park," *Newsweek*, October 3, 1977; "As the Korean Bribery Scandal Unfolds—," *U.S. News and World Report*, October 31, 1977; "Spooking Capitol Hill," *Time*, November 15, 1977, pp. 66–67.

justices; former agriculture secretary Earl Butz; Health, Education, and Welfare secretary Joseph Califano; and a score of senators and representatives. In all, federal investigators believe, Tongsun Park may have spent as much as $2 million on parties at the club he had founded and gifts for his friends."[22]

The House Ethics Committee moved slowly on the matter. It was a political hot potato. Few on Capitol Hill were interested in investigating a friendly government, and still fewer wanted to investigate themselves. Finally, in September 1977 the Justice Department brought a felony indictment against Park on thirty-six counts, charging conspiracy, racketeering, and bribery. By the time the indictment was issued, however, Park had fled to Korea.[23]

No extradition agreement exists between the United States and South Korea. Nevertheless, Jimmy Carter's secretary of state, Cyrus Vance, met in Washington with the South Korean foreign minister to urge Park's return to the United States. The effort was not met with success.[24]

It was clear that Korean president Chung Hee Park intended to influence the U.S. Congress on matters associated with foreign aid appropriations. The decision not to return Park for prosecution angered many on the Hill. Among those offended was Republican congressman Bruce Caputo of New York. Caputo introduced an amendment that would lop off $110 million earmarked for Korea in a foreign aid appropriations bill if Park was not returned. Caputo's amendment was defeated by a vote of 205 to 181.[25]

Bo Hi Pak   Much of the speculation concerning Moon and his organization involved Moon's interpreter, Bo Hi Pak. Pak, a diminutive man, was often pictured in the press with Moon during the 1972 "Day of Hope" tour. Captions under newspaper pictures of Moon speaking at rallies usually read, "Reverend Sun Myung Moon and an interpreter."[*]

The then unidentified Pak may well be the most important person in the Unification Church, perhaps even more important than Moon himself. Wook Hyung Kim, former director of the KCIA, told the *New York Times* that Bo Hi Pak is a very important man because he made Mr. Moon

---

[22]"The Swindler from Seoul," *Time*, July 4, 1977, p. 8.

[23]Cf. "Lid Finally Blows Off Korean Bribery Scandal," *U.S. News and World Report*, September 19, 1977, p. 29.

[24]Ibid.

[25]"Still Waiting for 'Harvest Time,' " *Time*, September 19, 1977, p. 22.

[*]A photograph that appears on page 30 of the *New York Times*, June 2, 1976, shows Pak's usual place during Moon's speaking engagements. See also "Sun Myung Moon Ends Ministry in the U.S. with Anti-Communist Speech in Capital," and photograph, *New York Times*, September 20, 1976, p. 18.

famous. "It was all his idea."[26] Kim further claimed that Pak was secretly an agent in the United States for the KCIA a charge Pak denies.[27]

The Unification Church claims that Lieutenant Colonel Pak, an army intelligence officer, joined Moon's movement in 1957. In 1961 he was assigned to the Korean embassy in Washington, D.C. He resigned his army commission in 1965 to become head of the Korean Cultural and Freedom Foundation. Richard Halloran, reporting for the *New York Times* in March 1978, noted that the foundation "eventually [recruited] former presidents Harry Truman and Dwight Eisenhower as honorary chairmen, into a KCIA front for fund-raising and lobbying efforts."[28]

During the mid-1960s, Pak told a friend, Robert W. Roland (an airline pilot), that he planned to use the foundation to gain influence with wealthy Americans and government officials. Roland also said Pak told him that while he was at the embassy, he acted as liaison officer between the Korean Central Intelligence Agency and the U.S. Central Intelligence Agency. Pak vehemently denies any link to the KCIA.[29]

Considering the testimony of Koreans in the know and Pak's former official position in the Korean intelligence community, did Pak, a master propagandist, join Moon organizations in an attempt to influence American public opinion and political leaders? Today, Pak oversees all the important, separately chartered Moon organizations—including a vast propaganda network, which is discussed later in this chapter.

Before Moon's arrival in the United States, the Unification Church in America had fewer than 500 members.[30] Nevertheless, as sociologist Max Weber said of sectarians, they were "true believers." When Moon took charge of his followers in this country, he told them to become politically active and they did.

Under the direction of Neil Salonen, an organization called American Youth for Just Peace was formed in the fall of 1969. The group supported the invasion of Cambodia and campaigned against groups opposed to the Vietnam War.[31]

Allen Tate Wood, a former member of the Unification Church, helped direct the activities of the organization. As a reward, Wood, eight other

[26]Richard Halloran, "Former KCIA Head Says Park Tong Sun Was Korean Agent," *New York Times*, June 5, 1977.

[27]Selwyn Raab, "FBI Holds 6 in Kidnapping of Moon Aide," *New York Times*, November 28, 1984.

[28]Richard Halloran, "Unification Church Called Seoul Tool," *New York Times*, March 16, 1978.

[29]Richard Halloran, "Inquiry Raises Possibility That U.S. Citizens Work Illegally for Seoul," *New York Times*, October 30, 1976.

[30]Bryjak and Macy, "The Fall of Reverend Sung Myung Moon and the Unification Church in America."

[31]Crittenden, "Moon's Sect Pushes Pro-Seoul Activities."

church members, and four nonmembers were given a trip to South Vietnam and Cambodia in the early 1970s. Some in the group continued on to Korea. In Seoul they toured the KCIA building, where an official of the Unification Church told them that the church wanted to make "friends" with the intelligence agency. According to Wood, "the American movement's strategy at that time was to make President Park feel that Moon was his greatest ally, not a threat. Moon told us that our [the Unification Church's] whole goal was to identify Park's goals and then serve them."[32]

The Diplomat National Bank   One of the most intriguing Koreagate inquiries centered on the attempted takeover in 1976 of the Diplomat National Bank in Washington, D.C. Federal investigators suggested that the Korean government wanted to establish a financial center in the United States as an apparatus for handling the large sums of media money needed to influence Congress and the American public on policies affecting South Korea.[33]

A direct link to the Korean government was never established. However, *Time* magazine reported in 1976 that agents representing Tongsun Park had a $249,000 interest in the Diplomat National Bank.[34] Other sources reported that Colonel Pak had assembled about half of the bank's initial $2 million capitalization. Some of the money belonged to the Unification Church, some to other investors, and a share of it (allegedly $75,000) belonged to Colonel Pak.[35]

Pak is reported to have taken $50,000 in cash to the National Savings and Trust Bank in Washington, D.C., where he bought a cashier's check. He then went to another bank, cashed the first cashier's check, and purchased a second cashier's check. The second cashier's check was later deposited in the Diplomat National Bank. Why Pak chose to route his cash through two banks before depositing the $50,000 is unclear. Such steps, however, are typical of a laundering operation.[36]

To satisfy the Securities and Exchange Commission, the Koreans withdrew from controlling interest in the bank.[37] In the years that have followed, however, Moon organizations have spent vast sums of money in the United States without identifying the sources of their income. As will be shown, Moon's business ventures in the United States have been abysmal failures, and the Unification Church in America does not generate enough income to cover its losses.

[32]Ibid.
[33]Cf. Richard Halloran, "Inquiry Suggests Korean Agents Tried to Gain Control of Bank in U.S.," *New York Times*, May 31, 1977.
[34]Cf. "Koreagate on Capitol Hill?" *Time*, November 29, 1976, pp. 14, 19.
[35]Cf. Halloran, "Inquiry Suggests Korean Agents Tried to Gain Control of Bank in U.S."
[36]Ibid.
[37]"Tongsun Park Settles an SEC Complaint," *New York Times*, October 4, 1977.

House Subcommittee on International Organizations   During May 1978, in conjunction with the investigation of Koreagate, Donald Fraser, chairman of the House Subcommittee on International Organizations, attempted to subpoena Reverend Moon's testimony pertinent to the Diplomat National Bank episode and other alleged ties to Tongsun Park. However, Moon took a trip to Europe before the subpoena was issued. Bo Hi Pak did testify before the committee and attempted to explain the purchase of the bank shares:

> Concerning the source of the funds, I can tell you, Mr. Chairman, not one penny came from either the KCIA or the Korean government or any other government for that matter. The source of funds was the Unification Church Pension Fund International, which had money here in this country for a long time prior to the birth of the Diplomat National Bank. . . . These are funds which have been set aside for the purpose of settling aged or dedicated members of the Unification Church who served many years without pay.[38]

According to Moonies whom I have interviewed, the Unification Church does not have a pension plan. Indeed, most believe that Reverend Moon will take care of them when they get old, but none are aware of a formal pension plan. Yet Pak's statement before the committee went unchallenged.

At the outset of the Fraser committee investigation, the Unification Church was not a prime target. The committee's interest in the church developed only after investigators uncovered an intelligence report from 1963 that read in part, "Kim Chong Pil organized the Unification Church while he was head of the ROK Central Intelligence Agency, and has been using the church . . . as a political tool."[39]

A former member of the KCIA, Sang Kuen Kim, testified that in 1974 truckloads of Moonies had been sent—at KCIA request—to Washington to demonstrate against Japan's alleged lack of cooperation in investigating a Korean-Japanese assassin who killed Chung Hee Park's wife. President Park, the intended victim, survived the assassination attempt. State Department officials learned of the planned protest and demanded that the Korean government call it off.[40]

The Fraser committee also learned that Reverend Moon's Tong-Il In-

[38]Bo Hi Pak, *Truth Is My Sword: Testimony of Col. Bo Hi Pak at the Korea Hearings, U.S. Congress* (New York: Unification Church of America, 1978), p. 101. The church also actively distributed a videotape of Pak's testimony before the Fraser committee.

[39]Richard Halloran, "South Korean CIA Extends U.S. Activities, Seeking to Influence Government Policies," *New York Times,* October 1, 1976. Cf. Richard Halloran, "Unification Church Called Seoul Tool," *New York Times,* March 16, 1978.

[40]"Panel Told Seoul Used Followers of Sun Myung Moon for Protests," *New York Times,* June 7, 1978.

dustries was manufacturing parts for the M-16 rifle and other weapons used by the Korean army. The committee report added that "executives from Tong-Il . . . traveled to Hartford, Connecticut, to seek permission from Colt Industries to export a version of the M-16 rifle made in Korea under a coproduction agreement. Colt said no."[41]

During this period, all government contracts in Korea were awarded without bid by Chung Hee Park's military government. At a time when opposition journalists were gagged and businesspeople, religious leaders, and rival politicians were jailed at the whim of President Park, Moon was allowed to travel the world freely and his Korean businesses flourished.[42] It appears that the South Korean government was not displeased with Moon's activities.

Pak spent much of his time before the Fraser committee complaining, claiming ethnic and religious bigotry. He stated, "I am here today because I am a Korean, a disciple of Reverend Moon and a member of the Unification Church, and a dedicated anticommunist. 'Korean' is a dirty word these days, and everything Korean is suspect. Also, to be a 'Moonie' in this country is very unpopular and the cause for anticommunism is practically dead now."[43]

On numerous occasions Pak called Fraser a communist bent on subverting Korean-American relations. He told the committee that Moon would not testify—not because he was afraid to testify but because the church would not allow him to be slandered. Pak stated, "Reverend Moon is not afraid of you. When he heard of your June 6 challenge he wanted to confront you himself, but we will not allow this. Why not? Our fight is a fight for principle. Reverend Moon is not a private person. He is a symbol of our church and religion. Once a religious leader becomes prey to a political opportunist [Fraser], every religion is threatened."[44]

In identifying members of the Korean extradiplomatic lobby, Richard Halloran wrote in a New York Times article in 1976 that "Mr. Moon is reportedly not trusted by the South Korean intelligence agency, which is said to consider him eccentric and opportunistic. But his organization has people and money that the Korean CIA is said to think useful."[45]

A later incident demonstrates the danger of allowing Moon to testify in a public forum. In late May 1982 a civil suit seeking $9 million in damages was brought by Anthony Colombrito against a deprogrammer,

[41]"Clouded Moon," Newsweek, November 13, 1978, p. 69.
[42]Cf. Halloran, "South Korean CIA Extends U.S. Activities, Seeking to Influence Government Policies."
[43]From video, Truth Is My Sword (Unification Church, 1978). Cited in Richard Halloran, "Aide in Moon Church Calls Inquiry 'Abuse,' " New York Times, March 23, 1978.
[44]Ibid.
[45]Halloran, "South Korean CIA Extends U.S. Activities, Seeking to Influence Government Policies."

Galen Kelly, whom Colombrito alleged abducted him in an attempt to make him renounce the Unification Church.[46] The case was heard in a Manhattan district court by Judge Richard Owen. Moon was subpoenaed and testified under oath—despite repeated and often angry objections by his lawyer—that he had met with and spoken to Christ, Buddha, and Moses. When defense attorney John Degraff asked Moon how he knew it was Christ, Moon responded, "I remember Him from His holy picture. . . . He said He was the Jesus Christ."[47] Moon, who seemed eager to testify, was scheduled to appear again in court the following morning. But, apparently embarrassed by his testimony, the church urged Colombrito to drop the case.*

In an unprecedented move, Judge Owens ordered the Unification Church, which was not a party to the case, to pay $79,000 in costs to Kelly and his attorney.[48] The Colombrito case was not the only case dropped by the church in an apparent effort to keep Moon out of a witness box.†

In November 1978, after eighteen months of investigation and hearings, the Subcommittee on International Organizations released its final report. The authors of the 447-page document concluded that the Moon organization was not a vehicle of the Korean government. However, the report emphasized that the church engaged in political activity and had attempted to gain control of American institutions.[49]

In conclusion, the Fraser committee recommended an interagency probe of the Unification Church and its activities, noting that there "was evidence that the church had systematically violated U.S. tax, immigration, banking, currency, and Foreign Agents Registration Act laws, as well as state and local laws relating to charity fraud, and these violations were related to the organization's overall goal of gaining temporal power."[50]

Foreign Agents Registration Act   Prior to World War II, Congress, fearing that Japanese and German business interests in the United States

---

[46]Marcia Chambers, "Moon on Stand, Tells of His Religious Beliefs," *New York Times*, May 28, 1982.

[47]Ibid.

*Moon can be capricious. In 1988 a Zimbabwean convinced Reverend Moon that he was a channel to Moon's seventeen-year-old son who was killed in an automobile accident in 1984. See Nancy Cooper and Mark Miller, "Rev. Moon's Rising Son: A Bizarre Tale Roils the Unification Church," *Newsweek*, April 11, 1988, p. 39.

[48]"Unification Church Told to Pay Fees," *New York Times*, July 4, 1984, p. B3.

†In 1980, Moon was not allowed to testify in a tax case in Westchester County, New York; the church argued that he was the equivalent of the Catholic Pope. See Edward Hudson, "Moon's Church Drops Tax Case in Westchester," *New York Times*, May 31, 1980.

[49]Richard Halloran, supplementary material from the *New York Times* News Service and the Associated Press, November 2, 1978.

[50]Ibid.

were attempting to buy political influence, passed the Foreign Agents Registration Act. The act states in part that any organization involved in political activities and controlled or directed by a foreign principal must do the following:

1. register with the Justice Department
2. make regular reports on its activities
3. provide detailed accounts of its foreign sources of funding.

The Unification Church may have been guilty in some measure of all the allegations found in the Fraser report; the report's evidence of violations of the Foreign Agents Registration Act seems strong. Why, then, was there no real investigation by the Justice Department?[51]

A *Frontline* special noted that "by the time Ronald Reagan was inaugurated, the idea of investigating Moon's political activities was a dead issue. Ronald Reagan's presidency was hailed as the beginning of a conservative revolution. . . . Ironically, with the revolution seemingly won, traditional sources of money for conservative politics, such as direct mail, began to dry up. But Moon, a VIP guest at the inauguration, soon became a major funder of Washington's new conservative establishment."[52]

During the Reagan and Bush years, the Moon organizations became more bold in their activities, operating virtually unchecked.

Fraser Defeated in U.S. Senate Race   In late March 1978 Pak testified before the Fraser committee that "my principles will not permit me to resort to methods such as buying influence with money. So I have never engaged in such activities."[53]

In September 1978 Donald Fraser was defeated in the Minnesota primary for the U.S. Senate by what amounted to one vote per precinct. Unification Church defectors reported that the church had sent 300 "missionaries" into Minnesota to campaign against Fraser and that $2 million was spent on the effort. It appears that Pak was not above buying influence with money after all.[54]

In the effort to defeat Fraser, the Unificationists waged a door-to-door campaign and the press was misused effectively. Articles branding Fraser a communist written by Walter Riley, a former convict turned journalist, appeared in Minnesota newspapers. The sign on the door of Riley's business in Washington, D.C., read:

[51]*Frontline*, "The Resurrection of Reverend Moon," Public Broadcasting System, January 21, 1992. Written and produced by Rory O'Connor, reported by Eric Nadler.
[52]Ibid.
[53]*Truth Is My Sword.*
[54]Anne Nelson, "God, Man and the Rev. Moon," *Nation*, March 31, 1979, pp. 325–28.

ELECTRONIC COUNTERMEASURES

TransWorld News Service

and

Korean Consumers Association

Riley's wife, a Korean, had at one time worked with Bo Hi Pak in the Korean embassy.[55] Donald Fraser served as mayor of Minneapolis from 1980 to 1993; removed from the national scene, he is no longer a threat to Moon, Pak, and the Unification Church.

Moon's Mass Media

The *Washington Times*   Despite Moon's problems with the Internal Revenue Service, the Unification Church did not retrench. In the same month that Moon was convicted of tax violations (May 1982), a new daily newspaper appeared in bright orange boxes in the nation's capital. The church, with Bo Hi Pak heading the World Media Association, had purchased the assets of the *Washington Star*, adopted the name *Washington Times*, and began competition with the *Washington Post*.[56]

The first editor of the *Washington Times*, James Whalen, a respected journalist, said the paper would emphasize "a conservatism we believe is as relevant and vital to the solutions of man's problems today as it was in the mind and struggles of Edmund Burke two centuries ago."[57] The *Times*, now over ten years old, has remained ultraconservative—but without Whalen.

Two months before publication of the first edition of the *Times*, the *Unification News* (an in-house organ) noted that "the newspaper is being funded by tax-paying businesses associated with the Unification Church . . . [but] the paper will be editorially independent from the church and [Whalen] has been given complete responsibility for the paper's design and contents." [58] Upon taking charge of the *Times*, Whalen said he had met with both Moon and Pak and the three had agreed that there would be a "high wall" between the newspaper and the Unification Church. According to Whalen, Moon breached that wall on many occasions. Upon tendering his resignation, Whalen told

[55]Ibid.

[56]Eric Alterman, "In Moon's Orbit: The Messiah with Money," *New Republic*, October 27, 1986, pp. 12–14.

[57]"Sun Myung Moon Paper Appears in Washington," *New York Times*, October 18, 1982.

[58]"Enter the *Washington Times*," *Unification News*, March 22, 1982, p. 4.

a press conference that the *Times* "had become a Moonie newspaper."[59] Whalen's successor, Arnaud de Borchgrave, denies that Moon influences the paper's content.

The *Times* competes with the *Washington Post* editorially, but it does not compete successfully for advertising dollars. The Unification Church has lost hundreds of millions of dollars on the *Times*. Its chronic lack of advertising would convince the dullest businessman to close shop. On the surface, there appears no reason for its existence.[60]

Although many newspapers take political postures, none is as unrelenting in its support of right-wing policies as the *Washington Times*. While Reagan was president, de Borchgrave bragged: "The *Washington Times* is the first thing that Ronald Reagan reads each morning. He called me up and told me so."[61]

Within days after taking over the *Times*, de Borchgrave published a front-page editorial seeking donations toward the sum of $14 million to aid the Contras. Congress had just turned down an appropriations bill that would have provided a similar sum to arm the guerrillas. The *Times* was the first contributor to the Nicaraguan Freedom Fund—$100,000![62]

In the months that followed, William Cheshire, chief of the editorial department, resigned along with four of his colleagues because de Borchgrave squelched an editorial that was critical of South Korea. A number of reporters (including Cheshire) contacted the Justice Department, arguing that the *Times* was in violation of the Foreign Agents Registration Act. The inquiries raise an interesting question: Are foreign-owned newspapers considered foreign agents and subject to registration? The inquiries went unanswered.[63]

Insight **and the** *World & I*   The *Washington Times* publishes a high–production cost weekly, *Insight*, which is similar in appearance to *Time* and *Newsweek* magazines. Like the parent paper, *Insight* does not have as strong an advertising base as its major competitors. Full-page ads promote trivial items such as language cassettes, Chinese exercise balls, and talking alarm clocks. The magazine also publishes advertisements for cigarettes and liquor. This seems odd coming from an organization that consistently exhorts against the evils of smoking and drinking.

Also produced by the *Times* is the magazine *World & I*, a monthly that runs to more than 700 pages and resembles *National Geographic*. Despite its

[59]*Frontline*, PBS.
[60]Alex Jones, "*Washington Times* and the Conservative Niche," *New York Times*, May 26, 1978. See also "The Unification Church Aims a Major Public Relations Effort at Christian Leaders," *Christianity Today*, April 19, 1985, pp. 50–51.
[61]Jones, "*Washington Times* and the Conservative Niche."
[62]*Frontline*, PBS. See also Jones, "*Washington Times* and the Conservative Niche."
[63]*Frontline*, PBS. See also "War of Independence," *Newsweek*, April 27, 1987.

polish and sophistication, *World & I* must be an economic failure, even at $10 a copy. The annual budget for the magazine is a whopping $10 million.[64] Circulation figures are not published for either magazine, but more than a few copies are given away. My first fifty-two issues of *Insight* came as a Christmas gift subscription paid for by the "Unification family."

The influence of these publications reaches far beyond the printed word. The newspaper provides a base for conservative columnists. Without the *Times,* would television be aware of and employ such personages as Pat Buchanan, William Rusher, and Mona Charen? In the case of Buchanan, the *Times* in essence was the launching pad for a presidential bid in 1992.[65]

The Unificationists are trying to reach as large an audience as possible. Pak's biography, which is distributed at CAUSA conventions, states that he is also publisher of the *New York City Tribune* and *Noticias del Mundo,* the latter purported to be the largest Spanish-language newspaper in New York.* The handout further notes that Pak is "Chairman of the Preparatory Committee for the World Media Conference and the annual fact-finding tour for journalists worldwide." Annual Tours for journalists involve sending media people to all-expenses-paid conferences similar to the CAUSA conferences.[66]

Paragon House   In 1984 the Unification Church founded an academic press, Paragon House, with longtime Moon friend Frederick Sontag as chairman of the editorial board. Sontag is author of *Sun Myung Moon and the Unification Church* (Abingdon Press, 1974). The book is used as a public relations handout by the church. Before joining Paragon, Sontag was Denison Professor of philosophy at Pomona College in California.[67]

The church guaranteed Paragon House $5 million for the first five years of its operation. One of its earliest publications was *Mind and Brain: The Many-Faceted Problems* edited by John Eccles, a 1963 Nobelist in the category of Physiology or Medicine. The press also published Morton Kaplan's *Science, Language and the Human Condition.* Kaplan, at the time a faculty member at the University of Chicago, is also on the editorial board of Paragon House.[68]

Edwin McDowell, reporting for the *New York Times* in April 1984, noted that Paragon's board of directors "consists of eighteen scholars from such prominent universities as Harvard, Yale, Columbia, Stanford,

[64]Alterman, "In Moon's Orbit," p. 13.

[65]*Frontline,* PBS

*The *New York City Tribune* ceased publication on January 4, 1990.

[66]Walter Goodman, "Ticket to Seoul, Journalists' Free Trip," *New York Times,* May 16, 1985.

[67]Edwin McDowell, "Unification Church Is Starting a Publishing House: 18 Scholars are Included on Board," *New York Times,* April 2, 1984.

[68]Ibid.

Princeton, Oxford, and Chicago." McDowell also stated that "Paragon House's $1 million-a-year financing will come from the International Cultural Foundation . . . incorporated by the Unification Church. The foundation's stated objective is 'to promote world peace through academic, scientific and cultural exchange.' Since 1972, it has sponsored an annual Conference on the Unity of the Sciences."[69]

In the late fall of 1990, I received a brochure advertising four Paragon textbooks. I ordered a review copy of one, *The Republic of Many Mansions* by Denise and John Carmody of Tulsa University. The book's dust jacket reads:

> In counterpoint to mainstream influences, the Carmodys [take into consideration] the responses of the many religious and secular groups that were not, and still are not, part of the primarily white, Protestant, male historical tradition: Catholics, Jews, Muslims, Buddhists, women, African-Americans, and others. *The Republic of Many Mansions* concludes that the future of American religious culture lies in a collective and ongoing dialogue among the many voices active in the American religious landscape.[70]

There is nothing in the Carmody text that is directly related to the Unification Church. Denise Carmody says that no pressure was put on her to include Moon's group as one that should be part of the "ongoing dialogue." She also says that all her dealings with Paragon were very professional.*

The theme of the Carmodys' book, though not specific to the Unification Church, is consistent with much of the literature produced by the church. The Carmodys did not write their book to suit the Unificationists, but what they wrote was suitable for publication by the church.

Dialogue and Alliance   Another publication meant to influence educators and the ministry is *Dialogue & Alliance*. It is billed as a "quarterly journal of interreligious wisdom and learning"; advertisements inform the reader that "one of the central goals of [the journal] is to promote interreligious exchanges among scholars and religious leaders." The brochure also promotes a number of books written by well-known authors in the field of sociology of religion. The books offered for sale are similar to the books distributed by Paragon House; minority religious viewpoints are stressed.

Dialogue & Alliance is offered by the International Religious Foundation (IRF). Had I not known that IRF was a front organization of the Unification Church and that the editor-in-charge, Frank E. Flynn, was a

---

[69]Ibid.
[70]Denise Carmody and John Carmody, *The Republic of Many Mansions* (New York: Paragon House, 1990), dust jacket.
*Telephone interview with Denise Carmody, 1991.

Moonie, I would never have guessed that the journal was a church publication. Nevertheless, *Dialogue & Alliance* is as professionally produced as *Insight* and *World & I*, and there is much of interest in the publication.

Television   The print media is not the only medium of interest to the Unification family. *Unification News* reported in November 1990 that Moon and his family had inaugurated the Washington Television Center in Washington, D.C., a studio with the capacity to tape any kind of commercial broadcast. The article further noted that "our rapid rise [is] a cause for concern and a target for attack from people in the media who misunderstand or are prejudiced by any success of the Unificationists."[71]

The studio is an offshoot of Atlantic Video, Inc., a taping studio in Alexandria, Virginia. The *News* stated, "Our true parents [Reverend and Mrs. Moon] recognized early on the importance of the television media in shaping the mores of the American public and the course of public affairs in America."[72] The Unificationists claimed contracts with the Discovery Channel and BET (Black Entertainment Television), a cable network with programs aimed at 25 million African-Americans. Also, Atlantic Video was said to have a "a myriad of other production clients including the U.S. government, local governments, the major broadcast networks, advertising agencies, political parties, political candidates, and many associations, corporations, and small producers."[73]

International Security Council

Before the lessening of tensions between the former Soviet Union and the United States, the Unification Church published booklets under the rubric International Security Council. Packaged to look like government publications, the books, which were distributed at a variety of Unification seminars, fueled support for reactionary attitudes toward the Soviet Union.

Among the titles were the following: *Negotiating with Marxists in Central America; The Strategic Stakes in the Sudan; The Brezhnev Doctrine and the Challenge of Soviet Imperialism; The Caribbean Basin and Global Security; Strategic Implications of the Soviet Threat; The Soviet Challenge in Central America and the Caribbean; The Soviet Challenge in East Asia; State Terrorism and the International System; The Geopolitics of Southwestern Africa; Proceedings of the*

[71]Jonathan S. Pak, "Inauguration of the Washington Television Center," *Unification News*, November 1990, p. 4.
[72]Ibid.
[73]Ibid.

First Pan-American Convention; The Soviet Union and the Middle East; The Soviet Union and the Security of East Asia; International Security and the Brezhnev Doctrine.

Citing conservative politicians, top military brass, and public officials, this odd lot of church literature took a hard-line approach to dealing with perceived communist threats. CAUSA International, not the Unification Church, was identified as sponsor of the publications. Much of what appears in some of the booklets was first published in the *Washington Times.*

The International Security Council (ISC) has sponsored a number of conferences around the world that are similar to the CAUSA conferences. Guests at ISC conferences, however, are mostly retired military brass. For example, 55 of the 100-plus participants attending an ISC conference in Paris during February 1985 held the rank of admiral or general. All 35 American officers in attendance were retired.[74]

The resolutions published at the end of the ISC conference stated that the nations of the Western hemisphere:

1. Denounce Cuba and Nicaragua as surrogate Marxist states adversely affecting the security of the Caribbean Basin.
2. Support the president of the United States as champion of democracy and democratic values and help him to inform the people of the United States of the critical situation in the Caribbean Basin.
3. Give full support to the OAS [Organization of American States] commitments and security objectives, including proper utilization of the Inter-American Defense Board.[75]

The effects of the Paris resolutions differed little from the "fight communism with Godism" pledge signed by most of the participants at the CAUSA convention in Los Angeles (described earlier in this chapter). An officer who attended a similar convention told me that his group was asked to do the same things that the ministers at the CAUSA convention were asked to do: write letters to their local newspapers, contact political leaders, support President Reagan's foreign policies, and ask their friends to do the same. They were told that CAUSA and ISC would be in touch.

God or Godism is not mentioned even once in the sixty-eight pages of the Paris proceedings. It is obvious that different themes were created for different audiences: Godism for ministers, a political declaration for military personnel. Nevertheless, the message was the same: support President Reagan's policies in Central America.

---

[74]*International Security Council: The Caribbean Basin and Global Security: Strategic Implications of the Soviet Threat* (New York: CAUSA Publications, International Security Council, 1985). The list of participants appears on pp. 63–65.

[75]Ibid.

It is common practice for the Unification Church to stage conferences to affect public opinion. At incalculable cost, the church has sponsored hundreds of events for journalists, political figures, scientists, and educators. Perhaps the most enduring and costly of these propaganda efforts has been aimed at the clergy.

Interdenominational Conferences for Clergy (ICC)

In May 1988 I was invited by the Unificationists to attend the thirty-third ICC held in Seoul, Korea. Some 6,000 ministers had preceded our group on similar trips, and 1,000 would follow before the conferences ended in July. Participants were asked to pay $400, about 10 percent of the cost of the trip. The ministerial composition at the Korea conference was statistically similar to the audience at the CAUSA seminar.

Most of the ministers represented conservative churches, including a variety of independent Apostolic, Pentecostal, and Baptist organizations. The largest single block of believers with us in Korea were Mormons. Nearly half the participants were black. In February 1988 *Newsweek* commented on Moon's unique coalition:

> Moon . . . has become active through a labyrinth of corporations, in funding two seemingly disparate interests: conservative organizations, particularly the religious right, and civil rights activists. One thing the organizations and the activists share is a need for fresh revenue. . . . Evangelist Robert Grant . . . predicts conservative activists in need of cash will have to close ranks with Moon—"even if they have to hold their noses." [In the pages that follow, it is shown that Grant had no problem holding his nose.] . . .
>
> Some old-line civil rights activists have swallowed their suspicions of Moon after being wooed by offers of help for their hard-pressed programs. Reverend Ralph Abernathy, for example, is on the board of [Robert Grant's American Freedom Coalition]. . . .
>
> What does Moon hope to achieve through the financial help he gives? It places him in position to influence grass-roots politics in the same way other lobbies do. Last August [1987], Col. Bo Hi Pak . . . said, "This extraordinary match [between the Christian Right and Moon] . . . shows what a great sense of humor God has."[76]

"Koreans Are a Small People"   On our first day in Korea, Unificationists at the seminar told the assembled ministers that "the Unification Church in Korea has more than 500,000 members."

---

[76]"Rev. Moon's Political Moves: He's Funding Both the Right and Civil Rights Leaders," *Newsweek*, February 15, 1988, p. 31.

On the following Sunday we were taken to the first Unification Church established in Seoul. It was a modest building, more house than church. One of the first-floor rooms, about the size of an average American living room, was—and still is—used for church services. In the early days Moon and his family lived in the rest of the house. Somehow, nearly a hundred of us managed to squeeze into the tiny place of worship.

At first I thought the church was atypical, retained as a museum. But Pastor David Hose told us that it was typical of the church in Korea today. "We have nearly 500 churches in Korea," he said. "And most of them are like this one or smaller. We believe in spending our money on people, not on buildings."

I was sitting next to Levy Daugherty, a Unification minister. I leaned toward him and posed a simple question. "Doesn't it get a bit crowded on Sundays for your half-million members, putting a thousand or so of them in a room as small as this?" Levy said without changing expression, "Koreans are a lot smaller than Americans." I am really not sure he understood the question.

On the return trip from the church to the hotel, I sat next to our travel agent, Do Pak, a church member who had not been in the meeting room. In response to questioning, he said he didn't know what the church membership was but that he had been told there were nearly 300 churches.

No real history of the Unification Church in Korea exists. Consequently, it is impossible to know if the church membership is growing or declining. One fact is evident, however: there are not 500,000 Moonies in Korea—nor a number approaching that figure. The Moonies simply wanted us to believe that the Unification Church is one of the largest churches in Korea.

How Rich Is Reverend Moon?   The Unification Church has always exaggerated its numbers. Just as size portends respectability, so does money. Do the Moonies exaggerate their wealth in the same way that they do their numbers? Moon's foundations such as CAUSA and ICC have pumped billions of dollars into a variety of propaganda efforts in the United States.

It is a common misconception that Moon's enterprises have had enormous success in the United States. The U.S. press has paid considerable attention to Moon's $30 million ship-building business (now defunct) and fishing fleet, neither of which ever turned a profit.[77] One of Moon's biggest boondoggles was the anticommunist movie *Inchon*, starring Sir

---

[77]Cf. Anson Shupe, "Sun Myung Moon's Mission in Retreat," *Wall Street Journal*, November 1, 1989. See also Art Toalston, "The Unification Church Aims a Major Public Relations Effort at Christian Leaders," *Christianity Today*, April 19, 1985, pp. 50–51.

Lawrence Olivier as General MacArthur. The church lost more than $30 million on the film.[78]

Americans who are interested in Moon's activities tend to believe that the money he spends in the United States comes from the profits of his Korean businesses—or from a wealthy Japanese industrialist. Moon's sources of wealth are not obvious.

With the help of an interpreter, I buttonholed Koreans in the lobby of the luxury Sheraton Walker-Hill hotel where we stayed. To my amazement, few of the Korean hotel guests knew anything about the Reverend Sun Myung Moon. My interpreter told me that most of the businessmen I had spoken with were well educated and fairly affluent. *It appears that Moon does not have the name recognition in Korea that he has in the United States! He is an American phenomenon!*

McCol   On our first day in Korea, the Unificationists told us something of Moon's businesses. Pastor Hose said that Tong-Il Industries in the port city of Pusan was making transmission parts for the hot-selling Hyundai automobile. Ilhwa Industries, a processor of ginseng tea and herbal medicines, had in the past year begun bottling a soft drink called McCol. "McCol," Hose said, "is already the third leading soft drink in Korea, trailing only Coca-Cola and Pepsi in sales." The following day we were taken to the McCol bottling plant.

McCol is a barley-based drink sweetened with fructose. Hose told us that Moon thought colas were bad for people, so he decided to produce a healthful soft drink. At the bottling plant a dozen or so neatly attired young women, dressed in red-and-white uniforms, served each of us a small bottle of McCol. There were a lot of crooked smiles and rolling eyes as the ministers politely tried to choke the drink down. The beverage may suit Korean tastes, but it will never be popular in America.

The Moonies told us that Ilhwa was producing 9 million bottles of McCol a day. Indeed, it was impressive watching the bottles jiggle down the production line—but 9 million bottles a day? Ilhwa was not exporting. If 9 million bottles a day were produced, then one of every four Koreans would have to drink a bottle every day. McCol is very expensive by Korean standards, the equivalent of sixty-eight cents a bottle. The average Korean earns $3,000 to $4,000 a year.

There were not a lot of production workers on the plant floor, perhaps two dozen. Certainly not enough to handle 9 million bottles of soda on that day. I asked an American-born Unification minister how so few employees managed so much production. The minister reminded me that it was Saturday and that the plant was operating with a skeleton crew. I learned later that the typical Korean works seven days a week

[78]Ibid.

with every other Sunday off. The McCol bottling plant is not modern by American standards, and it is unlikely that production ever approaches what the Unificationists would have had us believe.

A Charismatic Church—When It Wants To Be   I had attended many Unification Church meetings before going to Korea. Such meetings were usually semiformal and followed a lecture format. But the church can be something of a chameleon and will play to an audience. As shown earlier, the CAUSA conference catering to ministers had a Godism pledge, and the ISC chose a political posture to convince admirals and generals to support Reagan's policies.

Apart from a significant number of Mormons among our group, many of the ministers attending the ICC convention were pastors of "charismatic," tongues-speaking churches. Most of the remainder pastored churches in which emotion runs high in both pulpit and pew. Surprisingly, a number of the Moonies said that they too spoke in tongues.

The Unificationists tend to draw pastors that are particularly prone to emotional messages. For example, during Sunday service at the headquarters church several elderly Korean women sobbed, shouted in Korean, and waved their arms, much in the spirit of a charismatic meeting. The services were conducted in Korean by a Korean pastor with an interpreter at his side. After every few sentences the interpreter would translate the message into English.

On one occasion the pastor spoke for an extended period without translation. A number of the American pastors, caught up in the spirit, began waving their arms and speaking in tongues as though language barriers had been removed. When the Korean minister finally concluded, the interpreter informed the congregation that the pastor had just read the church announcements and meetings scheduled for the upcoming week.

Unless dedicated anticommunism can be considered a religion, our week in Korea was more political than spiritual. Every effort was made to involve us emotionally in what we were seeing and doing. For example, one of our guides at the first church in Seoul said, "Everything in here is original except for Reverend Moon's desk, which had to be replaced. Father Moon shed so many tears for humanity over the desk that the veneer cracked and peeled."

During Sunday service at the headquarters church, Reverend Hosea Williams, pastor of the Martin Luther King, Jr., People's Church of Love (Atlanta), was asked to speak. Williams called himself Martin Luther King's "personally chosen top field general." The Unificationists provided handouts: brochures and copies of the *People's Crusader*, Williams's church newspaper. The following attack on Jesse Jackson is excerpted from a lengthy article published in the *Crusader*: "Democratic presidential candidate Jesse Jackson continues to claim that the late Dr. King died while cradled in his arms. . . . Reverend Williams said . . . the only people who got close to King were Andrew Young, Ralph Abernathy and himself. Jesse got that blood and scraped it off the floor."[79] (Williams was referring to a blood-stained T-shirt worn by Jackson on a *Today* show interview.)

Like Martin Luther King, Jr., Jesse Jackson, Andrew Young, and most members of the Southern Christian Leadership Conference of the 1960s, Hosea Williams had been a Democrat. When Reagan was elected president, Williams bolted from the Democratic party. For a short time he was one of Reagan's advisors for minority concerns.

Williams no longer had access to the Oval Office, but he didn't blame that on Reagan. "It's those sleazy people around him, especially Meese and Deaver,*" he complained to a group of us idling in the hotel lobby before a meeting. "The president is getting bad advice." He went on to tell us that "Bush is a good man; and if you really want to help poor people, you should vote for him."

Williams was one of the few speakers who did not address the issue of communism. His focus was on domestic and racial concerns, and how churches should unite in response to growing social problems. His solutions were conservative in keeping with Reagan's domestic policies. Preaching from the pulpit, Southern Baptist style, Williams said:

> We need what you [Moon] have to offer—unity and solidarity. Graduates of the Unification Seminary are sowing seeds along the highways and byways of our nation. We owe a debt to Moon and the Unification movement for bringing together God's forces. Stop conflict between different religious groups. I am sorry to have to come halfway around the world to have such a religious experience—to find such love. America, the richest nation in the world, is one of the most disturbed nations. We have become a morally despicable and disrespected people.

Prominent civil rights leader Ralph Abernathy, who died in 1991, made several trips to Korea with the ICC as a "special guest" of the Unification Church.

The Unification Church in Pusan   On May 10, 1988, our group flew from Seoul to Pusan to visit the Unification Church museum at the site of Reverend Moon's first church in South Korea. According to church history, Moon began his ministry in Pyongyang, North Korea, in 1945. Allegedly, because his teachings were anticommunist, he was arrested in

---

*Edwin Meese III and Michael Deaver held several offices in the Reagan administrations. Both served as chief of staff.

[79]*People's Crusader*, April 29, 1988, p. 12. (The newspaper notes that the article was first printed in the *Travelers Rest Monitor*, Greenville County, South Carolina, date not shown.)

1948 for "advocating social chaos." He was sentenced to five years in prison in the Hungnam concentration camp. In the autumn of 1950 he was told to prepare for his execution. Before he could be executed, however, U.N. forces liberated the camp in October 1950.[80]

Moon fled to Pusan, South Korea, arriving in January 1951. The trip, which took most refugees ten days to two weeks, took Reverend Moon, Won Pil Kim (an early follower), and a Mr. Pak (first name unknown, not Bo Hi) more than three months. Pak had two broken legs and was carried by Reverend Moon. The museum has a picture of Moon carrying a man piggy-back across a stream. The man wore a heavy parka with an extremely large pack on his back.[81]

On July 4, 1955, Moon was arrested in Seoul, South Korea. Published sources state that he was held for twenty days, after which he was charged with draft evasion. The charges were eventually dropped.[82]

Mose Durst, former president of the Unification Church in America, wrote in his book *To Bigotry, No Sanction* that "since Moon was imprisoned in a North Korean concentration camp during the war, he could not have been available for conscription by the South Korean army."[83] The hole in that argument is that the war ended in 1953, but Moon was free and in Pusan, South Korea, by January 1951. It is quite possible that Sun Myung Moon was a draft dodger.

Now, atop a craggy hill behind the Pusan museum is a rock that is special to the Moonies—the Rock of Tears. "It's the same as the Mount of Olives," said Levy Daugherty, a former Apostolic minister from Virginia. Soon a number of American pastors sobbed and dropped to their knees to kiss the rock. Togetherness was prayed for, and Hosea Williams was again called on to denounce the moral degeneracy of America. America had to return to conservative values if it was going to survive.

The DMZ   On May 12, our last day in Korea, we traveled north from Seoul to the DMZ (Demilitarized Zone), the sharply drawn line between North and South Korea. We were told with a sense of urgency not to shout or wave our arms, that peace between North and South was delicate and care was necessary. Everyone was given a blue armband, U.N. color, to signify that we had come in peace. After we had been provided with army helmets, a Korean army captain led us down into one of three tunnels purportedly dug by the North Koreans as an attack avenue to the South. At the bottom of the tunnel was

[80]Cf. Mose Durst, *To Bigotry, No Sanction: Reverend Sun Myung Moon and the Unification Church* (Chicago: Regnery Gateway, 1984).
[81]Ibid.
[82]Ibid.
[83]Ibid. p. 74.

an armed South Korean soldier; facing him was his counterpart from the North.

The air in the tunnel was stale, and I was delighted when that part of the tour was over. Our next stop was a glassed-in tower overlooking North Korea. From the tower we took turns looking at North Korea through swivel binoculars, the kind found atop skyscrapers. The army captain told us that the clean, modern-looking community to the north was a propaganda village, maintained by the communists so observers would think that North Korea was prosperous—nobody really lived there.

Unificationists mingled with the crowd and told us of communist atrocities, attempted assassinations, bombings, and the killing of innocent children. We were provided with a propaganda brochure that confirmed what we were being told. Near the end of the tour, there was a shout. "Over there! Over there!" All binoculars turned in the direction toward which one of the ministers was pointing. The pastor had spotted a genuine communist in the artificial village. He was carrying something—a gun!—no, a shovel.

The Little Angels   The "love bomb" that I had first encountered in my walk in the woods with the Moonies eight years earlier was practiced on a grand scale during the ICC conference in Korea. Along with our political education, we were made to feel important. To that end, our last evening in Korea was made special by our hosts.

After a sumptuous meal served in the banquet hall of the Little Angels Art School, we were guests at a performance of the troupe. Selected from a student body of 4,000 gifted and talented children, the Little Angels are a troupe of three boys and twenty-five girls, ages seven to fifteen. Since 1965 the group has taken sixteen world tours and performed more than 2,000 times in forty countries. *New York Times* dance critic Anna Kisselgoff wrote of a performance at Hunter College, New York: "these children should shame all the cute but uncoordinated mice, candy canes and toy soldiers of the 'Nutcrackers' of the earth. . . . Every detail in their performance, from eyebrow-raising to intricate footwork and some complex drum-beating, has been worked out to perfection."[84]

In Korea the troupe performs in its own on-campus theater, the Little Angels Performing Art Center. Opened in 1981, the architecturally perfect theater is decorated in brilliant red with white-and-gold trim. After dinner we were led into the theater from a door off-stage. It was a packed house, except for the first four or five rows of seats, front center—our seats.

---

[84]Quoted in "The Little Angels" (Seoul, Korea: Korean Cultural Foundation, Inc., undated). Twelve-page theater glossy, pages not numbered.

After we were seated, we were introduced as visiting dignitaries from the United States. The Korean audience rose and clapped; we in turn stood, faced the audience, and bowed. The experience was new and strange for most of us, perhaps all of us. It was difficult not to feel important in that setting.

As a memento of the evening we were given a glossy, twelve-page program produced by the Korean Cultural Foundation, Inc., the organization that Bo Hi Pak headed after resigning from the Korean army. In the program are pictures of the Angels meeting dignitaries from around the world. Although he is not mentioned by name, Bo Hi Pak is pictured introducing the Angels to the Queen of England, British prime minister Heath, and presidents Nixon and Eisenhower.[85]

In a number of places the program refers to the ideas of the founder of the Little Angels Art School, but the name of the founder is not mentioned. During the banquet I told one of the Moonies waiting on tables that I thought the newly redecorated facilities were beautiful. He said his arms were so sore that he felt he had painted most of it himself, even though dozens were involved in the restoration. I asked him why he had any part in painting the school at all. I learned then that Reverend Moon was the unnamed founder mentioned in the program. Was it quiet philanthropy on the part of Reverend Moon? Or was his name withheld because it could have had a negative effect on Pak's propaganda machine, the Korean Cultural Foundation, Inc.? We knew who our host was. But what about Truman, Eisenhower, Nixon, Queen Elizabeth, and other luminaries approached by Pak? Did they know who their host was?

It is quite possible that Moon supports the arts as a vehicle for co-mingling with the elite. After all, opera, classical music, and ballet are elite pastimes in the United States. What better places for meeting powerful, influential people than in boardrooms supporting the arts? To that apparent end, Moon founded the Universal Ballet Academy in Washington, D.C. In December 1989 he hired a Russian, Oleg Vinogradov of the world-famous Kirov Ballet, to direct the academy.[86]

At the academy's inauguration ceremony, "letters of congratulation from President Bush and John Frohnmeyer, former chairman of the National Endowment for the Arts, were read." [87] Moon is also responsible for a major portion of the funding for the New York City Symphony.[88]

---

[85]Ibid.

[86]"Dance and the New Culture: Universal Ballet Academy Opens in D.C.: President Bush and NEA's Frohnmeyer Send Congratulations," *Unification News*, November 1990, p. 1.

[87]Ibid.

[88]David Eaton, "NY City Symphony Opens 1989–90 Season: Performance Receives Favorable Reviews in NY Papers," *Unification News*, December 1989, p. 10.

American Seminars and Tours

The Unification Church is full of surprises; but none took me aback as much as learning (nearly two years after the fact) that while I was in Korea, the Unification Church had as guests in Washington, D.C., a contingent of Koreans studying the United States.

According to the December 1989 edition of *Unification News*, 7,000 Koreans attended such conferences in the first two years of the program. The first guests invited to tour the United States were college professors; but with student protests and anti-American sentiment on the upswing in South Korea, the church changed its focus and invited a greater number of student leaders. *Unification News* said this of the students:

> In light of the history occurring now in otherwise oppressed nations, our student guests are the most interesting. They are not ordinary students. They are generally student activists; students who are leaders on their respective university campuses. As can be imagined, some of them have strong anti-American sentiments. And some of them have been strongly influenced by leftist thought.
>
> Happily we can report that once the students get out of their familiar environment and see the United States for themselves, their intense emotions and keen intelligence begin to take a different direction. Following are statistics for fifty-three seminars held during the period July 1987 to December 1989:
>
> Professors: 3,628
> Religious Leaders: 400
> Civic Leaders: 997
> Military Leaders: 528
> Writers: 30
> High School Principals: 560
> Family Roots Chairmen: 278
> Government Administrators: 269
> Student Leaders: 310
> The total number of participants: 7,000[89]

It is clear that the seminars had no religious function whatsoever. The Unification Church was used as a political instrument to build and cement relations between the governments of Korea and the United States.*

---

[89]Betty Lancaster, "7,000 Korean Guests Hosted in America," *Unification News*, December 1989, p. 25.

*While I was in Korea, a Unificationist told me that the church had "educational" centers that focused on training low-level officials for the Korean government. Participants were taught theoretical rebuttals to Marxism, so they could "improve their performance in governmental activities." See also "Seoul Officials Deny Links to Moon Sect," *New York Times*, May 26, 1976.

Citizens for Reagan

After the ICC conference, participants received mailings from organizations and groups endorsed by the church. One such group was Citizens for Reagan. Eric Bobrycki, the local Moonie supporting the American Freedom Coalition, said that Unificationists were working with the group.

Bulletins from Citizens for Reagan sought aid for the Contras by making outlandish charges against House Speaker Jim Wright, who was touted as Reagan's number one enemy. The June 1988 bulletin bannered Wright as "The Most Corrupt House Speaker in History" and added, "as long as Somoza was a source of cash for Democratic politicians, Wright was happy to do his bidding. Today, as long as the demand of the Democratic Caucus is that the Resistance not be aided, Wright is willing to do Ortega's bidding."

Another bulletin began, "[Y]ou know the reason for this alert. Ollie North has been indicted! . . . The Sandinistas are trying to wipe out the Freedom Fighters. Your help is urgently needed! . . . After you have contacted your Representative and two U.S. Senators, send a letter to your local newspaper. If you would like to tell Jim Wright what you think of his support for the communists, his office number is 202-225-8040."[90]

American Freedom Coalition   For the most part Unification operatives work behind the scenes, providing money and labor for conservative groups. For example, during Desert Storm the American Freedom Coalition (AFC), founded by evangelist Robert Grant, promoted rallies in each of the fifty states. Where possible, AFC tied its activities and financial support to well-known patriotic organizations such as the American Legion and Veterans of Foreign Wars. In most cases the veterans groups had no knowledge that the AFC had ties to the Moonies. Moon organizations have pumped hundreds of millions of dollars, perhaps billions, into operations such as the AFC.[91]

Christianity Today reported in February 1988 that Robert Grant solicited CAUSA USA president Philip Sanchez and CAUSA International president Bo Hi Pak for help in promoting the AFC. Sanchez and Pak agreed to assist Grant in the following ways:

1. Time on the program agenda of all CAUSA conferences to enable AFC board members to present the goals of the AFC and to solicit members.
2. Access to the names of thousands of attendees who have participated in previous CAUSA conferences.

[90]Citizens for Reagan, March 1988.
[91]*Frontline*, PBS.

3. The services of one staff member per state to help in reaching out to the CAUSA "graduates" and to encourage them to join the AFC, as well as the services of several others to help the new AFC office in Washington, D.C.[92]

The original board roster of the AFC listed Robert Grant as president; Grant was also founder and chairman of the political lobby group Christian Voice. The Southern Christian Leadership Conference's Ralph Abernathy was vice president. Former congressmen Richard Ichord (Democrat, Missouri) and Bob Wilson (Republican, California) cochaired the board. The organization's first secretary was Richard Viguerie, a prominent conservative fund raiser. Most AFC administrative officers, including the executive director, administrative director, and publications director, were members of the Unification Church. By 1987 the AFC boasted a membership of 300,000.[93]

In an interview with a Montana minister, *Christianity Today* reported that the pastor "received an unsolicited AFC promotional mailing that talked about God, traditional values, and the moral and spiritual foundation of the nation. A letter responding to his request for more information mentioned Christian Voice, Ralph Abernathy, and the fact that Ichord and Wilson are Baptist and Viguerie is Catholic. It never mentioned the Unification Church."[94]

The AFC has been involved in a number of far-reaching events. Among these were the telethons to absolve marine colonel Oliver North for his part in the Iran-Contra affair, and George Bush's 1988 election campaign. Hosted by Jerry Falwell, the "Olliethons" were produced by the AFC. During the 1988 presidential campaign, AFC published 30 million pieces of campaign literature. Douglas Weed—former special assistant to President Bush, whose job it was to act as liaison between the president and conservative groups—said that AFC's campaign literature was the "slickest and a real boon to the campaign because it was free."[95]

Another important AFC project was the promotion of the "Star Wars" Strategic Defense Initiative (SDI). In an effort to sell SDI to the public, a film narrated by Charlton Heston was produced at a cost of $200,000.[96]

Moon organizations are major contributors to AFC, and there is no doubt that AFC's goals are political. When ties between the AFC and the Moonies were first made public, Grant was reluctant to disclose the extent of their help. He later told the *Washington Post* that more than $5 million came from church business interests.[97]

[92]"Unification Church Ties Haunt New Coalition," *Christianity Today*, February 5, 1988, p. 46.
[93]Ibid.
[94]Ibid.
[95]*Frontline*, PBS. See also "Rev. Moon's Political Moves," *Newsweek*, February 15, 1988, p. 31.
[96]*Frontline*, PBS.
[97]Ibid.

Although ministers may individually support whichever candidates or whatever political parties they please, if a church per se becomes political, it may lose its tax-exempt status. Clearly, organizations with ties to the Unification Church are politically active. At the bottom of a solicitation I received from the AFC during the Oliver North campaign is the following admission: "The American Freedom Coalition is a 501 C4 political lobby organized to influence legislation. According to IRS regulations, contributions to this nonprofit corporation are not tax deductible."

Reverend Tim LaHaye   Carolyn Weaver, a Washington-based freelance writer, ran out of recording tape while interviewing evangelist Tim LaHaye's wife, Beverly. LaHaye's public relations director provided Weaver with a backup from his desk.[98] Later, while searching the tape for the interview with Mrs. LaHaye, Weaver stumbled upon a letter written by Tim LaHaye to Bo Hi Pak. At the time (early 1985), LaHaye "was riding high on the success of his new American Coalition for Traditional Values (ACTV). ACTV, whose executives included television evangelists Jerry Falwell, Jim Bakker, and Jimmy Swaggart, claimed to have registered 2 million new Christian voters for the 1984 elections."[99]

The letter expressed LaHaye's thanks to Pak for his "generous help" in promoting his work. He noted that moving ACTV to Washington had been "extremely expensive." He went on to suggest that they try to "sit together at the first CBS shareholders' meeting when Jesse Helms makes his move to take it over."[100]

In later interviews with both Pak and LaHaye, Weaver was unable to get either man to acknowledge a strong tie between their respective organizations, despite what was on the tape. Nowhere on the tape is the nature of Pak's generous help specified. LaHaye would later state that the help involved introductions in Washington. However, the Unificationists do not get involved in halfway measures. They have also made sizable financial contributions to right-wing organizations. For example, in 1984 CAUSA contributed $500,000 to New Right leader Terry Dolan.[101] Another conservative leader, David Finzer, took $400,000 from Moon to combat South Africa disinvestment campaigns.[102]

The Christian Right and Reverend Moon seem strange bedfellows, but each has political aspirations. For some conservative Christian leaders, it is enough that Moon has the money to support their activities. For

[98]Carolyn Weaver, "Unholy Alliance," *Mother Jones,* April 1986, pp. 14, 16–17, 44, 46. See also "Magazine Says Tim LaHaye Received Help from Unification Church," *Christianity Today,* January 17, 1986, pp. 40–41.
[99]Ibid., p. 14.
[100]Ibid., pp. 14–16.
[101]Ibid., p. 16.
[102]*Frontline,* PBS.

Moon, Pak, and whoever else is involved in shaping public perceptions, it is enough that the Christian Right adopts their agenda. No other payback is required.

Foreign Investments

In the past few years the Moon organization has purchased a hotel, a daily newspaper, and the third largest bank in Uruguay. The properties cost $70 million. The Unificationists used the newspaper as a propaganda tool in support of an anticommunist military junta that was forced in 1984 to participate in a democratic election or risk revolution. Opposition leader Julio Sanguinetti won the election despite the newspaper's opposition. Sanguinetti said of the church, "the Moonies are a suspicious presence. They are religious fanatics with no religious activities."[103] In rigidly Catholic Uruguay, officials in the mid-1980s reported that there were no more than twenty converts to the Unification Church in the entire country.[104]

Some critics of the church argue that Moon organizations work to promote right-wing extremist groups. For example, Chris Bryson reporting for *Lingua Franca* writes that "a Moon organization reportedly funnels money to Latin American . . . extremist groups [including] death squads in Honduras, and the officers who organized the 1980 putsch in Bolivia, which replaced a democratic government with a military junta. (According to German press reports, a top Moon official worked with Klaus Barbie on the coup.)"[105]

Propaganda efforts by foreign nationals to control politics in Latin America are not new. In 1973 our own Central Intelligence Agency manipulated the overthrow of Chile's socialist president, Salvadore Allende, by funding a massive propaganda campaign and providing financial support to the opposition.

Panda Motors   During the summer of 1990, Moon stunned the business world by announcing that he would spend $1 billion to build Panda Motors, an automobile manufacturing plant in China fifty miles north of Hong Kong. The church claims to have spent more than $100 million on the project to date. As of 1990, all it had to show for its money was a steel frame erected on the site. The money was said to have been donated by Japanese, West German, and Korean members of the church.[106]

[103]Edward Schumacher, "Uruguay Is Fertile Soil for Moon Church Money," *New York Times*, February 16, 1984.

[104]Ibid.

[105]Chris Bryson, "Heavenly Deception," *Lingua Franca*, September/October 1992, pp. 37–42.

[106]Frank Gibney, Jr., "A Panda of a Different Sort: Can the Reverend Moon Build Cars in China?" *Newsweek*, August 13, 1990, p. 45.

In August 1990 *Newsweek* noted that Panda management had not yet decided on a design, nor had they identified a market for their cars. The Chinese government made it clear from the outset that Panda would not be allowed to sell cars in China. Foreign investment is welcome in China, but not at the expense of competition with domestic production. Panda must export, but to whom? Protectionist policies in nearby Korea and Japan are such that these countries are unlikely markets. An automobile expert interviewed by *Newsweek* stated, "For anyone in the automobile business in China, this [Moon's plan] does not look commercially viable."[107] *Newsweek*'s expert was right. By April 1991 Moon had dropped plans to produce automobiles in China and was seeking a partner to produce auto parts at the plant location.[108]

In 1989 sociologist Anson Shupe, writing for the *Wall Street Journal*, discussed a variety of business failures of the Unification Church and questioned the efficacy of Moon's pending investment in China.[109] In response, Tyler Hendricks, vice president of the Unification Church, wrote a letter which both the *Wall Street Journal* and the *Unification News* published. In it he noted that sociologists have been "consistently wrong" about the church.[110] It is here to stay.

Hendricks argued that "secular sociology cannot explain religion."[111] What Moon does with his business enterprises does not always involve a profit motive. Hendricks further stated that "[Moon's] 'losses' in America represent his giving to America."[112] Hendricks found it unfortunate that people in this country do not take advantage of Moon's enterprises, "for they exist for the benefit of our nation and our children."[113] Hendricks concluded that Reverend Moon has the same "ideal" for China as he has for the United States. His plan is to "create a God-centered vision and an economic foundation completely for the benefit of the Chinese people."[114]

Shupe was wrong. The Unification Church survives. But how? Perhaps it is time for the U.S. government to make inquiries into Moon's sources of funding.

RYS Syndrome   In 1986 Moon announced the organization of the Religious Youth Service (RYS). *Unification News* called it "the beginning of a

[107]Ibid.
[108]Richard L. Holman, "Panda Seeks Partner in China," *Wall Street Journal,* April 24, 1991, p. 11.
[109]Anson Shupe, "Sun Myung Moon's Mission in Retreat," *Wall Street Journal,* November 1, 1989. p. 14.
[110]Tyler Hendricks, "Rev. Moon Eclipses Secular Predictions," *Unification News,* December 1989, p. 5.
[111]Ibid.
[112]Ibid.
[113]Ibid.
[114]Ibid.

religious Peace Corps. Young people will travel to various parts of the world with a willingness to serve and a commitment to hard work. The projects that develop will be done with the cooperation of local and national governments."[115] The church promoted RYS as an ecumenical foundation and solicited volunteers from outside the Unification Church. Few accepted Moon's invitation to join, and RYS is now wholly a Unification organization.[116]

The first RYS project involved sending eighty young people to Senegal in the western part of Africa. Their projects included refurbishing schools and medical dispensaries as well as planting 600,000 seedling trees in an effort to control drought.[117]

There is no question that RYS has been a benefit to a number of underdeveloped nations. But, given Moon's proclivity for turning apparent largess into political activity, does RYS serve other purposes?

Education

Moon has always needed an echelon of people who are capable of running his businesses and managing his seminars. For the most part, the brightest and best of the Unificationists are graduates of the Unification Theological Seminary at Barrytown, New York. The school was purchased in 1974 from the Christian Brothers, a Roman Catholic teaching order. In the first year of operation, fifty students enrolled in a two-year Religious Education program. In 1980 a three-year Divinity program was added.[118]

After establishing the seminary, administrators and faculty thought that state accreditation was just around the corner. But that was not to be. For a variety of reasons, accreditation was denied. For example, a provisional charter was denied in 1984 because, according to evaluators, "Prior to coming to the seminary, none of the senior administrators had experience in theological education. The president was a government administrator, the executive vice president was a businessman with a doctorate in economics, and the academic dean was in nursing education. None of them holds a degree in theology or any related discipline."[119]

After years of struggle, the Unification Theological Seminary was fully accredited on January 17, 1990.[120]

[115]John Gehring, "Religious Youth Service: From Dialogue to Action," *Unification News*, May 1986, p. 5.

[116]Ibid.

[117]Ibid.

[118]Jennifer P. Tanabe, "UTS Awarded Its Absolute Charter," *Unification News*, February 1990, p. 1.

[119]Ibid.

[120]Ibid.

University of Bridgeport   Following a twenty-year slide in enrollment and a faculty strike that began in 1990 at the University of Bridgeport (Connecticut), the Unification Church attempted to buy a controlling interest in the school. Despite the school's problems, Bridgeport's board of trustees at first declined the $50 million offered by the Professors World Peace Academy (PWPA), a Unification Church organization. The board feared that the association might damage the credibility of the university, and there was a possibility that the state of Connecticut might help with funding.[121]

Colin Gunn, chairman of the board of trustees, said that PWPA intended to develop four universities around the world and that Bridgeport was in their plans as the flagship campus. PWPA, founded in 1973, is primarily funded by the church's International Cultural Foundation. Until buying control of the University of Bridgeport became a possibility, PWPA functioned in a way similar to ICC, hosting political conventions for professors.[122]

PWPA guaranteed the trustees that there would be no interference with academic freedom and additionally promised that it could influence an increase in enrollment by at least 1,000 students. Despite PWPA's assurances, townspeople, students, faculty, and alumni urged the trustees not to accept Moon's offer.[123] Nevertheless, forced with accepting church money or closing, the trustees reluctantly struck an agreement with the Unification Church in August 1992 which allowed the university to remain open. The final arrangement guaranteed Bridgeport at least "$50.5 million over the next five years in exchange for control of the university's board of trustees, oversight of its budget, and the chance to offer advice on its curriculum."[124]

Hillsdale College   An invitation from Dr. George Roche, president of Hillsdale College in southern Michigan, appears in full-page ads in many issues of *Insight* magazine. An 800 telephone number is provided for anyone who is interested in learning more about the college. A call will get you Dr. Roche's book, *One by One: Preserving Values and Freedom in Heartland America* (1990).

Roche's book is a tribute to the Reagan years. Dedicated to liberal-bashing, every chapter emphasizes the abrasiveness of the media. In Roche's words, "there was no moment when the successes of the Rea-

[121]John T. McQuiston, "U. of Bridgeport Refuses Aid from Moon's Group," *New York Times,* October 22, 1991, p. B1.
[122]Ibid.
[123]Ibid.
[124]Courtney Leatherman, "After Brush with Extinction, Bridgeport Resumes Classes amid Many Questions," *Chronicle of Higher Education,* September 2, 1992.

evolution, or the philosophy under which it operated, were fairly
r---nted in the American press, especially the electronic media. Until
the media gives up their suffocating liberal bias, they will remain an
enemy, and a potent one, of change toward a freer, more morally responsible society."[125]

Roche attempts to prove the liberal bias of the press by listing
grants to so-called liberal-left groups made by the New York Times
Company Foundation. Included in Roche's list are donations made to
the following:

American Friends Service Committee (Quakers)
National Audubon Society
Conservation Foundation
National Public Radio
King Center for Nonviolent Social Change
Children's Defense Fund[126]

Roche credits another conservative organization, MediaWatch, for "dig-
ging out" the donation figures. Based in Alexandria, Virginia, MediaWatch also advertises in Moon's publications.[127]

Hillsdale refuses to comply with civil rights reporting requirements,
choosing instead to forgo federal funds.[128] Its campus provides a forum
for conservative speakers and writers, some of them well known, others
not so well known. Among the well known are Charlton Heston, William F. Buckley, Jr., Jeane J. Kirkpatrick, and Robert Novak. Like the
Washington Times, Hillsdale speaks to a wide audience.

Every month Hillsdale publishes a bulletin, *Imprimis*, which highlights
the writings, speeches, and visits of notables to the campus. The bulletin
is sent free to anyone who contacts the college, contributor or not. Apparently, advertising pays off. I received my first copy of *Imprimis* in
December 1990. Circulation at that time was 270,000. By March 1994
circulation had increased to 510,000.

Bo Hi Pak Kidnapped

A bizarre chain of events began on September 23, 1984. After eating
dinner at the Grand Hyatt Hotel in New York City, Bo Hi Pak was

[125]George Roche, *One by One: Preserving Values and Freedom in Heartland America* (Hillsdale,
MI: Hillsdale College Press, 1990), p. 27.
[126]Ibid., p. 161.
[127]Ibid., p. 160.
[128]"Hillsdale College: A Beacon of Freedom," *Imprimis*, October 1992.

kidnapped by six Korean nationals. Two kidnappers were members of the church; all resided in the United States.[129]

Blindfolded and handcuffed, Pak was taken to a residence in Wawa-yanda, a small town about eighty miles from Manhattan. Beaten and tortured for two days, Pak pleaded with his abductors to let him go so he could obtain the million dollars they demanded. Two days later he was released at LaGuardia Airport in New York and permitted to travel unescorted to Washington, D.C.[130]

Pak did not immediately report his abduction. Instead, he first went to a bank and tried to transfer $500,000, the first of two promised installments, to an unnumbered Swiss bank account.[131]

Members of the church had reported Pak missing, and FBI agents were waiting for him at his office, ready to intercept the transfer. Pak cooperated and told agents the details of his abduction. He explained that he had not contacted the FBI because threats had been made against his wife and eight children.[132]

On November 27, 1984, all six kidnappers were arrested. One of the kidnappers pleaded guilty and received a minimum sentence of fifteen years.[133] Some years later I asked a church field representative what ultimately happened in the kidnapping cases. He stated, "Colonel Pak is a compassionate man. He asked the government to forgive his kidnappers. I think they were released and they returned to Korea."

Moon's International Relations

Moon over Russia   The May 1990 issue of *Unification News* may be the most remarkable issue ever. Included with the usual news is a twelve-page supplement featuring Reverend Moon's visit to Moscow the previous month.

During Moon's visit, the Unification Church hosted three conferences: the Eleventh World Media Conference, the Third Summit Conference for World Peace, and the Ninth AULA (Association for Unity of Latin America) Conference. According to the *News* there were "500 participants from 60 nations. There were 41 former presidents, heads of state and government, and prime ministers who attended the Summit and AULA

---

[129]Selwyn Raab, "FBI Holds 6 in Kidnapping of Moon Aide," *New York Times*, November 28, 1984.
[130]Ibid.
[131]Ibid.
[132]Ibid.
[133]Ibid.

meetings." The meetings centered on the implications of glasnost and perestroika.[134]

On April 10 Moon addressed the World Media Association. With the victory over world communism a near reality, Moon's message was religious, typical of the kind of lecture I have heard dozens of times at church events. It must be remembered while reading the following excerpt from the address that Unificationists consider Reverend and Mrs. Moon their "True Parents":

> True love always travels the shortest distance with the fastest speed. Therefore, true love coming from God to the earth travels the shortest distance—a vertical line. The love between man and woman also travels the shortest distance, forming a horizontal line. When the vertical true love meets with the horizontal true love, the crossing point must absolutely be 90 degrees. There is no other way these love lines can intersect.
>
> Who is God? God is the vertical True Parents centered on true love. He is intimately close to each of us because He is our vertical parents. When we welcome the perfected human ancestors—perfected Adam and Eve—as True Parents, we create a 90 degree crossing point between the vertical true love of God and the horizontal true love of True Parents. We have two sets of True Parents. From them we receive true love, true life, and true blood lineage. This creates one world totally resonating with true love.[135]

The following day, Moon, along with a delegation of newspaper publishers and former heads of state, met with President Mikhail Gorbachev of the Soviet Union. During the conference, Moon pledged that he would support President Gorbachev in his reform efforts.[136]

Much was made in the Soviet press of a new era of cooperation between the Soviet Union and South Korea; it was even noted that Korean Air Lines had begun regular flights to Moscow the previous week. Tass called the meeting between Moon and Gorbachev a "very important element of cooperation."[137] To cement the cooperative bond, PWPA (Professors World Peace Academy) established an office at Kalinin State University.[138]

Also, within months of Moon's visit the *New York City Tribune*, under the direction of Ambassador Sanchez, reported the establishment of a "bureau in Moscow just in time for the convening of the Soviet Parliament. . . . The *New York City Tribune* is something of a curiosity in the Kremlin. It is the smallest and arguably most conservative foreign newspaper accredited in Moscow. It is also the only paper with an office

---

[134]Antonio Betancourt, "Rev. Moon in Moscow," *Unification News*, May 1990, p. 1S.

[135]Sun Myung Moon, "True Unification and One World," *Unification News*, May 1990, p. 3S.

[136]"Meets with President Gorbachev," *Unification News*, May 1990, p. 1S.

[137]Ibid.

[138]Gordon L. Anderson, "PWPA Opens a Chapter in Moscow," *Unification News*, May 1990, p. 6S.

across the street from Mikhail Gorbachev's residence. (Contrary to rumor, no coin-operated telescope has been installed in the office.)"[139] Unfortunately for the Moscow bureau, even Moon's resources could not sustain the losses of the parent paper. The *New York City Tribune* ceased publication on January 4, 1990.[140]

Writing for *Unification News,* Antonio Betancourt noted that "the Miracle in Moscow came about as the culmination of years of work by our movement led by Reverend Moon. The final details were carried out with meticulous planning and preparation directed by Dr. Bo Hi Pak, who with enormous sacrifice crafted the whole strategy."[141]

The Moscow conference closed with Raisa Gorbachev, as the honored guest of Reverend and Mrs. Moon, attending a performance of the Little Angels held at the Moscow State Children's Theater.[142]

Moon over the Middle East   Unificationists have become so adept at putting together conferences that such affairs can begin with very little notice. In the fall of 1990, as tensions were building in the Middle East, Frank Kaufmann reported in *Unification News* that Moon "even in his distant land of Korea . . . could not sleep knowing that such tragic potentialities were at large."[143]

To avert possible disaster, Moon sent Reverend Hwan Chung Kwak to Syria, where he met with Grand Mufti Ahmad Kuftaro to "present Moon's vision, and discuss strategies for serving the Divine Will at this crucial time. . . . In Syria, Reverend Kwak also met with a number of political officials."[144]

Although the mission failed (war was not averted), it is interesting to note the church's ability to quickly gather together a discussion group:

> The second stop on the peace mission was the Muslim Leader's Summit. . . . Despite the short notice [less than one week], a serious and influential group gathered to discuss the present emergency and to hear the message of Reverend Moon. Among those represented were two Grand Muftis [Syria and Yemen], several faculty and department heads from the El Azhar University, sheiks of major movements, an Egyptian former ambassador, the former prime minister of the Sudan, journalists, financiers and others.[145]

---

[139]"*NYC Tribune* Moscow Bureau Opens with a Splash," *Unification News,* August 1990, p. 13.

[140]"*NY City Tribune* Closes after 14 Years," *Unification News,* February 1991, p. 16.

[141]Betancourt, "Rev. Moon in Moscow."

[142]Ibid.

[143]Frank Kaufmann, "Muslim Leaders Receive Rev. Moon's Vision," *Unification News,* December 1990, p. 1.

[144]Ibid., pp. 1, 4.

[145]Ibid., p. 4.

Mentioned in Kaufmann's article, along with the Council for the World's Religions, was the input of the Inter-Religious Federation for Peace, and the Assembly of World's Religions.[146]

Reviewing Unification literature is mind-boggling. The church has established literally hundreds of subgroups to carry out its missions. Some of these groups were shortlived and had a limited function. Others persist to this day, and hundreds of millions of dollars, perhaps billions, have been spent on their activities.

In the months that followed the crisis in the Middle East, *Unification News* reported on a myriad of church-sponsored conventions held around the globe under a variety of rubrics. Reverend Moon's Peace Corps, RYS, was active. Moon's eldest son, Hyo Jin Nim, was given more responsibility in the church, possibly in light of his father's future retirement—Sun Myung Moon is nearly seventy-three years old. During this period the church was also actively recruiting members in the Soviet Union, exhibiting the same vigor shown in the United States twenty years earlier. The next major Unification event, however, occurred when Reverend Moon was invited by his archenemy, Kim Il Sung, to visit North Korea.

Moon over North Korea   On November 30, 1991, Sun Myung Moon returned to North Korea—ostensibly to visit his birthplace—as the guest of North Korea's president, Kim Il Sung. At Pyongyang Airport, Moon and his entourage were met by Deputy Prime Minister Da' Hyun Kim and Chairman Yoon of the Committee on Foreign Affairs.[147]

From a verbal account given the *Unification News* by Peter Kim and Bo Hi Pak, it appears that Moon's encounters with Sung's underlings were less than friendly. Yet it appears that Moon and President Sung met amiably.[148]

For the record at least, Moon and Sung discussed family and fishing. Reunification plans for the Koreas, trade agreements, politics, and the like were not reported as part of their conversations. Considering the situation objectively, however, there was no reason for President Sung to invite Reverend Moon home, even for just a few days. It is quite possible that in private Moon and Sung laid the groundwork for later dialogue between the governments of North and South Korea.

New Birth Project

Following Moon's release from prison in 1985, the church began its New Birth Project, an all-out effort to absolve Moon of any guilt associated

[146]Ibid., pp. 1, 4.
[147]Peter Kim and Bo Hi Pak (transcripts of verbal reports), "True Parents in North Korea," *Unification News*, January 1992, pp. 1, 5.
[148]Ibid.

with his conviction. Church leaders used the media to blame the media for bias in reporting Moon's activities. To make its point, the church purchased full-page ads in leading newspapers asking "Who's Next?" Few religious leaders were interested in having the federal government examine their books; and, ironically, Moon did become something of a martyr to religious bigotry.[149]

In keeping with church practice, a number of organizations were established to assist Moon with the purification process. One such organization was the Committee to Defend the U.S. Constitution. David Finzer, the man who managed a campaign to manipulate public opinion concerning South Africa, was asked to be a member of the board. All the papers necessary for incorporation were signed the very next day. According to Finzer, "that was the last I heard of the Committee to Defend the U.S. Constitution for about two years."[150]

Finzer claims he did not learn that the committee was a Unification Church front until much later. Concerned, he reviewed the organization's accounts and found that all the money that was spent was used to advertise or arrange events that supported Reverend Moon. Finzer further stated that "the real purpose of the [organization] was not to support religious liberty. What it was was to support and sanitize Reverend Moon's name to give the appearance of independent support instead of wholly owned, bought support to make him some kind of First Amendment hero."[151]

Presidential Pardon   To clear his name, Moon has been seeking a presidential pardon. Max Hugel, a former Reagan campaign official, was asked to use his influence on behalf of Moon. Early in Reagan's first term, CIA director William Casey hired Hugel as his deputy director in charge of covert operations. Hugel resigned that position in July 1981 in the wake of an alleged stock scandal. A year later he was in the teleproduction business with Bo Hi Pak's son, John Park.[152]

In April 1988 Hugel sent a memo to church member Mark Lee, proposing to arrange a meeting between George Bush and Bo Hi Pak. One of the suggested mechanisms for staging the event was for Pak to pay $50,000 to have his picture taken with Mr. Bush. There is no evidence that the fee was paid, but the meeting apparently took place.

The following letter was aired as part of the PBS documentary "The Resurrection of Reverend Moon:"[153]

---

[149]Cf. John McClaughry, "Pyrrhic Victory over Moon," *New York Times*, May 20, 1984.
[150]*Frontline*, PBS.
[151]Ibid.
[152]Ibid. See also "Reagan's CIA Troubles," *Newsweek*, July 27, 1981, p. 18.
[153]*Frontline*, PBS.

Dr. Bo Hi Pak
President and CEO
Insight Magazine
3600 New York Ave., N.E.
Washington, D.C., 20002

Dear Dr. Pak,

Max Hugel has told me of your friendship and he is indeed a great friend to have. I share his high regard for your publications and much of the work you have done in our community. I hope we can meet again soon.

Sincerely,

George Bush

Bush noted that Hugel was a great friend to have. The extent of the friendship between Bush and Hugel is not known, but they did have a common tie.* Bush had headed the CIA during 1976 and 1977. It is not known if a pardon for Reverend Moon was discussed when they met. The PBS producers received a "no comment" response to their inquiries.[154]

Hugel also tried to promote Moon's pardon by hiring a law firm in which one of Reagan's closest friends, former senator Paul Laxalt, was a partner. The firm was paid $100,000 up front and $50,000 per month plus expenses while the pardon was pursued. A petition for executive clemency was filed with the Justice Department. Accompanying the petition were letters recommending the pardon written by Senator Orrin Hatch (Republican, Utah), author-publisher William Rusher, and Ralph Abernathy. Despite the church's high-powered efforts, both Reagan and Bush left office without taking action on the clemency petition.[155]

---

*According to news accounts, Hugel was something of a loose cannon as director of covert operations for the CIA. His CIA activities are not open to public scrutiny, but his actions on behalf of Reagan during the 1980 campaign were observable and apparently impressed William Casey, the man who was to become director of the CIA.

Newsweek reported that while he was working on Reagan's campaign, Hugel "quickly impressed Casey with what other aides thought were 'hairbrained' schemes to mobilize volunteers and voters. He was 'a bull in a china shop,' one Reagan worker recalled. 'People who saw him in action would say, Christ, you guys need help.' " See "Reagan's CIA Troubles," *Newsweek*, July 27, 1981, p. 18.

[154]Ibid.
[155]Ibid.

The Impenetrable Church

Moon and Pak have insulated themselves and their church from serious investigation by building walls that sociologists and other serious investigators cannot climb without appearing to be prejudiced.

For example, when officers of the church are taken to task for questionable activities, there is always the cry of racial and religious bigotry. You will remember that Pak, testifying before the Fraser committee, said, "I am here today because I am a Korean, a disciple of Reverend Moon and a member of the Unification Church, and a dedicated anticommunist." Three years later, upon his indictment for tax evasion, Moon told an audience in Foley Square Park, New York, "I would not be here today if my skin were white and my religion Presbyterian."

In harvesting religionists to their political causes, the Moon organizations have found allies among black religious circles, Protestant fundamentalists, and Mormons. By arguing that *"they got us, you may be next,"* these minority groups respond to Unificationist claims of racial and religious persecution. In the past Moon's church was open to critical review; today it is not. The church now reduces questions it does not want to answer to charges of bigotry against all races and minority religions.[156]

Pak also testified before the Fraser committee that "Korean is a dirty word these days and everything Korean is suspect. Also, to be a Moonie in this country is very unpopular and the cause for anticommunism is practically dead now." A master at creating impressions, Pak not only put Congressman Fraser on the defensive by turning legitimate questions concerning church activities into accusations of bigotry, but he also implied that Fraser was a communist conspirator. In the months that followed Pak's testimony, Moonies actively campaigned against Fraser in Minnesota. Publicly pilloried, Fraser, a shoo-in to win a Senate seat, went down to defeat. It is little wonder that political figures are hesitant to challenge the church.

Church Allies   A great many people have enjoyed the hospitality of the Moonies: pastors, educators, journalists, scientists, government officials, politicians, and a myriad of others. By providing free trips for everyone, a publication source for many, and money for others, the church has built an enormous number of allies. Critics of the Unification Church often find themselves at odds with colleagues who have supped at the church's table.

General wisdom holds that one should never look behind a waving flag. It is not politically correct; in fact, it is considered unpatriotic. Many

---

[156]Cf. McClaughry, "Pyrrhic Victory over Moon."

Moon-supported organizations—such as CAUSA, AULA, AFC, and a seemingly endless number of similar organizations—survive on American patriotism. But patriotism for the sake of what? Why? Who pays the tab? Politically correct or not, there are many questions that should be answered.

Brainwashing of America   Citizens in this country have the right to know if foreign citizens are exporting money to manipulate public opinion here. The Korean government has apparently done this in the past, as evidenced by the Koreagate scandal.

Until the early 1980s, Unification Church operations in the United States were modest. Political activity for the most part was centered on creating and maintaining harmonious relations between the U.S. government and the government of South Korea. With Moon's tax indictment, however, other political agendas took the fore. Particularly noteworthy was a massive propaganda effort aimed at gaining support for military efforts in Latin America. Reasons underlying this operation are not immediately apparent.

Full-Scale Investigation

Upon disbanding in 1978, the Fraser committee called for a full-scale investigation of the Unification Church involving a variety of government agencies. For political reasons, no such investigation ensued. Since the early 1980s Moon's organizations have become richer and bolder, spending billions on propaganda, while reports indicate that church businesses in the United States are having difficulties.

There is no question that Moon's organizations have been a source of support for three Republican presidents. In the 1970s, Moon met with President Nixon and used church money and organization in an attempt to keep Nixon from resigning. During the 1980s, Moon's propaganda machine, particularly the *Washington Times*, spent billions of dollars to develop support for most of Reagan's major initiatives, both foreign and domestic. When Bush sought the presidency in 1988 and again in 1992, he had the full support of Moon's media.

There is no doubt that before 1965 Colonel Pak was an intelligence officer assigned to the Korean embassy in the United States, and that one of his functions was to act as liaison officer between the Korean and U.S. intelligence communities. His former bosses confirm this fact.

Pak resigned his army commission to become a propagandist, promoting the Korean government. He next turned up as an interpreter for Sun Myung Moon. During the period just prior to Moon's imprisonment and while Moon was in prison, Moon's organizations expanded enormously; and an apparent influx of money enabled Pak to build a large and effective media. It is obvious that Moon is following a political agenda in the United States. The full-scale investigation that the Fraser committee called for in 1978 is long overdue.

INDEX